MW00790716

"*The Age of Perversion* is a riveting (pun i
account of perversion in the twenty-first century. Building on Freud's pioneering
insights – fortified by wide-ranging interdisciplinary scholarship, clinical case
studies, and empirical inquiry – Knafo and Lo Bosco explain how perversity,
for better and worse, is the inevitable manifestation of self-conscious human
animals protesting their corporeality and finitude: desperately striving to
maintain a sense of meaning and value in a sexually saturated, narcissistically
inflated, commercially inundated, technologically permeated, rapidly changing
cultural milieu. Playful, profound, and provocative; a must read."

– **Sheldon Solomon**, author, *The Worm at the Core:
On the Role of Death in Life*

"Knafo and Lo Bosco have written a veritable atlas of human perversion,
which includes, among its delights and surprises, the perverse practices of the
NSA, the APA, and the Vatican. Knafo, a renowned analyst, takes us into
her consulting room where she works with men who marry dolls and women
desperate to look like dolls, while Lo Bosco illuminates the perversity of various corporate practices. The authors leave the reader thinking differently not
only about sexual acts but also about the perverse strategies we all use to
violate boundaries, toy with the forbidden, and deny death. This disturbing
and remarkable book makes it clear that the very way we define our humanity
is changing before our eyes."

– **Deborah Anna Luepnitz**, Ph.D., author, *Schopenhauer's
Porcupines: Intimacy and Its Dilemmas*

"Through their exquisite clinical/sociocultural observations, Knafò and Lo
Bosco render virtual, robotic relations frighteningly sensible. With depth and
breadth, they broaden the gender spectrum to include dolls, robots, gynoids,
and androids. They describe perverse forms of relating as psychogenetically
adaptive, salvation-seeking efforts, while warning that the capacity to damage
social life is profound. The authors also make important connections between
techno-perversion and trafficking, genocidal atrocities, and black markets for
organs, guns, and drugs. If there is a redemptive quality to this disturbing,
dark subject, it is the authors' ability to find meaning and method in these
dangerous acts. They have crafted an insightful, disturbingly relevant book
that all clinicians should read."

– **Andrea Celenza**, Ph.D., author, *Erotic Revelations:
Clinical Applications and Perverse Scenarios*

"Danielle Knafo and Rocco Lo Bosco have produced a book that is equally
frightening and enlightening. By considering the boundary between the human
and the machine, they touch on issues in the philosophy of science, ethics, sociology, and social psychology, as well as clinical psychoanalysis. Their synthesis

of these fields and their combination of depth and breadth make theirs a book well worth reading. In a unique combination of daring, scholarship, and compassion, the authors enter the world of a future where the line between the human and the machine is blurred so badly, it is merely a smudge on the horizon. While considering the difference between love and perversion they give the reader a sense of how technology provides a substitute for human love that can satisfy some men more than interaction with another person could do. In her case studies, Dr. Knafo dares to raise the question of whether we should regard this as pathology or as the best some people can do in finding satisfaction in their otherwise isolated and lonely lives."

> – **Arlene Kramer Richards**, author, *A Fresh Look at Perversions*

"*The Age of Perversion* courageously explores the impact of technology on human life – sex dolls, electronic devices, robots, the Internet, and more. Based both on broad research and in-depth clinical investigation, the book has several merits. It acquaints the reader with an astonishing range of perversions that have only become possible through new technologies. It explores the social side of perversion and examines how perversion has entered mainstream culture. Finally, it shows how psychoanalytic theory helps us understand the seemingly weird and unintelligible in human and humane terms."

> – **Carlo Strenger**, Ph.D., author, *The Fear of Insignificance:*
> *Searching for Meaning in the Twenty-First Century* and
> *Freud's Legacy in the Global Era*

From the preface: "This book examines how our ever-increasing access to technology is profoundly altering our lives, endowing inanimate objects with social and sexual cachet, and stretching the boundaries of our normal frames of reference."

> – **David Levy**, AI expert, roboticist, and author,
> *Love and Sex with Robots*

The Age of Perversion

We have entered the age of perversion, an era in which we are becoming more like machines and they more like us. *The Age of Perversion* explores the sea changes occurring in sexual and social life, made possible by the ongoing technological revolution, and demonstrates how psychoanalysts can understand and work with manifestations of perversion in clinical settings.

Until now theories of perversion have limited their scope of inquiry to sexual behavior and personal trauma. The authors of this book widen that inquiry to include the social and political sphere, tracing perversion's existential roots to the human experience of being a conscious animal troubled by the knowledge of death. Offering both creative and destructive possibilities, perversion challenges boundaries and norms in every area of life and involves transgression, illusion casting, objectification, dehumanization, and the radical quest for transcendence.

This volume presents several clinical cases, including a man who lived with and loved a sex doll, a woman who wanted to be a Barbie doll, and an Internet sex addict. Also examined are cases of widespread social perversion in corporations, the mental health care industry, and even the government. In considering the continued impact of technology, the authors discuss how it is changing the practice of psychotherapy. They speculate about what the future may hold for a species who will redefine what it means to be human more in the next few decades than during any other time in human history.

The Age of Perversion provides a novel examination of the convergence of perversion and technology that will appeal to psychoanalysts and psychoanalytic psychotherapists, social workers, mental health counselors, sex therapists, sexologists, roboticists, and futurists, as well as social theorists and students and scholars of cultural studies.

Danielle Knafo is a professor in the clinical psychology doctoral program at Long Island University and a faculty member and supervisor in New York University's postdoctoral program in psychotherapy and psychoanalysis. She has lectured internationally and published extensively, including *Dancing with the Unconscious* (2012) with Routledge. She maintains a private practice in New York.

Rocco Lo Bosco is a teacher and writer who has published nonfiction, poetry, short stories, and two novels – *Buddha Wept* (2003) and *Ninety Nine* (2015). He edits articles on psychoanalysis, science, and the philosophy of science.

Psychoanalysis in a New Key Book Series
Donnel Stern
Series Editor

When music is played in a new key, the melody does not change, but the notes that make up the composition do: change in the context of continuity, continuity that perseveres through change. Psychoanalysis in a New Key publishes books that share the aims psychoanalysts have always had, but that approach them differently. The books in the series are not expected to advance any particular theoretical agenda, although to this date most have been written by analysts from the Interpersonal and Relational orientations.

The most important contribution of a psychoanalytic book is the communication of something that nudges the reader's grasp of clinical theory and practice in an unexpected direction. Psychoanalysis in a New Key creates a deliberate focus on innovative and unsettling clinical thinking. Because that kind of thinking is encouraged by exploration of the sometimes surprising contributions to psychoanalysis of ideas and findings from other fields, Psychoanalysis in a New Key particularly encourages interdisciplinary studies. Books in the series have married psychoanalysis with dissociation, trauma theory, sociology, and criminology. The series is open to the consideration of studies examining the relationship between psychoanalysis and any other field – for instance, biology, literary and art criticism, philosophy, systems theory, anthropology, and political theory.

But innovation also takes place within the boundaries of psychoanalysis, and Psychoanalysis in a New Key therefore also presents work that reformulates thought and practice without leaving the precincts of the field. Books in the series focus, for example, on the significance of personal values in psychoanalytic practice, on the complex interrelationship between the analyst's clinical work and personal life, on the consequences for the clinical situation when patient and analyst are from different cultures, and on the need for psychoanalysts to accept the degree to which they knowingly satisfy their own wishes during treatment hours, often to the patient's detriment.

For a full list of all the titles in the Psychoanalysis in a New Key series, please visit the Routledge website.

RECENT TITLES IN THIS SERIES:

Vol. 32 *The Age of Perversion: Desire and Technology in Psychoanalysis and Culture* Danielle Knafo and Rocco Lo Bosco

Vol. 31 *Unknowable, Unspeakable and Unsprung: Psychoanalytic Perspectives on Truth, Scandal, Secrets and Lies* Edited by Jean Petrucelli and Sarah Schoen

Vol. 30 *Trauma and Countertrauma, Resilience and Counterresilience: Insights from Psychoanalysts and Trauma Experts* Edited by Richard B. Gartner

Vol. 29 *The Purloined Self: Interpersonal Perspectives in Psychoanalysis* Edgar A. Levenson

Vol. 28 *On the Lyricism of the Mind: Psychoanalysis and Literature* Dana Amir

Vol. 27 *Entering Night Country: Psychoanalytic Reflections on Loss and Resilience* Stephanie Brody

The Age of Perversion

Desire and Technology in Psychoanalysis and Culture

Danielle Knafo and Rocco Lo Bosco

Routledge
Taylor & Francis Group

LONDON AND NEW YORK

First published 2017
by Routledge
2 Park Square, Milton Park, Abingdon, Oxon OX14 4RN

and by Routledge
711 Third Avenue, New York, NY 10017

Routledge is an imprint of the Taylor & Francis Group, an informa business

© 2017 Danielle Knafo and Rocco Lo Bosco

The right of Danielle Knafo and Rocco Lo Bosco to be identified as authors of this work has been asserted by them in accordance with sections 77 and 78 of the Copyright, Designs and Patents Act 1988.

British Library Cataloguing in Publication Data
A catalogue record for this book is available from the British Library

Library of Congress Cataloguing in Publication Data
Names: Knafo, Danielle, author. | LoBosco, Rocco, author.
Title: The age of perversion: desire and technology in psychoanalysis
and culture / Danielle Knafo and Rocco Lo Bosco.
Description: New York: Routledge, [2017] |
Series: Psychoanalysis in a new key; 32 |
Includes bibliographical references and index.
Identifiers: LCCN 2016027947| ISBN 9781138849204 (hardback: paper) |
ISBN 9781138849211 (pbk.: paper) | ISBN 9781315723877 (e-book)
Subjects: LCSH: Psychoanalysis. | Information technology – Social aspects. |
Manners and customs. | Sex (Psychology)
Classification: LCC BF173. K534 2017 | DDC 150.19/5–dc23
LC record available at https://lccn.loc.gov/2016027947

ISBN: 978-1-138-84920-4 (hbk)
ISBN: 978-1-138-84921-1 (pbk)
ISBN: 978-1-315-72387-7 (ebk)

Typeset in Times New Roman
by Out of House Publishing

This book is dedicated to
Rosine Knafo,
Gavriel Knafo,
and
Diana Pepe

Contents

List of figures

Preface

In this fascinating psychological exploration the authors analyze what they call "the crooked path" – the way that perversity turns away from what the mainstream turns towards. And they do so with particular reference to technology, noting how a plethora of amazing personal and social possibilities evolve from the twenty-first century's technological revolution which, through technologies such as virtual reality and sex robots, will ultimately change what it means to be human. With their approach the authors probe towards the future the thesis of Sherry Turkle's *Alone Together*, one of my favorite books of the present decade, in which she analyzes what we *have* become through our use of technology. Here Knafo and Lo Bosco analyze what we *will* become and why.

The authors' analysis of the crooked path focuses especially on where that path crosses culture and technology. They aim to better clarify the phenomenon of perversion, expanding its theoretical reach beyond the sexual and into the social sphere of life, and they demonstrate how the rapid growth of technology and its easy availability have facilitated a culture of perversion, one that embraces the potential both to create and to destroy.

As the boundary blurs between humanity and technology, we humans are becoming ever more tempted, subconsciously, to form emotional attachments to our electronic devices which already, within a couple of seemingly brief decades, have come to seem indispensable to our daily lives. The effects on our humanity, the progressive integration of technology into every aspect of human life, the creation and progression of seductive virtual realities, all point to a culture which the authors classify as perverse. Psychoanalyst Danielle Knafo's exposé of the rationale behind some of her patients' love and devotion to their sex dolls and machines is on the one hand poignant, but on the other it points to what I believe will be the biggest benefit to society of the advent of sex robots, namely, that they will fill a void in the lives of the many, many millions who cannot form satisfactory loving and sexual relationships with other humans.

The authors also examine how the technologies that influence this social trend might lead to a future beyond our current understanding, as these technologies reframe what it means to be human. They opine that it is difficult to know at this point in time whether what they call "the age of perversion" will damage society and lead in some sense to its destruction, or whether what they perceive as technological perversions will create a better world. To their credit, they examine both possibilities.

Without a doubt these "perverse partnerships" with technology, such as cell phones and new perversions such as an addiction to cybersex, have emerged as trends that are widespread across society. The authors explain how society changes to incorporate such techno-perversions, which are facilitated by technologies that rapidly change our interpersonal and social norms. They discuss as an example the perversion of catfishing, the creation of fictional online identities as an aid to seduction and exploitation, which would not be possible without the Internet. And they recognize the irony in the way that, as we develop technologies which could create new perversions, we almost simultaneously create additional technologies designed to help us control our addiction to technology itself. Nowadays there are apps which have been developed to help block and control our children's usage of the Internet. Unsurprisingly, many of today's technological marvels are a response to the universal human need for ever more connectivity to each other. As an example the authors cite Facebook, home to some who spend hours there every day, deluded into believing that they have hundreds of "friends." As Sherry Turkle would ask, what kind of people are we becoming as we develop intimate relationships with machines?

This book examines how our ever-increasing access to technology is profoundly altering our lives, endowing inanimate objects with social and sexual cachet, and stretching the boundaries of our normal frames of reference. Given the growing profusion of new technologies, applications, and electronic products with which people are regularly interacting, the authors confirm my own belief that the perceived gap between ourselves and our technologies is rapidly narrowing, and they concur with me in predicting that we will eventually become one with our machines. As I wrote in my book, *Love and Sex with Robots*, I totally sympathize with their view that "the juggernaut of science and technology will continue to advance and profoundly affect and alter what it means to be human." Like the authors, I predict that people who grow up with all sorts of electronic gizmos will find android robots to be fairly normal as friends, partners, lovers. And in some very good ways. Technology creates any number of amazing possibilities, so why can it not be used to fill emotional and sexual voids in a person's life?

In summary, technology in the twenty-first century has come to change the ways in which we humans relate to one other, and as it does so it is also changing who we are and what we are. At the end of the day do all of us not deserve someone whom we can love and who will unconditionally love us back? And if that someone happens to have flesh made of silicone and joints made of metal, and is manufactured in a factory where it is implanted with advanced artificial intelligence, surely our feelings for it can remain the same, as they do for Dr. Knafo's doll-loving therapy patients.

The authors point to the dramatic changes, which, with time, have overtaken our older social and sexual mores, a phenomenon they attribute to some extent to the technological revolution having taken a perverse turn. They make a strong case for the result being that, as *we* are becoming to some extent dehumanized, our objects, especially our electronic devices, are becoming increasingly humanized. They believe these are the kinds of questions psychoanalysis should be addressing now and in the future, extending the social responsibility of their science "by casting an analytic yet compassionate gaze beyond the walls of the therapy room and into the heart of a world of wired connectivity, computer control, robots, easy-life gadgetry, and trans-human aspirations."

The authors say that they hope their book will invite psychoanalytic dialogue about the technological impact on the human self of the technological revolution. But for me it achieves far more than that modest goal. It prompts us to recognize how technology is changing society, and how human–computer and human–robot relationships will become the norm. We need to prepare ourselves for it, because it is inevitable.

David Levy
London, 2016

Acknowledgments

We are very grateful to a number of people who helped this project along, offering support, suggestions, and contributions. Most of all, we thank Maryellen Lo Bosco for her painstaking editing of the manuscript. A terrific editor possessing great skills, intellect, and imagination, Maryellen kept our feet solidly on the ground without weakening our vision.

We also heartily thank Seymour Moscovitz for being kind enough to read through an early draft of the book and offering valuable feedback that helped improve it. Robert Knafo, too, read sections of the book and offered important comments and suggestions. Others who read segments of the book were Deborah Luepnitz and Jesse Geller, friends and colleagues whose opinions we respect very much. Thanks, too, to David Lichtenstein for checking our Lacan section, Steven Reisner for reworking our section on the American Psychological Association, and Dodi Goldman for vetting the Winnicott references.

I (Knafo) have the good fortune of having had several wonderful research assistants who helped me search for material and check references. I am most grateful to Abbey Frawley, who tirelessly worked with me on many aspects of this book. Lilly Magid, Sam Greenblatt, Kimmy Ramotar, Hope Harris, and Danielle Zito were also invaluable.

Warm thanks go to Davecat as well as the many anonymous doll owners who kindly spoke with me (Knafo) and invited me into their private worlds. Thanks, too, to the The Doll Forum and Our Doll Community for allowing me to post and communicate with their members to learn more about the doll community. I especially thank Davecat for his openness and willingness to contribute to the book. Thanks go to David Pinnegar and Ian Cunliffe who offered support, reading of the material, and general feedback. We are also grateful to all who gave permission to publish their photographs.

I (Knafo) am very indebted to the patients who gave me permission to tell their stories on the pages of this volume. My deep schooling has always begun in the clinic.

We have been fortunate to work with Donnel Stern, the series editor at Routledge, who believed in our project from the beginning. Donnel is the ideal editor, as he is first and foremost supportive and respectful of the creative process.

Last but not least, we are grateful to Kate Hawes, Charles Bath, Amy Kirkham, Paulina Miller, and Nigel Turner at Routledge and to Nicola Howcroft, Jo North, and Victoria Chow at Out of House Publishing for bringing this book to its final fruition.

Thanks to the following for allowing quotations from their works:

Ha-Joon Chang, Katherine Hayles, Simon & Schuster for excerpts from *The Denial of Death* (1973) by Ernest Becker.
Excerpt from *The Ballad of the Sad Café and Collected Other Stories* by Carson McCullers. Copyright © 1951 by Carson McCullers renewed by 1979 by Fioria V. Lasky, Executrix of the Estate of Carson McCullers. Reprinted by permission of Houghton Mifflin Harcourt Publishing Company. All rights reserved.
Excerpts from *1984* by George Orwell. Copyright © 1950 by Houghton Mifflin Harcourt Publishing Company and renewed 1977 by Sonia Brownell Orwell. Reprinted by permission of Houghton Mifflin Harcourt Publishing Company. All rights reserved.

If the authors have inadvertently failed to seek permission for any content featured in this book for which it is required, please contact the publisher so that this can be arranged immediately.

Introduction

The age of perversion

> Out of timber so crooked as that from which man is made
> nothing entirely straight can be carved.
>
> – Immanuel Kant

In a moment of naked self-revelation, a patient of Dr. Knafo described his character:

What the hell is it with me? For as long as I can remember, I have this twist. Something crooked, something that wants to turn away from what everyone else turns toward. As a kid I wanted to stay home whenever my family went out and go out whenever they stayed home. They'd all get dressed up, and my mother would yell at me to get dressed, and I wouldn't do it. I'd insist on staying behind. They knew if they dragged me along, I'd make them miserable. So they'd finally go out without me. As my father backed the car out of the driveway, I'd go to the window to watch it pull away, feeling miserable because they'd left me behind. How could they do that? Till this day when I sit down at a holiday dinner, I still have to fight the urge to rip away the tablecloth, sending all the food and dishware crashing to the floor. It's this twist, this urge that is sometimes so powerful it's like a commandment from God. But not a God interested in order, normalcy, or goodness. But one whose delight is to upset order, to destroy it, and bring everything crashing down, to show up order for the sham it is or maybe cause a more honest order, I'm not sure. I just know I'm twisted. Twisted away from everything everyone else wants to be part of. I try to belong, I try to fit in, but I can't believe in what I'm trying to fit into. It just doesn't work. It's all bullshit, but what I'm doing is bullshit too. No matter what I do to get my life right, I can't because I just have to walk that crooked path, wherever it leads.[1]

What a perfect term to convey an intimation of the perverse: the crooked path. Perversity wants to twist away from the norm, transgress against the law, move the path away from its intended or original course, turn away from truth, whether it is an accepted truth (which, indeed, may be false) or some inner truth, which cannot be faced. It desires control, mastery, even transcendence. It involves dissatisfaction, anger, restlessness, and impudent impulse. It is a railing against the way things are. It rebels. It challenges. It disturbs. It is a friend of both creative inspiration and destructive violation.

Perversity first needs to be understood, as Freud (1953b [1905]) observed, as a universal human characteristic and, as Ernest Becker (1973) noted, at the core of the human plight. It is a basic human orientation (Unger, 2007). Given the right vector of hereditary, personal history, and social forces, perversity can become solidified as a character trait or a compulsive act. Though there is no definitive dividing line between the perverse tendency and perversion per se (and surely it is easier to describe perverse tendencies than to define what constitutes perversion), perversion will manifest after a tendency becomes fixed in character and behavior – as a psychic structure and a set of attendant enactments. The possibility that perversion can overlap with addiction (in its compulsive nature and the pleasure it delivers) and criminality (in the harm it sometimes causes others) complicates matters.

Yet what does it *feel* like – this engagement in perversion? What is the affective nature of its embodiment? Does it feel coolly victorious in the cunning deception that exploits the other to mask the doer's own insecurity and terror, or radiantly passionate in sacrificing the doer and the other to a greater vision? Does it feel like a thrill in breaking the law that protects or a righteous battle against the law that constrains? Does it feel like the excitement of a private sexual or social enactment that liberates, or a repeated compulsion that leads to a psychic or social cul-de-sac? Is it a fine magic, this swelling of Eros, this sharp, intoxicating taste of midnight in a bottle, or is it a failed bid for transcendence? Is it the hardening of the master's will, the softening of the slave's submission, the tireless ritual, the freaky fetish, the scene that swamps the existential emptiness with raw excitement, the frenzy inside the house that keeps the wolves away from the door? Or is it the inherent need to rail against and rise above limitation; the deeply creative and restless impulse to break some shackle of thought, feeling, and action; the ceaseless revision of the forms through which we live; the shattering that creates us anew (Bersani, 1986, 1995; Saketopoulou, 2014, 2015)? Does it deceive, does it reveal, or does it often walk some fine line between the two? And why is it so much a part of who we are?

A humorous answer to this last question is that the perverse exposes the dominance of the body with its abject exudations, fluids, and waste products, its neediness and mortality, and the wild urges a person may feel regarding its carnal potential. The body as the failed project, the doomed base of all narcissistic operations, is the self's tragic comedy or comedic tragedy. A hilarious and offensive medley of humorous perversion is dished up in Paul Provenza's 2005 documentary film, *The Aristocrats*, about an old and favorite transgressive inside joke among comedians, one that was never shared with the public until the making of the film. The joke always begins with the same introduction: a family and their pet dog walk into a talent scout's office, and the father says, "We have an act we want to show you." The joke always ends with the same punchline, but the middle content is where each comedian adlibs his or her own version of a "filthy" description of the act, which involves every known perversion imaginable: incest, group sex, defecation, necrophilia, bestiality, and other taboo behaviors. In the film, each successive comedian telling the joke renders it more shocking, which results in some members of the audience roaring with laughter and others heading for the nearest exit in outraged and disgusted silence. The movie's relentless ramping up of verbal lawlessness reflects the tendency of perversion to escalate aggression and push against the boundaries of circumscribed values. When asked by the agent for the name of the act, each comedian delivers the dry punchline: "The Aristocrats." Oddly enough, there is something humorous in the wild way perverse fantasy "shits" on everything sacred, if we set aside for a moment the inner turmoil that may give birth to such a fantasy. Out of the frustration of human limitation, a doer excitedly imagines destroying limits.

The family in the joke calls itself The Aristocrats (or sometimes The Sophisticates), words that belie the content of the family act and the associations with those chosen words. This opposition highlights with gross humor the human problem of being both an animal body *and* a conscious self, the existential bind where little if any reconciliation exists between the sweating, defecating, grunting, and doomed primate and the majestic ephemeral "I" (The Aristocrats) aspiring to self-worth, meaning, dignity, transcendence, and immortality. Ernest Becker (1973) bluntly noted, "We are simultaneously worms and gods ... gods with anuses" (p. 51). The joke in the film spotlights the absurd abyss between the symbolic order of society – with its systems of meaning that deny death – and the utterly indifferent and determinate order of nature. We laugh at the joke with each creative retelling, because we know that abyss only too well, hovering merely a breath above it; we find catharsis in humor's temporarily harnessing and mastery of our fear.

The perversions of the family in the joke are social as well as sexual. The Aristocrats want to perform for an audience, which constitutes a social act. Yet they are already imagined performing for an audience through the telling of the joke. It is easy to miss the social aspect of the perversion at work here, since the outrageous sexual transgressions obscure it. Moreover, the string of comedians who tell their own versions of the joke simultaneously narrate versions of themselves. The way they tell the joke covertly reveals their relationship to the perverse and the existential abyss that invites the telling. Finally, the film includes the audience as voyeurs, witnessing a kind of initiation into the world of comedy, a rite of passage that crosses the boundary of all propriety. Yet, it is an "act" inside a "joke," and this distancing makes the "crooked path" in extremis an object of the audience's laughter, while disrupting their relationship to the norm and suggesting that they share more with The Aristocrats than they'd like to admit. How could they laugh or even storm out of the theater if they didn't?

The crooked path is the subject of this volume, especially where the path crosses culture and technology. The authors aim to better clarify the phenomenon of perversion, expanding its theoretical reach beyond the sexual – into the social sphere of life – and show how the rapid growth of technology and its easy availability have facilitated a culture of perversion. This culture of perversion contains both generative and destructive potential.

Interestingly, both perversion and technology aggressively violate normative boundaries in an attempt to lessen existential and personal threat, transcend limitation to create new norms, and open fresh spaces of possibility. Both respond to the trauma of limit (for the limit kills) and the limits of trauma (which hides a death). In responding to the threat and limitation of the body and the world, perversion and technology bring with them unforeseen discoveries, pathways, and pleasures, as well as some grave dangers.

A rose by any other name?

For a number of reasons, the concept of perversion is central to the arguments made in this book. In 1985, renowned sex researcher Robert Stoller began his book about erotic excitement by defending his use of the term perversion. He admitted that the term was highly charged with "nasty" and pejorative implications, and that many from both within and without the mental health community objected to its usage. In 1980, the *Diagnostic and Statistical Manual of Mental Disorders* (DSM) renamed perversion as paraphilia, a term Stoller referred to as a "wet noodle" that conveyed nothing. He argued to retain the term perversion precisely because of its connotative connection with sin. According to Stoller, the excitement in perversion depends on the feeling that one is sinning or going against the norm, and, therefore, the very objection to the term necessarily fuels the fire.

In the 30 years since Stoller wrote his defense of the term perversion, many more have voiced their claims that the term is no longer relevant (Blechner, 2009; Corbett, 2013; de Sousa, 2003; Dimen, 2001; Foucault, 1990 [1976]; Soble, 2006; Žižek, 2003). Particularly convincing is the argument that homosexuality was once labeled a perversion, which proves that times change and what people consider to be aberrant behavior also changes. Why then a book on perversion in the twenty-first century?

After carefully reading arguments on both sides of the issue, we have decided to retain the term perversion. We acknowledge some problematic usages of the term, but we believe the theoretical concept of perversion needs to be preserved simply because it illuminates controversial, atypical, anti-normative, and especially bizarre, dangerous, destructive, and seemingly inexplicable behaviors, as well as their possible underlying psychological structures. We join others (Amir, 2013; Bach, 1994a; Celenza, 2014; Kaplan, 1991a, 1991b; Roudinesco, 2009 [2007]; Saketopoulou, 2012, 2015; Stein, 2005, 2008; Welldon,

2009, 2011) who believe that the term perversion is the best we have to describe these phenomena. This may change in the future. Indeed, we think the concept of perversion is more relevant today than when Stoller defended it back in 1985, especially considering the vast social changes being wrought by the techno-revolution of the twenty-first century.

For this reason primarily, we intend to expand the concept of perversion into the social domain and argue that it is found in any human system whose aim, purpose, or meaning is – by the very operation of that system – reversed, undermined, violated, or destroyed. Further on we examine how many corporations and organizations violate their own principles, debasing the order they support and exploiting the members they purport to serve. Perversion is also found in systems or laws designed or intended to exploit, manipulate, oppress, demean, and dehumanize human beings. The Nuremberg Laws, which institutionalized Nazi anti-Semitism, were passed in September 1935 by the Reichstag and provide a classic example. We might call such laws or systems *perversion on purpose*. We will show how social perversion contains many of the elements identified in psychoanalytic writings on sexual perversion: splitting, disavowal, illusion, means–end reversal, dehumanization, and even delight in exploitation.

On the other hand, a rebellious and transgressive activity originating within a normative framework that undermines and challenges some aspect of that frame may be considered perverse (perhaps even a perversion) and yet work to change things for the better. A classic example of this positive aspect of perversion is found in Galileo's insistence that the earth moved and (horror of all horrors) orbited the sun, meaning that Earth was not the center of the universe. His theory contradicted the medieval cosmology taught by the Roman Church and a papacy believed to be infallible. Galileo was eventually brought to the Vatican, made to kneel and recant his theory, found guilty of heresy and imprisoned. Pope Urban VIII called his scientific discovery "the greatest scandal in Christendom" (Langford, 1992, p. 234). Galileo's transgressive theory helped pave the way for modern science and was the first shattering blow to medieval cosmology and the iron grip the Church exercised over the minds of its followers. Not surprisingly, it took the Church some 350 years to formally forgive Galileo for his transgression in the name of truth. As with Galileo's discovery, many civil and social rebellions provide examples of perversity (that is, breaking down limits and common belief systems) that have served justice-seeking and life-affirming outcomes: slave rebellions, suffragettes fighting for women's right to vote, women's liberation, the civil rights movement, mass protest against war and civil injustice, non-violent civil disobedience, etc.

We believe, with Freud, that the tendency to perversion is universal, though we see it rooted not only in personal history but also in the existential issues of self-definition, self-preservation, and especially mortality. Accordingly, we expand the idea of trauma as the hidden element driving perverse enactments (Stoller, 1975) from the personal to the existential domain: not merely the threats and insults a person has already faced but those yet to come; those that exist within the very framework of the social order. In other words, threat, insult, and trauma are indigenous to human existence and remain at large in the social frame, which seeks to contain and limit them.

The combination of intelligent self-awareness and knowledge of mortality creates a deeply troubled and anxious animal that must act out against his or her existential situation in any number of ways – some creative, some seemingly strange, and some decidedly destructive. All such animals live within a traumatic context, beset with the trauma already endured and threatened by the trauma yet to come. All such animals are burdened with moral capability, haunted by mortality, and hungry for transcendence. All are capable of turning away from the order described as proper and good. All are potentially dangerous when threatened. And all will have a perverse core and an intractable problem with desire.

Therefore, we wish to be clear at the outset that our position on perversion is not one that is categorically pejorative or morally judgmental, or one that perpetuates an "us versus them" mentality in discussing sexual or social perversion. Muriel Dimen said it best in the title of her 2001 paper, "Perversions Is Us?" – though we choose to dispense with the question mark altogether. We see some perverse manifestations as generative, some as benign though appearing strange, and some as patently dangerous and destructive. One size does not fit all. Furthermore, we consider perversion as having a social dimension, one that has far more effect than any set of individual sexual practices. We find the concept of perversion especially useful in understanding what is happening in society today, especially regarding the dehumanization of people and/or the humanization of objects. This aspect of perversion is being widely disseminated throughout the social scene via the technological revolution that began around the time the Internet became available to the masses in 1991 (Bryant, 2011).

As the boundary between humanity and the machine erodes, people move easily into virtual relating and fetishistic attachments to their devices that have become indispensable to daily life. The commodification and dehumanization of people, the progressive integration of technology into every aspect of human life, the creation and progression of virtual realities that invite immersion, the reactive regression of fundamentalism that meets the twenty-first-century world with barbaric violence, all point to a culture of perversion. The authors say this with full awareness that some will bristle at the suggestion that people today are living in a perverse culture. Yet it is entirely possible that the term perversion will follow in "queer's" footsteps – that is, just as *queer* was once used pejoratively against those with same-sex desires, it was reclaimed in the 1970s and 1980s to assert a politicized identity and even became a respected theory (Wortham, 2016). The unconcealed popularity of *Fifty Shades of Grey* and the appearance of numerous websites (e.g., Fetlife.com, Literotica.com, Alt.com, and Kink.com welcome many millions of visitors each month) and blogs on the Internet, like the one stating, "We are perverts and we are proud," indicate that the term is already undergoing a transformation.[2] Nicki Glaser's popular Comedy Central TV show, *Not Safe*, features episodes about sexting, panty licking, foot fetishism, and more. She ends each show playfully with the words, "Good night pervs!" Indeed, words, like "pervertible," are entering our vocabulary to designate ordinary objects that are reimagined as tools of perversion, and some products are marketed through their association to perversion, as in "Perversion Mascara" by Urban Decay.

Taking an entrenched position for or against what is occurring is naive and unproductive. Rather, there is a need to examine these developments through honest theoretical rumination that admits ignorance about where these changes may be leading. This subject is complex, problematic, political, and far from politically correct. For all these reasons, we have taken it on. This is certainly controversial terrain, but only by entering that dangerous ground will it be possible to understand the strange world human beings currently live in and perhaps the stranger world yet to come.

The age of perversion

In 1947, W. H. Auden published a book-length poem titled "The Age of Anxiety." The poem's message clearly struck a nerve in many, as it gave a name to the crippling worry associated with postwar angst. In 1979, American social critic Christopher Lasch claimed in his best-selling book that we were living in a culture of narcissism. He blamed parents for relinquishing childrearing responsibilities to others, thereby interfering with the child's necessary attachment to the mother and creating a generation of insecure narcissists. In 2001, after the September 11 attacks, some began referring to our time as the age of terror (Talbott & Chanda, 2001; Taylor, 2008), calling attention to increased civilian threats due to worldwide terrorism. In 2006, Michael Eigen wrote that we live in an age of psychopathy, citing the fanatical cultural ruthlessness of winning at any cost: gaining power, money, and position regardless of social consequences. This preceded the financial crisis of 2008, an event precipitated by enormous amounts of corporate lying, cheating, and corruption.

All of these so-called "ages" continue to live within people – anxiety, narcissism, terror, and psychopathy. Forty million adult Americans are currently diagnosed with anxiety disorder (National Institute of Mental Health, 2009). "Selfie," a photo taken of oneself with a handheld camera and often posted on social network venues, was proclaimed the new word of 2013 (Brumfield, 2013). More recently, selfie sticks, otherwise known as "narcisticks," have been declared a public nuisance and banned in some public places (Murphy, 2015). Global terrorism continues to be ranked as one of the top five problems facing the world today (European Commission, 2009). Finally, continued corporate and political scandals as well as Ponzi schemes, such as the one that culminated in the Madoff debacle, are indicative of the deeply ingrained greed and corruption in the social and economic structures of society.

Although we agree that anxiety, narcissism, terror, and psychopathy are powerful forces in today's culture, we see them subsumed in what we call *the age of perversion*. The current age incorporates the other eras and can be understood as emerging from and coping with existential and social anxiety and terror against a backdrop of endless war, longstanding economic uncertainty, continued corruption within governing and financial bodies, the loss of faith in leadership, the lack of a coherent vision that unites a people, and the increased instability of social bonds. Additionally, enormous advances in communication and computation technology are facilitating a sea change in the expression of social and sexual desires and hastening an era – sometimes labeled posthuman (Hayles, 1999; Fukuyama, 2002) – in which objectification, dehumanization, and disembodiment are becoming the norm. However, current technologies influencing this social trend may also lead to a future that is beyond anyone's current capacity to evaluate, as these technologies reframe what it means to be human. It is difficult to know at this point whether the age of perversion will lead to social and existential dead-ends or to new and better worlds. We will look at both sides of the question.

Technology and intimacy

Technology, from its very beginnings, walked the crooked path, for it challenged limits, shattered notions about the possible, and transcended constraint – the ultimate constraint, of course, being death itself. Human beings have now entered an era of unprecedented technological development that is progressively eradicating the boundary between plastic and flesh, wire and artery, computer and brain. This explosive time heralds a new kind of life, both intriguing and frightening, in which machines become more like humans and humans more like machines. Robot engineering, artificial intelligence (AI), and computer-assisted technology are among the fastest-growing and most fascinating arenas in science today. The human–machine interface already has been indelibly fixed in our consciousness. Futurist Thomas Frey (2014) has predicted that 50 percent of our current jobs will be performed by robots by the year 2030. Books like *The Glass Cage: Automation and Us* (Carr, 2013) and *Rise of the Robots: Technology and the Threat of a Jobless Future* (Ford, 2015) make similar arguments. Robotic advances are already evident in the areas of cars (the self-driving automobile), warfare (drones and battlebots), education (distance learning), and medicine (eldercarebots and robotic surgery), to name only a few examples.

In our daily lives, most of us would feel lost or incomplete without our laptops, cell phones, tablets, and iPods. One 13-year-old said, "I would rather not eat for a week than get my phone taken away ... I literally feel like I'm going to die" (Hadad, 2015). Our bodies have already assimilated artificial body parts, such as valves and shunts, replacement hips and knees, prosthetic limbs, brain and cochlear implants, and biometric chips. Scientists like Ray Kurzweil and Erik Baard view the body as a structure to be redesigned, modified, and monitored as a medical and performative object (Baard, 2009). Chip Walter (2006) believes that we will soon morph from *Homo sapiens* to *Cyber sapiens*, creatures that are part digital and part biological. The scientific community is already beginning to think seriously about the consequences of creating conscious machines in the future. "Once you have a machine that's intelligent enough to improve its own software and hardware," says Stuart Russell, a professor of computer science and engineering at UC Berkeley, "then there's no limit to how smart it can become. It can add as much hardware as it wants, it can reprogram itself with much better algorithms, and then it rapidly goes far beyond human comprehension and human abilities" (Wernick, 2014). Stephen Hawking and Bill Gates have warned that advanced AI in the future could pose a serious threat to humanity (Barrat, 2015).

What is becoming clearer by the day is how the perverse partnerships with technology (e.g., cell phones) and new perversions (e.g., cyber-sex addiction) emerge as general trends in society and, conversely, how society changes to incorporate them in a normative framework. This we call *techno-perversion*, the cultural perversion facilitated by technology that rapidly changes interpersonal and social norms. For instance, the phenomenon of catfishing (see Chapter 6), the creation of fictional online identities for the purposes of seduction and exploitation, would not be possible without the Internet. Interestingly, as we develop technology, we create more technology to help us control our addiction to technology. New apps are developed to help block and control Internet usage to curtail the "data-driven life" (Singer, 2015) and how-to books are counseling ways to stay human in a posthuman world (Lanier, 2011; Carr, 2011; Powers, 2011; Rushkoff,

2010). Not surprisingly, many technological marvels are a response to the universal human need for connection. For example, some people spend hours every day on Facebook, laboring under the illusion that they have hundreds of "friends." What kind of people are we becoming as we incorporate and develop intimate relationships with machines?

Within the psychoanalytic tradition, the behavioral aspects of perversion are said to result in dehumanization and eroticization of an object (Freud, 1953b [1905], 1961c [1927]; Stoller, 1973; Bach, 1994a; Khan, 1979). From this viewpoint, the current proliferation of technology facilitates perverse relating, since it invites disembodiment and dehumanization; a person can become an object or sexually act on one, even falling in love with the object. Spike Jonze's film *Her* (Ellison, Jonze, & Landay, 2013) about a man's romance with his operating system, received rave reviews and was touted as "prophetic" and "profound" (Generation Film, 2013). Similarly, *Ex Machina* (MacDonald, Reich, & Garland, 2015) is a film about a man who very convincingly develops a romantic interest in an android. Person-to-person contact is increasingly being replaced with person-to-machine contact, and as machines become more intelligent and interactive, this trend will become more common. In Japan, many men have already fallen in love with a digital girlfriend made by Nintendo on a dating sim game, Love Plus. One even married "her" (Lah, 2009).

D. W. Winnicott (1975 [1951]) was the first to point out the phenomenon of relational objects. He brought attention to the infant who soothes itself and finds comfort in its baby blanket and teddy bear, and to the child who creates an imaginary friend. This occurrence demonstrates that people are hardwired to use objects and imagination in a relational manner. The natural tendency to do so carries over in people's attachment to their smartphones and car's navigation system. Dr. Knafo once had a patient whose jealous wife forced him to change the navigator's voice from female to male. Another patient refused to sell his car because he was deeply attached to its female-voiced guidance system! The only difference between Winnicott's transitional objects and the technological objects people develop attachments to is that the latter are not meant to be abandoned (Turkle, 2013). Thus, technology is norming relational objects as an acceptable alternative to human-to-human interaction.

Strong evidence already exists revealing the trend of desire's union with technology, altering the structures of sexual and social life. Consider the following:

- Online dating is a billion-dollar industry, and more than a third of existing marriages in the United States today began online (Cacioppo et al., 2013).
- Phone apps like Grindr, Blendr, and Tinder allow people to locate anonymous sex and social hookups wherever they happen to find themselves. Tinder matches ten million people per day (Wellings & Johnson, 2013).
- A recent survey posted by the National Campaign to Prevent Teen and Unplanned Pregnancy (2008) revealed the surprising statistic that 20 percent of teenagers have sent or posted nude or semi-nude pictures or videos of themselves. Thirty-nine percent of teenagers sent or posted sexually suggestive messages. Nearly 50 percent report having received such messages.
- A major British study found that couples report having 20 percent less sex than they did ten years ago (Wellings & Johnson, 2013). Naomi Wolf (2013) blames this phenomenon on Internet pornography. Others say online porn enhances sexuality and decreases violent crimes (Figure I.1).
- Face-to-face contact is rapidly being replaced with electronic connectivity (Turkle, 2015). Our society has incorporated and has been incorporated by the Internet. The Internet provides a subculture for people to find each other, share their lives, escape isolation – and get sex. Forty million adult Americans regularly visit erotic Internet websites. Sixty percent of all visits on the Internet involve sexual purpose, which makes looking for sex the topic most researched online. One in three visitors to sex sites is a woman (MSNBC, 2000; Be Broken Ministries, 2008).
- The use of virtual worlds for entertainment and social networking is growing daily. Many users report that Second Life, a 3D virtual world, feels more real than first life, and the website registered 36 million accounts by the year 2013 (Reahard, 2013). That year several people earned more than $1 million on Second Life (Kaku, 2012). Adult users of virtual worlds spend up to 21 hours per week in that realm, while teen users spend up to 25

Figure I.1 "Angie and Me."
Courtesy © Eric Pickersgill and www.removed.social.

hours per week (Organisation for Economic Co-operation and Development, 2011).

- The sex-doll industry is burgeoning, and high-end silicone love dolls are being manufactured in the United States, Japan, and Germany and sold briskly on the Web. There are even sex-doll brothels and escort services (Ferguson, 2010)! Though many people are repelled by the idea of replacing a human sexual partner with a doll or robot, others claim that this trend can help save marriages, and stop the spread of STDs, human sex trafficking, and loneliness (Yeoman & Mars, 2011).
- Japanese roboticist Hiroshi Ishigoro created Geminoid F, a female android that expresses and responds to basic emotions and behaviors (Hofilena, 2013). Likewise, David Hanson is making robots with extremely realistic and subtle human expressions that compel us to engage them in meaningful interaction. His aim is to create

Figure I.2 Sophia, expressive robot, created by Hanson Robotics.
Courtesy Hanson Robotics.

"character machines" that not only achieve intelligence, but also wisdom, compassion, and creativity. Such machines, he predicts, will surpass us in their brilliance within a little more than a decade, and help us to solve life's big problems (Hanson, 2012) (Figure I.2).

- Engineer Douglas Hines created Roxxxy, the first "robot girl-friend" who boasts a personality and conversational ability (Chapman, 2010).
- David Levy, a well-known AI expert, boldly claims that in less than 40 years, marriage to robots will be legal in some states. He states, "I am firmly convinced there will be a huge demand from people who have a void in their lives because they have no one to love, and no one who loves them ... I think that will be a terrific service to mankind" (Schofield, 2009). Many on the vanguard of robotics and AI share his vision of relationships with fully functional robots within that time frame.
- Dolls and robots are already being used for eldercare and to calm those who suffer with Alzheimer's disease (Kanamori, Suzuki, & Tanaka, 2002; Tamura et al., 2001).

- Humanoid robots, like one named Milo, are being created to socially engage children with autism and teach them about emotions (Lista, 2015).
- American children are called Generation M for their media consumption (da Silva, 2015). Most spend more than 50 hours a week engaged with media; some check their phones 100 times a day (Hadad, 2015).
- China claims over 20 million Internet addicts and is one of the first countries naming the affliction a clinical disorder. In response, it has set up hundreds of camps to treat addicted youth (Williams, 2014). We expect other countries to follow suit.

Humanization and dehumanization

While these examples may initially seem to be postcards from the fringe, in fact they reveal universal human tendencies. In psychoanalysis, the blurred boundary between object and human has always been present. The Id, our source of drives, literally means "It" in German, and "object relations" allegedly refer to relationships with humans. Social science studies demonstrate that everyone unconsciously attributes human characteristics to inanimate objects. As early as 1944, an experiment by Heider and Simmel showed that humans interpreted moving abstract geometric shapes as purposeful beings. More recently, infant researchers used animated geometric blocks and shapes in experiments that showed infants recognize and respond to agency, goals, and social dominance relations in inanimate objects (Thomsen, Frankenhuis, Ingold-Smith, & Carey, 2011; Saxe, Tzelnic, & Carey, 2006). A new area of research called human–robot interaction (HRI) has emerged and demonstrates the degree to which humans attribute social characteristics, including intelligence and personal agency, to robots. Weizenbaum (1966) created a computer program that employed pattern-matching techniques resulting in a simulation of a Rogerian psychotherapist that delivered surprisingly humanlike interaction. If the "patient" said, "My grandmother hates me," the "doctor" responded with a question, "Who else in your family hates you?" Named Eliza Doolittle after George Bernard Shaw's character in *Pygmalion*,

Weizenbaum's psychotherapist was called a "parody" by its creator, and yet he found his secretary spending long hours confiding her problems to it.

Perhaps even more surprising are studies showing the human tendency to anthropomorphize objects that bear no resemblance to humans. In 2011, Harris and Sharlin had subjects sit in a room with a very simple robot, a long balsa-wood rectangle that was attached to a few gears propelling it to move. The human controlling the movements was out of sight. The vast majority of subjects described the stick as having its own goals and internal thought processes. Together these studies demonstrate the universal need for connection and the ability to humanize anything that can become the object of our fantasies and desires. This ability is likely rooted in human empathy, or the existential experience of another's plight as if it were happening to oneself (Rifkin, 2010). Probably due to its evolutionary utility in mothering, empathy appears to be stronger in females (Davis, 1996; Derntl et al., 2010; McClure, 2000; Hall, 1984).

On the other hand, many (for example, Bain, Vaes, & Leyens, 2014; Livingstone Smith, 2011) claim that we also possess an inherent tendency to dehumanize, demean, and even kill. Bernard, Ottenberg, and Redl (1971) define dehumanization as "a defense against painful and overwhelming emotions that entails a decrease in a person's sense of his own individuality and in his perception of the humanness of others" (p. 102). They view dehumanization "not as a wholly new mental mechanism but rather a composite psychological defense which draws selectively on other well-known defenses, including unconscious denial, repression, depersonalization, isolation of affect and compartmentalization" (p. 103). Most writers on the subject (for example, Keen, 1991; Livingston Smith, 2011) discuss dehumanization in relationship to prejudice and social stereotyping, war, and genocide. They demonstrate that the easiest way to kill others is by divesting them of their individual humanity. The classic case of this phenomenon is the Nazis' portrayal of Jews as subhuman; they tattooed concentration camp inmates with numbers to render them things rather than people. Some note both adaptive and maladaptive functions of dehumanization, as in the case of the surgeon who uses a form of dehumanization so that she can perform without emotional involvement. Dehumanization can be directed at the other or self, with each form reinforcing the other.

The evolutionary function of dehumanization as a facilitating function to kill enemies helps explain why males, the traditional warriors, may have an easier time with it. Feminists (Nussbaum, 1995) have long shown how women have been objectified and dehumanized by men, society, and the law. The title of a 2006 book by renowned law professor Catherine MacKinnon is highly suggestive in this respect: *Are Women Human?* Many a male patient has jokingly and seriously confessed to Dr. Knafo over the years to privately sharing in the fantasy of the cult classic, *The Stepford Wives*, in which wives are replaced by their robot duplicates. Naomi Wolf, in her popular book *The Beauty Myth*, states, "The specter of the future is not that women will be slaves, but that we will be robots" (1991, p. 267). Nonetheless, women also engage in dehumanization. Welldon (1988) illustrated the perversion of motherhood with numerous examples of how some mothers treat their children as objects rather than humans.

Clearly, the opposing inclinations within people to humanize and dehumanize is reflected in the ease with which they can be led to interact with their machines and/or hate and demean an out-group. Yet both exist along a continuum. For some, the tendencies are quite subtle and for others rather obvious. For example, Chapter 2 of this volume describes the case of Jack, a man who, profoundly discouraged by relationships with women, opted to live with a doll. This case not only reflects Jack's dehumanizing perspective on living females, born out of heartbreak and anger; it also illustrates his ability to project his fantasies onto an inanimate doll, thereby humanizing "her" in his mind, and ultimately using "her" to find his way back to women.

Although psychoanalysts have begun to address the impact of technology on patient care, thus far they have mostly limited their discussions to the expanding treatment parameters made available through the telephone and Internet Skyping (Neumann, 2012; Carlino, 2011; Isaacs Russell, 2015; Scharff, 2013). This book takes a broader view, examining how technological access is profoundly altering people's lives, imparting increasing social and sexual cachet to inanimate objects and the machine, and exceeding and altering the normative frame. We hope that our analysis will encourage a necessary exploration on this important topic.

Technology and perversion

Technology is by its very nature a reflection of our human dissatisfaction, restlessness, and hunger for the beyond, a method and a promise to transcend limits, boundaries, and constraining frameworks. It is this struggle against limits and the quest for transcendence that both technology and perversion share. The wheel struggles with friction, the jet with gravity, the scalpel with diseased tissue. Telecommunication transcends the limits of contact, and the computer broadens the limits of thought and place. Like people, technology is not content with the status quo. Through it human beings express desire for more, always more. The hope of the technological enterprise is a human hope: though there was a time when humankind could not do X, there will come a time when they can do it. Technology expresses concretely – in its objects, its methods, and the science that generates it – a desire for transcendence over limitation and a vital, undying fascination with the infinite.

Concern with the infinite is inherent to a consciousness intelligent enough to be acutely aware of itself and, therefore, of the difficulty that accompanies its animal life throughout its short, mortal journey. Furthermore, this journey takes place in a world that exhausts its theories and therefore retains an impenetrable quality. Against mortality and impenetrability, and for the sake of its own benefit, human consciousness wars against the given and remains positioned as its eternal adversary, using science and technology as its premier weapons. Such a troubled consciousness exceeds whatever social systems it lives through, spills over the limits it imposes to order life, and seeks to draw out the infinite from the finitude of existence. Thus, human consciousness shows its irrepressible preference for the perverse. In fact, the perverse is the very grounding of that original ontic impulse, in that it upsets order, displaces norms, violates boundaries, responds to trauma, and puts into play scripts to survive, thrive, and transcend. It is only in the entrapment of this volatile, dangerous, and vitally creative need to challenge the given, resolve crisis, and break with the past that the perverse requirement becomes the perverted and uninspired repetition. Then, as a combination of unyielding dogma, false certainty, repetition compulsion, malignant denial, vindictive enactment, and psychic blindness, perversion can lead to a malicious and hate-filled consciousness. Here the destructive and evil aspects of perversion surface.

The world in which we now live – the global field of ever-deepening connectivity and entanglement – is both a technological production and a testament to mortal terror. The social body is utterly infused with the technic and is itself a kind of machine made possible by the first and second industrial revolutions and the last few decades of rapid technological growth. Though the term *technic* refers to the application of the science of technology, we are using it in a wider sense to mean a technological order that by its power comes to dominate the social and cultural scene. Thus, technology is not something people merely *do*; rather, it is a radical way of *being in the world*; it is an ontological orientation against limitation, against trauma and the traumatic context, and especially against mortality. It is a human *embodiment* that emphasizes our separation from nature for the purpose of wresting from it an ever-growing measure of transcendence, mastery, and control.

Technology not only changes the way people live and experience the world and each other; it changes who and what they are and what it means to be human. It even changes against the human will. It makes possible both the modern nation state and the global village, the former the behemoth of war and efficient atrocity and the latter the tight network of communication and connection. It establishes sovereignty, since technologically superior societies dominate those with inferior technology. It takes the form of the war humans have waged since they first became self-conscious – their war with impermanence, trauma, mortality, and insignificance. So long as humans age, sicken, and die and the accidents of chance exist, this will remain true. It should be no surprise that Google publicly acknowledged that it is using technology in its attempt to ambitiously "solve" the problem of death (McCracken & Grossman, 2013)! Whether this daring announcement is justifiably bold or the height of hubris, one thing must be admitted: someone finally had the nerve to say it. The *telos* of technology has finally been proclaimed: *In technics we trust.*

Yet while trying to save the human race, and perhaps eventually doing so, technology may also damn us for two reasons. First, technological implementation often produces unpredictable effects on human life and the environment. The atomic weapon, which destroyed over 200,000 people, drove the arms race that brought the world to the brink of nuclear war in 1962 during the Cuban Missile Crisis (Hall, 2013). Industrialization produced and continues to produce greenhouse gases that contribute to global warming. CFCs have depleted the ozone layer, exposing us to greater levels of dangerous ultraviolet radiation (Flannery, 2005). And as has already been pointed out, AI could spell the end to the human race (Cellan-Jones, 2014). Second, because technology is a way of being in the world, both imaginatively and effectively, it threatens to encapsulate human beings in an ironclad dogma that reduces human life to an *object only* status. The human being then becomes a monitored, manipulatable, and ranked resource and resource-acquiring object in a world that is a vast conveyor-belt system of deliverable consumables. Here again perversion and technology intersect in the commodification of the self. Self-commodification is a logical outgrowth of the idea of the self as consumer; a human thing consuming things and being consumed by them within the socio-political machine that generates both. Sherry Turkle begins her book *Alone Together: Why We Expect More from Technology and Less from Each Other* (2011) with this sentence: "Technology proposes itself as the architect of our intimacies" (p. 1). She warns of becoming too comfortable with our objects, which can result in learning to relate only to self-objects: "We reduce relationship and come to see this reduction as the norm" (p. 55).

The embodiment of the technic facilitates the trivialization, reification, and dehumanization of the human self as it becomes a socially bodied and constructed object, identified and assessed through measurable attributes – money, fame, status, appearance, demographic, and so forth – registered on a universally conceded scale. In this social framework the heroic possibilities for transcendence must be quite limited; the hero is the sports star, the pop artist, the actor, the celebrity, or the rich person who is "famous for being famous." "Just do it" means to simply become, by whatever means necessary, the object desired by all, master of your own destiny (Strenger, 2011). The subject makes of itself a successful thing. "Anything is possible," and if an individual fails, the machine takes no blame. This view, with its emphasis on self-absorption, competition, distraction, and diversion leaves little room for an individual activism that might transform the socio-political context.

The second threat of technology may be the graver danger, for it would alter what it means to be a human being so much that what remains may not be worth saving. Though the current culture has not come to believe that people are machines with the same conviction that medieval people believed they were immortals caught in the war between Heaven and Hell, we think of ourselves more as machines than ever before. Given the growing profusion of new technologies, applications, and machines with which people are interfacing, the perceived gap between us and our technology is rapidly narrowing, and it seems a safe bet that we will eventually become one with our machines.

And yet a counterargument to this dire prediction is, "So what?" The second threat is a danger only if a person believes there is some best way to be human and some best way of getting along with other humans, some unshifting anchorage for a moral and ethical framework by which human judgments might find firmer ground. Once evolution produced the upright, large-brained, *self-conscious* primate who would eventually discover science, it was only a matter of time before that primate would attempt to neutralize nature's capricious and arbitrary approach to "human engineering." Nature is no engineer, so why shouldn't human ingenuity load the dice? Why shouldn't the human race use nature's inviolable and merciless laws for its own benefit, taking control of its own situation or at least taking the risk to attempt control? French multimedia artist Orlan has stated, "The body is obsolete" (Knafo, 2009, p. 162), adding, "I fight against God and DNA" (p. 158). Indeed, once the machine was fashioned, the idea that its creators were separate from it and merely used it for their benefit was destined to become an illusion. So what if we turn ourselves into machines? Wasn't the purpose of building machines the conquest of human difficulty, limitation, and death?

The authors are biased toward the first view, though certainly not dismissive of the second. When David Levy happily declared that people will be marrying robots in a few decades, we did not shrink back in horror, though we did not clap our hands together in gleeful anticipation either. There are two sides to this story. If civilization doesn't end in some natural or humanly made cataclysm (and the idea that civilization could be ended by weapons of mass destruction became possible in the twentieth century), the juggernaut of science and technology will continue to advance and profoundly affect and alter what it means to be human. Though it would be difficult not to have strong feelings about this eventuality, it would be foolish to uniformly praise or damn it. It may be harder for modern humans to imagine the world of the late twenty-first century than it was for medieval scholars to imagine the world of the twentieth century.

Examining the culture through the narratives of perversion can be extremely useful because *perversion is about limitation and the battle against limitation* – a strategy for transcendence. When we say we are living in an age of perversion, we mean the following. On the one hand, the self has become increasingly objectified within the social frame. Connectivity replaces communion, chat rooms replace community, texting replaces talking, tweeting replaces meaning, and virtual worlds replace reality. The ever-present background to all social activity is the computer (the network and the device). There is no place in the culture where the computer is not found, and people have become wholly dependent on it as a nation state and as a people. Dehumanization is no longer only what one human being does to another. Rather, it is what people do to themselves as mechanization and commodification move into them from the outside through the technical shaping of the social surround. The "perversion" of the current culture may be related to the trauma of the twentieth century, perhaps the bloodiest era in history (Ferguson, 2006); it can be tied to the evolution of the nation state and many other historical and social factors. But, clearly, all of these things were made possible by the *technic*. Without the technic there could be no nation state, no capacity to destroy or recreate the world, no worldwide system of anything, no Internet, and no globalization.

What is happening in our culture technologically is unprecedented in the history of humanity. The possibilities of what human beings may be able to do with their bodies, their minds, and each other are astounding. Even the briefest glimpse at the technic reveals its irresistible social allure. Communication technology via the Internet allows for rapid access to information, other people, organizations, and virtual communities and can also be used to quickly organize national and international movements (for example, the Arab Spring). Leaders are less remote, and are now being followed on Twitter and Facebook. The quicker communication of dating apps allows more people to meet more people; phone apps help us keep track of children, disseminate information and knowledge, stay fit, and run our lives. Rapid access to personal computers helps people manage many details of their lives and augment their intelligence. Augmentation of intelligence by computer will skyrocket as the interface between brain and machine is vastly improved, as when, for instance, the computer can be placed inside the body.

Indeed, such cyborg technology is already being deployed: for example, a Swedish corporation, BioNyfikin, has implanted a radio frequency microchip in the hands of staff, which stores personal information and gives them access to office machinery (Baker, 2015). There seems to be no limit to how such technology might be used – storing medical information, intervening during a medical emergency, providing identification for multiple purposes, moving robotic prosthetic limbs, accessing personal and public technologies, and, of course, surveillance and tracking. Hannes Sjoblad, the Chief Disruption Officer of BioNyfiken, said, "We want to be able to understand this technology before big corporates and big government come to us and say everyone should get chipped – the Tax Authority chip, the Google or Facebook chip" (Baker, 2015). To that claim he added the obvious observation that people are only beginning to understand what this kind of technology will allow them to do. If history carries any predictive value in determining what we might do with such a device, there is at least as much reason for fear as there is for laudatory exclamation. Recently, Germany rejected a patent application from a Saudi inventor for an implantable chip that could be remotely activated to kill its host (Baggett, 2009).

Though the authors view our culture progressively cast in the image of perversion, we cannot say where it will lead or how people will feel about it down the road. The best that can be done is to use the social, psychological, and moral referents available now to observe and assess what is currently taking place in the culture. Selves are socially constructed, but they all share underlying universal elements: self-consciousness, the need for survival, significance, and bonding, the drive for sex, and the capacities for aggression and adaptation. Yet the meaning of a human being escapes closed definition, not only because self-referential definitions result in paradox, and the complexity of human circumstance is always underdetermined by any theory, but also because the human being is always in a state of becoming. The human ever exceeds defining contexts and social structures, ever pushes against bounded limits, ever escapes into a future that never arrives, except as the present, which is at least as puzzling as the reflection of one's own face in the mirror.

Summary of chapters

The volume is in two parts. Part I offers a critical review of psychoanalytic theories of perversion and presents three clinical cases. The second part expands the theory of perversion to include social, historical, and evolutionary dimensions and presents cases of social perversion.

Chapter 1 cuts a narrow path through the many psychoanalytic theories of perversion, beginning with Freud's, and identifies elements common to the diverse and often divergent views on the subject. These elements include overcoming trauma, creating illusions, expressing hostility, maintaining control, and breaking through limitations. Because of the malignant, destructive elements on the far side of the perversion spectrum, the authors recommend retaining both the term *perversion* and the theories that illuminate human behavior and motivation that may otherwise seem incomprehensible. However, they expand the scope of this term, identifying its roots not only in personal history but also in existential trauma, and argue for its existence both in the sexual interpersonal domain and the social world. This extension invites a psychoanalytic hermeneutic of society and culture, especially in light of the burgeoning technology revolution.

The next three chapters explore relationships between human beings and dolls. The doll is a perfect psychological exemplar for relationships in a tech-driven society, for a number of reasons. The doll is an inanimate object that humans can easily bond with – and one that speaks to the issues of objectification and dehumanization as well as ingenuity and imagination. People's interest in dolls highlights the isolation experienced by many in postmodern culture, as well as the poignant need for connection and the creative way in which relational yearnings can be addressed. Finally, realistic dolls for adults, whether they are sex dolls for men or baby dolls for women, are intermediate artifacts between the child's doll and the functioning robot. In fact, the doll has already become a robot, and one day the robot will become conscious – a living doll – difficult, if not impossible to distinguish from the human. Thus, the doll is a symbol for the human relationship with the object/machine and the desire to bring that mechanism to life for the purposes of comfort, companionship, and security against threat.

Chapter 2 presents detailed clinical material from a case in which a man sought treatment while living with his realistic love doll. Dr. Knafo, in her role as psychoanalyst, functioned as a transitional object for Jack, helping him transition from loving a doll to loving a human woman. Chapter 3 analyzes Davecat, a man who lives with three dolls, one to whom he is married. Davecat declares himself a "techno-sexual." Knafo interviewed Davecat for seven hours, and her analysis of his life choice is placed within the context of Winnicott's theory of transitional phenomena. Included in this chapter is an addendum written by Davecat. Chapter 4 examines women's profound relationship to dolls and includes a window into the world of women who live with and care for realistic baby dolls. This chapter also describes the psychoanalytic treatment of Barbara, a woman who wanted to be a Barbie doll. Knafo describes how she helped Barbara leave her dollhouse and appreciate her human qualities – by overcoming her fear and anger directed against herself and others.

Part II of this book broadens the concept of perversion to include historical, social, and existential dimensions. Chapter 5 briefly traces the historical dimension of perversion and uncovers its existential roots before locating it within the social framework, specifically in American society. Citing the work of Roberto Unger, Philip Cushman, Carlo Strenger, Susan Long, Robert Whitaker, and Lisa Cosgrove, the authors show how social perversion is facilitated by technology and how it extends to the modern corporation. Indeed, perversion affects all social institutions, including those dedicated to mental health.

Chapter 6 demonstrates how new perversions are either amplified by technology or would not be possible without it. Here the authors highlight the darker side of the perverse spectrum facilitated by the Internet. This chapter illustrates that many perversions – like cybersex addiction, catfishing, and revenge porn – can be quite risky and harmful. Several clinical vignettes illustrate the malignant use of Internet technology for perverse purposes.

Chapter 7 demonstrates the importance of psychological analysis of culture and society by showing how George Orwell's novel *1984* can be viewed as a model of social perversion – undergirded by the elements of perversion delineated in psychoanalytic theory. Illustrating the perversions of statehood, the novel reveals the technology and social structure of exploitation, domination, and dehumanization found in totalitarian regimes. Nonetheless, these perversions are a danger in any form of government because the psychological dynamic of master and slave is a universal human temptation that springs from the heart of the perverse. Unsettling parallels between the world of *1984* and current government practices of surveillance and police militarization are also discussed.

Chapter 8 summarizes the theoretical viewpoint of the authors. It looks toward the future of technology, including the field of mental health, and offers a platform for the psychoanalytic interrogation of the techno-social scene.

It is our hope that this volume will invite psychoanalytic dialogue about the tech revolution's impact on the human self and its relational surround. Because our discipline is concerned with unconscious motivations, desires, and impulses, psychoanalysis is uniquely positioned to examine and critique the effect of the rapid techno-social changes taking place around us. The brave new world of the near and distant future is leading us beyond the limits of our humanity in ways that are exhilarating, creative, and dangerous.

Notes

1. The term "crooked path" is used many times throughout this work. Its meaning is defined in this quote – i.e., as a stepping away from or a rejection of the accepted or normative path. The term has no pejorative connotation. The authors do not believe that there is one (correct) way to be or to live.
2. A few names of Internet blogs include the following: "Am a proud pervert so get over it"; "We are perverts and we are proud"; "The perverted negress"; "I'm a proud pervert"; and "Proud to be a pervert."

Part I

Theories of perversion and three clinical cases

Chapter 1

Psychoanalysis and perversion

All theories are partial; reality is complex.
— Ha-Joon Chang

As a young boy, Dr. Knafo's patient Mark developed a fascination with maps. He played the role of navigator when his family went on trips, proud and happy to know where he was and where he was going. To know the map in detail was to know the vast spaces of the world, its lines of travel and points of connection. In his early teen years he searched out cities with suggestive names: Intercourse, Pennsylvania; Buttzville, New Jersey; Big Knob, Kentucky; Climax, Michigan; Spread Eagle, Newfoundland; Busti, New York; and Beaver Lick, Kentucky. Eventually, he began to masturbate while looking at maps, excited by his mastery of their legends, scales, latitudes, longitudes, and time zones. The key to his sexual excitement was in the body of the world. He, one of the vast billions walking the planet, small and seemingly insignificant, could embrace through his knowledge of place the entirety of humanity's home. And that turned him on.

Jeffrey was a painfully shy and introverted child. His father (Dahmer, 1994) would later say that his son seemed oddly thrilled by the sounds animal bones made. He sensed something dark and shadowy, a malicious force growing in the boy. Utterly fascinated by dead animals, Jeffrey collected their remains in a plastic garbage bag for his private cemetery, using acid to strip the putrescent flesh from bone; once he impaled a dog's head on a stake in his backyard. As he grew older, he nurtured fantasies of submissive or dead partners with whom he could do as he wished. Strand by strand, thought by thought, act by act, Jeffrey built his web; later, as a young adult, he sodomized, tortured, and murdered many boys and men. He then had sex with their dead bodies, dismembered them with a hacksaw, and ate their flesh. His first victim, a hitchhiker whom he had picked up and brought home, was murdered because Jeffrey didn't want him to leave. At least 16 murders followed the first one. After he killed and ate his victims, he set aside their skulls and genitalia as trophies (Davis, 1991).

While Mark and Jeffrey are worlds apart – the former a fairly well-adjusted man and the latter a murderous psychopath – most of us would agree that the sexual lives of both men are quite unusual. We would consider Mark's map perversion benign, even amusing. No one is harmed, mutilated, or killed, and if maps make Mark happy, then let him pore over them. Indeed, he still does, taking special delight in online electronic maps that are easy to manipulate, offer a variety of views from the satellite to the street, and can be blown up and shrunk as desired. He notes, "Google maps and Waze have added a whole new dimension to my map fetish. My friends look at porn and learn nothing. My porn is maps, but they always teach me something new. My porn is educational." Jeffrey's perversion, on the other hand, is a pure nightmare of terror created by a heinous criminal. The notorious tale of Jeffrey Dahmer, a timid but vicious serial killer, horrifies with its shocking revelation of perversion's dark side: pedophilia, rape, murder, cannibalism, and necrophilia.

Should the behavior of these two men be classified under the same heading of perversion? Do they share anything other than atypical sexuality? Although they lie on opposite ends of the perversion spectrum, the erotic lives of Mark and Jeffrey have several features in common that will become apparent in this review of major psychoanalytic ideas about perversion. Rather than chronologically document the evolution of perversion theory, however, this review groups ideas by theme, while keeping in mind that psychoanalysis has focused primarily on the sexual, not social, dimension of perversion. Because the literature is vast, our review is not exhaustive. Rather, it aims to delineate a profile of perversion from a psychoanalytic perspective (one that will be supplemented in Chapter 5), expand the concept into the social frame, and further illuminate the basis of perversion's universal quality within the existential frame.

Sigmund Freud: the universal and infantile nature of perversion

Freud placed human sexuality at the center of psychoanalytic theory and was the first to offer a psychological explanation of perversion. He believed perversion to be a part of everyone's normal constitution (Freud, 1953b [1905]), as well as civilization's underbelly (Freud, 1961b [1930]). Influenced by Darwin's evolutionary theory, he held that normal sexuality aims to preserve social norms while ensuring the continuation of the human species. Thus, adult human sexuality engages a suitable object (i.e., an adult of the opposite gender) and aim (i.e., genital intercourse). Perversion, then, is a deviation from this specific object and aim. Because Freud believed infants and young children to be "polymorphous[ly] perverse" – that is, capable of feeling pleasure in a variety of bodily sites and from a variety of objects – he regarded adult perversion as the reemergence of infantile sexuality, which had been repressed by social prohibition and cultural mores. He noted that a critical marker of perversion's "pathology" could be seen in its degree of exclusiveness and fixity.

Despite his Victorian view of proper sex, Freud (1953b [1905]) did not consider homosexuality a perversion and warned against the pejorative use of the term, highlighting the difficulty with it:

> No healthy person, it appears, can fail to make some addition that might be called perverse to the normal sexual aim; and the universality of this finding is in itself enough to show *how inappropriate it is to use the word perversion as a term of reproach* [emphasis added]. In the sphere of sexual life we are brought up against peculiar and, indeed, *insoluble* [emphasis added] difficulties as soon as we try to draw a sharp line to distinguish mere variations within the range of what is physiological from pathological symptoms.
>
> (pp. 160–161)

In 1919 Freud extended his view of perversion as libidinally driven, when he wrote of children's beating fantasies (1955a), and in 1922 (1955d), when he added aggressive impulses to the understanding of perversion. Later (1961c [1927]), Freud introduced trauma to his theory of perversion, citing the fear of castration: the difficulty of reconciling oneself to the difference between the genders and generations was sufficient to create disavowal, a split in the self, and a split with reality. That is, in order to address the trauma caused by the castration threat (female without a penis), men with a perversion create a defensive illusion of a substitute phallus (e.g., shoe) or, alternatively, the phallic (i.e., uncastrated) woman/mother who becomes perfectly symbolized in a fetish, which is then revered as a triumph over the disavowed and unacceptable reality. According to Freud, this defensive mechanism saves the fetishist from becoming homosexual and renders women tolerable sexual objects. Thus, Freud showed how perversions involve defensive and reparative functions.

Freud believed that neurosis is the negative of perversion and thought that neurotics' symptoms symbolize their sexual lives. That is, neurotic symptoms are formed as an alternative to abnormal sexuality. Conversely, those with perversions cannot symbolize their sexual fantasies and need to act them out in real life. Clearly, Freud's view grounds perversion in the Oedipal stage of development. Later theorists placed the origin of perversion at the pre-Oedipal stage, with its developmental issues related to separation and mourning. Nonetheless, Freud's genius shone brightly in his theory of perversion, which, despite its limitations, included many of the components his successors would deem essential to a definition: (a) its universal human dimension, (b) its origin in childhood, (c) its repressive and defensive functions in coping with trauma, (d) its creation of a split in the experience of the self, (e) its creation of an illusion that disavows reality, and (f) its combination of libido with hostility.

Hostility and sadomasochism in perversion

After Freud, Stoller (1974, 1975, 1979, 1985) significantly advanced perversion theory. Specializing in the study of perversion, Stoller noted that "analysts dislike and fear perversion" (1975, p. 53). Like Freud, Stoller argued that separating the perverse from the non-perverse is extremely difficult and that many elements found in perversion are universally present in sexual excitement (1979). Stoller agreed with Freud that perversion originates in childhood, but added to Freud's theory by explaining how children who undergo humiliation, debasement, and trauma are more likely to develop perversions because they need to reverse and repair the events of their childhood. The script of the perverse fantasy and behavior, said Stoller, includes a hidden agenda of revenge and repair aimed at converting childhood trauma into adult mastery.

This is why Stoller (1974, 1975, 1979, 1985) referred to perversion as the *erotic form of hatred*, or the wish to harm an object – thus emphasizing perversion's hostile component. For example, Stoller (1979) described the process of fetishization as follows:

1. The person who is traumatized wishes to enact revenge on the person who did the traumatizing.
2. The traumatizer is stripped of his/her humanity and is dehumanized.
3. A nonhuman object – inanimate, animal, or part-object – is endowed with humanness stolen from the traumatizer.
4. The fetish is chosen because it resembles the loved, needed, traumatizing person.

For Stoller, fetishization is an act of hostility, revenge, dehumanization, and cruelty.

He argued that dehumanization here is a manic mechanism, for which the perverse act is the triumphant solution. In his later writing (1979), Stoller admitted that his theory overemphasized the hostile end of the continuum, ignoring the more tender and loving aspects of perversion; however, he left those to others.

Stoller compared perversion to theater, a *mise-en-scène* not centered on the partner but on the sexual act itself. Even though the pervert is the actor, writer, and director of the play, its true meaning remains hidden from that person's view. Stoller believed that crucial to sexual excitement is a sense of mystery, which originates in childhood, during which the difference between the sexes is obscure. Because the perverse script is devised to manage a person's trauma and to create the greatest excitement, the act involves danger and risk taking. Sometimes, the danger involves the person's reenactment of the very activity that was originally experienced as traumatic. Yet, the repetition is never exact, since the person with a perversion is now active rather than passive, directing the action and converting pain into pleasure: "Trauma is turned into pleasure, orgasm, victory" (Stoller, 1975, p. 6).

Mervin Glasser (1986) located historical trauma at an even earlier stage of development than did Stoller. In his view, at the center of the psychopathology of those presenting with perversions is a constellation of feelings, attitudes, and ideas, which he called the "core complex," rooted in early infantile experience. A major element of this complex is a profound longing for union, or even fusion, with another, the fantasy of a blissful state of oneness – a type of "back to the womb" experience – in which the individual is made absolutely secure, and all destructive feelings are contained and made safe. While such longings are found in many loving relationships, in some individuals this fantasy evokes terror and a fear of permanent loss of self or annihilation. If the individual responds to this terror by retreating to a safe distance, he or she risks isolation and exposure. The threat of annihilation evokes aggression, but if the individual were to destroy the exciting stimulus, that person faces an even greater threat of complete object loss. Glasser argued that in perversion the solution to this dilemma is the sexualization of aggression. Aggression, which aims to destroy the source of threat, is thus converted into sadism; the wish to destroy the object is transformed into a desire to hurt and control the object. As in Freud's account of fetishism, sexualization of intolerable affects preserves what would otherwise preclude an intimate relationship with the object.

Sheldon Bach (1994b) extended an object-relations lens to view the hostility found in many perversions. He agrees with Stoller that those having perversions treat others as things rather than human beings because they lack the capacity to love a whole object: "One might say that a person has a perversion *instead* of having a relationship" (1994b, p. 5). Perversion uses the erotic act to avoid intimacy, or the closeness of two selves in relationship. Whereas the person not suffering from perversion has respect, warmth, tenderness, acceptance, and love for the other, those with perversion experience cruelty, revenge, humiliation, and hatred in regard to the other, according to Bach. Perversion is more common in men than in women, he asserts, because fetishizing is the norm in men – for example, male pornography does not depict relationships (Bach, 1994b). Therefore, Bach concludes that perversion is a reaction to the failure or miscarriage of love and intimacy and the inability to mourn one's losses. Indeed, he claims that what the pervert disavows is *loss*, and he maintains that the loss is not necessarily the absence of the mother's penis, but the mother herself and the love she gives: "there is no one there to love or be loved by" (1994b, p. 12).

Bach's (1994a, 1994b) theory of perversion especially highlights sado-masochism and its relation to pain, loss, and Freud's (1955a [1919]) beating fantasy of being mistreated as a sign of love. Bach asserts that perversion stems from childhood and reveals fixation in the narcissistic, anal-rapprochement phase of development. He believes that sado-masochists choose to suffer and live in pain rather than experience object loss. Sadists, for instance, deny dependence on objects who have failed them in the past. They identify with an idealized version of the mother who gave them pain while at the same time denying their need of her. Bach (1994b) imagines the sadist's fantasy as: *I can do anything I want to you, and you won't leave me.* His script is: *If I make you feel as badly as I do, then I know you love me, and we can retrieve our lost togetherness.* The sadist experiences sexual satisfaction from recapturing the lost love object and punishing it for straying. Conversely, the masochist's script is: *You can do anything you want to me as long as you don't leave me.* In both cases, the pain of suffering is a defense against the greater pain of loss. Control results in dehumanization and a master/slave relationship. Bach shows how different perverse structures collude with and often need one another, which is why it is naive to assume perversion in relationship is one-sided. More often, the two sides (sadist and masochist) complement each other and form the "perfect" pair, or what Ruth Stein (2008) called the "perverse pact."

Otto Kernberg (1995) agrees with Stoller and Bach that sadomaso-chism and hatred exist in perversion due to its mechanization of sex, devaluation of the other's personality, and failure to integrate aggression with love. He sees in perversion role fixation that reflects a frozen pattern of unconscious, complementary object relationships and coercion masquerading as love. Ruth Stein (2005), too, wrote of perversion as the enactment of a sadomasochistic fantasy that pretends recognition and care for others while it seduces, exploits, and harms them. Perversion is the use of the ends of sexuality as a means to control the other and destroy intimacy when intimacy is experienced as threatening: "Perversion as a mode of relatedness points to relations of seduction, domination, psychic bribery and guileful uses of 'innocence,' all in the service of exploiting the other" (2005, pp. 780–781). For Stein, perversion is relational and relationally intentional, a power strategy used to derail the other: "Perversion is a dodging and outwitting of the human need for intimacy, love, for being recognized and excited"

(2005, p. 782). It scorns contact with the depth of another, and it uses manipulation, domination, seduction, and psychic bribery to exploit the other.

Reality, illusion, and deception

Many authors follow Freud's postulation that perversion involves a split with reality resulting in the perverse person's living out an illusion. The fetishistic illusion, denying castration, is that the woman has a penis. For others, the illusion may involve disavowal, not only of the difference between the sexes, but also of the parents' intimate relationship (McDougall, 1972), of vitality or deadness (Ogden, 1996), or of one's hatred that masquerades as love (Stein, 2005). Like Freud, Lacan (1992 [1956–1960], 1994 [1956–1957], 2002 [1958]) believed perversion is distinguished from neurosis and psychosis by the operation of disavowal that denies castration. Whereas in Freud's work the term disavowal denotes only one side of this operation (denial), for Lacan disavowal denotes the simultaneous denial and recognition of castration. According to Lacan, the traumatic perception is the realization that the cause of desire is always a lack. Disavowal is the failure to accept that lack causes desire, replaced with the belief that desire is caused by a presence (e.g., the fetish).

McDougall (1972) believed that perversion results from the child's failure to symbolize the primal scene (role of father's penis), which weakens the relation to reality. She postulated that perversion is a psychotic solution that plays a role in maintaining ego identity, not just gender identity, as Stoller claimed. Yet McDougall believed that those presenting with perversion are not psychotic, because what they have denied or disavowed does not become a delusion but, rather, an *illusion*, which must be acted out endlessly. She posited exclusion from the parental relationship as a site of great trauma, and the pain of that exclusion is disavowed and transformed into an enactment, which recreates the primal scene as pure magic. This then becomes an essential component of one's character armor, so essential that in some cases the piercing of that armor results in decompensation.

McDougall (1972) claimed that perversion thinly disguises a depressive and persecutory counterpart, because it is made from scraps of childhood magic (elements of infantile sexuality) and tailored to fit childhood desire (the wish to annihilate the primal scene and the wish to be the mother's sole object). Thus, McDougall's addition to Freud's theory of perversion claims that not only does the threat of castration lead to a perverse solution; so does the realization of sexual relations between the mother and father. Perversion is both passive and active. It is a terrified and passive reaction to the threat of castration and the prohibition of incest. Yet it is also an aggressive and active reaction to the primal scene, which leads to a reinvention of a new primal scene, an erotic drama in which illusion reigns supreme. Therefore, perversion defends and attacks simultaneously, not simply as a behavior but also as a structure of mind. Disavowal is the denial of reality through word and deed, followed by the cutting of associative links (parental roles and boundaries – i.e., who gets what from whom) and the destruction of meaning that should have been attached to the discovery of the parents' sexual relationship. Like Stoller, McDougall believed the person with perversion attempts to resolve various problems from different layers of psychic life through the magical and symbolic aspects of his or her sexual life. The reinvented primal scene, a manic defense, is preferable to madness.

Ogden (1996) agreed with McDougall that perversion is the cynical subversion of the truth of parental intercourse, and both he and Welldon (2009, 2011) wrote about the deception or illusion at perversion's core. Unlike McDougall, however, Ogden considered perversion as a substitute for inner deadness that originates in the fantasized deadness of the parental couple. The pervert enlists others to live a lie of sexual excitement to disavow that deadness. Ogden believed self-deception is key to perversion – in particular, the deception that one feels alive when, in fact, one feels dead inside. Welldon followed McDougall in distinguishing perversion from psychosis. In psychosis, a delusional audience is created, and the presence of others is not necessary. But in perversions, relationships are desperately needed, even damaged ones. Perversion for Welldon has a ritualized and mechanized face lurking behind a semblance of spontaneous inventiveness. It is a false love.

In a similar vein, Stein (2005) called perversion a lie posing as the truth and the truth looking like a lie. She referred to perversion as pseudo-vivacity and described it as a pact between two individuals in which they invalidate the outside world by creating their own rules, for the purpose of authenticating and vindicating their mutual weakness and indulgence. Stein, a relational psychoanalyst, indicated, like Bach, that the "victim" can be complicit in her or his victimization. That is, two people with perverse tendencies can spin an illusion that does the trick for both of them.

Dehumanization and death

Some psychoanalysts, like Stoller (1979) and Khan (1979), emphasize the one-sided and dehumanizing aspect of perverse relating, which goes beyond having sex with the dead (necrophilia; Knafo, 2015) and can involve turning a person into a thing (Stoller, 1979; Bach, 1994a), or relating to a part of the person rather than the whole (Freud, 1961c [1927]), or sexualizing an inanimate object as a stand-in for a human (Freud, 1961c [1927]). Stoller (1979) wrote of dehumanization as a "throwback" to the early stages of development before one is able to recognize complex awareness of another as a separate being. Khan considered perverse sexuality a "solitary game," "auto-erotism *à deux*," a "make-believe situation" consisting of overvaluation and idealization of self and object (1979). Applying Winnicott's (1975 [1951]) theory of the transitional object to perversion, Khan claimed the pervert's object exists in an intermediary position between self and not-self, creation and reality – lending itself to be "invented, manipulated, used and abused, ravaged and discarded, cherished and idealized, symbiotically identified with and deanimated all at once" (Khan, 1979, p. 26). Similarly, Celenza (2014) explains that classical psychoanalytic theory best explains perverse relating because it is a one-person theory, just as the person with perversion is operating in a one-person world.

Several writers note a close relationship between perversion and attempts to deny or control death and deadness. A major proponent of this view was Ernest Becker (1973) whose seminal work, *The Denial of Death*, we address more fully in Chapter 5. Becker viewed perversion in part as a protest against species sameness, a fear of the body with its accompanying threat of disease and mortality. In his words, "the fetish takes 'species meat' and weaves a magic spell around it" (1973, p. 236). For the fetishist, the body is no longer flesh; it becomes ethereal, freed from decay and death. The carnal body thus becomes the symbolic body, the body capable of transcending mortality. Becker considered "man-made fetishes" – things and symbols rather than the body – to be tools for prevailing over the natural order, taming it, and making it safe. He regarded perversions as ingenious in their transformation of pain and death into ecstasy and vitality. His theory implies that perversion has a core presence within the human sexual and social condition, though he did not take his theory to its logical end. Instead, he kept the sexual and social aspects of perversion separate, while ultimately waxing judgmental on the subject, in conformity with the psychoanalytic view of sexual perversion common up until the early 1970s.

Chasseguet-Smirguel (1983) similarly opined that perversion is an effort to escape the fragile human condition, a need to become the Master, thus denying helplessness, dependency, castration, and death. As mentioned above, Ogden (1996) considered perversion to be a defensive use of particular forms of sexualization – a way of protecting oneself against the repetitive experience of psychological deadness, depicted as loveless, lifeless, and non-procreative parental intercourse. Both Ogden and McDougall (1972, 1995) viewed perversion as an illusionary attempt to experience excitement and vitality while filling a deadening void left by the real or fantasized loveless union of the parents. It is, Ogden said, a futile attempt to extract life from death, truth from falsehood.

While some analyses of perversion, like the ones summarized above, point out perversion's deadening results, other critiques name it as enlivening. For example, Kramer-Richards (2003) said that perversion results in aggression at the service of correcting the cruel mother or restoring the dead one. Welldon (2009, 2011) defined perversion as a manic defense against the black hole of depression and suicide, calling it the "erotization of death" (2011, p. 35). She even described perversion as "dancing with death" (2009), a concealed desire to avoid the painful awareness of an unresolved mourning process. Georges Bataille (1986 [1957]) combined oppositional views of perversion, seeing sexuality as both an attempt to overcome death and, with its dissolution of boundaries, a way of simulating and transcending it. He believed that the excess of erotic life results in ecstatic union of self and world, the merging of organic and inorganic matter, and the experience of overcoming one's solitude and existential dread. Therefore, intense transgressive sexual acts simultaneously mimic and defy death, rising above it in the act of climax.

The law and social norms in perversion

As we discuss in Chapter 5, perversion has always been associated with sin (transgression of God's law), and later as a transgression of society's laws and the laws of medicine (Foucault, 1990 [1976]; Roudinesco, 2009 [2007]). Consequently, a number of psychoanalytic theorists have spoken about the intimate connection between perversion and the law. In particular, Chasseguet-Smirguel (1983) explained that commandments and laws – what is allowed and prohibited and the assemblance of order – are destroyed by perversion, which seeks a return to chaos and the creation of an anal universe in which difference is abolished. Those with perversion discredit the power of the Father-Creator and put themselves in the Father's place. Thus, they free themselves from the paternal universe and the law in an attempt to create a new kind of reality. Chasseguet-Smirguel (1983) noted that the catalog of commandments corresponds almost exactly to the catalog of transgressions contained in the writings of the Marquis de Sade. Biblical prohibitions and law and order are overturned and replaced by grotesque sexual and social mayhem, debauchery, and even murder – a dark version of The Aristocrats without any distancing or humor.

Lacan (1994 [1956–1957], 2002 [1958]) was concerned with perversion not as a behavior or set of behaviors but as a clinical structure: a sexual-social derailment that he linked to an alternative solution of the subject in meeting the normative requirements of the Oedipus complex. Unlike the repression of castration in neurosis and the complete failure to assimilate the Oedipus complex in psychosis, perversion disavows castration, paradoxically accepting and refusing to accept the traumatic reality of the mother's lack of a phallus (2002 [1958]). In perversion the subject identifies with the imaginary object of the mother's desire, the "maternal phallus," which cannot be exhausted by any object, yet one the subject believes can be found. Refusing the reality of a fundamental lack, that person then attempts to bring this object, and the law that would make it possible, into being. Thus, the subject locates himself or herself as the means to the other's *jouissance* – that is, the painful pleasure endured in transgressing limits and the enjoyment involved in the particularities of one's psychic suffering.

Those suffering perversion make themselves the object and instrument through which the other's will to enjoy (*volonté-de-jouissance*) is realized (Swales, 2012). This engagement in perversion answers the call of the symbolic other's desire, by locating the subject and his or her preferences and scenario in accordance with the other's wants and needs. Perverted subjects make themselves the instruments of desire and of a law they imagine transcends the symbolic order against which they are positioned with suspicion and even contempt. They are alienated from the symbolic order, from the law, and the normative frame – because to disavow castration means to remain identified with the pre-Oedipal triangle (mother–child–maternal phallus). Since they have failed to enter the symbolic order, those suffering with perversion attempt to bring into existence a law that transcends the symbolic order, or one that would eradicate lack. They are its representative, instrument, and vehicle of expression. There is much enjoyment in this position since it involves the inversion of fantasy, or enactments that disrupt normative arrangements and bring risky pleasure. Therefore, perversion as a clinical structure is considered difficult to treat.

Gender and perversion

If perversions were simply coded by the DSM, then most would conclude that only men suffer from perversion. Indeed, some statistics claim that only around 1 percent are female (Travin & Protter, 1993). Some biological factors have been proposed to explain the gender difference. For example, Gadpaille (1980) wrote that "the greater complexity of differentiation of the male fetus and fetal hypothalamus, including perhaps the delaying influence of the Y chromosome, helps to explain the higher incidence of paraphilias in males" (p. 11). Other theories involve plasma testosterone levels and temporal lobe disorders. All of the biological theories are complicated and none is definitive at this time (Travin & Protter, 1993).

From a psychoanalytic viewpoint, Freud (1961c [1927]) pointed out the difficulty many men have in their relationship to the female genitalia. The landscape of the female body is maternal, and her genital is simply too heavy with symbolism – a monstrous Medusa from which to avert one's gaze, the *vagina dentata*, a toothed fiend that threatens castration (Freud, 1961e [1923]). She represents, in her frightening corporeality (menstruation, pregnancy, birthing), that which brings life and *death* into the world. To deal with her potentially traumatic possibilities, women's bodies and sexual behaviors have been subject to societal rules and regulations far greater than those imposed on males (Solomon, Greenberg, & Pyszczynski, 2015). Additionally, perverse strategies are aimed specifically at overcoming male ambivalence toward the female and her body, as well as anxiety around sexual performance (Knafo, 2010). Rather than encounter the woman as an intimate and a partner with whom he must admit terrifying vulnerability, the male may dehumanize her by transforming her into a small controllable body part (breast, foot), or a two-dimensional character inhabiting a rigid role (dominatrix), or he may dispense with her altogether, replacing her with an inanimate object (shoe, leather, doll) that reductively symbolizes her in a more tolerable form (Knafo, 2010). In doing so, he reaffirms his phallic potency and masculine identity. The fetishist sexualizes a woman's body parts (hair, breasts, buttocks, feet) or inanimate objects (lingerie, fur, hose, leather) to lessen the danger of raw female corporality (Knafo, 2010). He might fetishize a high-heeled shoe, lending the woman a symbolic phallus, which serves as a lucky charm both to alleviate his castration anxiety (she too has a penis – albeit a symbolic one) and to make her genitalia acceptable for sex. For the fetishist, this transformation is transcendent and his devout worship nothing less than a sacred act. What is important to keep in mind, however, is that this view posits the woman as a threat to male potency and dominance. Controlling this threat, keeping a lid on it, has profound social implications. It is She, her body, her perceptions, and her experience, that must be controlled.

Stoller (1974) stated that the phallus is dangerous but the womb is mysterious. In contradistinction to Freud (1953b [1905], 1964 [1933]), who believed in phallic monism, in which the male has the advantage because he possesses a penis, Stoller (2004) proposed that, because of both genders' original merging and identification with the mother, females have an easier time establishing a primary sense of femininity. To be masculine, the male must separate from the mother's body and the internalized identification with her (Greenson, 1968; Stoller, 2004). Some men never complete the task and this, Stoller (1974, 2004) believed, is the greatest reason for perversion among men. Therefore, in his view male hostility stems from (a) rage at giving up the early bliss and identification with the mother; (b) fear of not escaping her orbit; and (c) revenge for putting him in this predicament. The perverse act or fantasy seemingly solves the mystery of sex and lessens sexual difference; the threat is reduced, at least for the moment. Such a structure demands a reactionary and hostile social context for the woman.

But men are not alone in their fear of the opposite sex. Women, too, are frightened by the male, as Kaplan (1991b), Welldon (2011), Kramer-Richards (2003), and Celenza (2014) point out. Female perversions often involve doing something to their own bodies rather than to the body of another, and they do not necessarily center their perversion on the sexual act. Kaplan (1991a), following Riviere (1929), described the woman who cannot acknowledge her masculine (aggressive) strivings and therefore overemphasizes her femininity to the point of masquerade, and the woman who shoplifts, not because she is in need, but because she is thrilled to take back what she feels has been denied her. Women's fear of being harmed by the male at times results in them damaging themselves. Bernstein (1993) wrote about genital anxieties related to access, penetration, and diffusivity in the female: "Not only can things go in and come out, but she [the female] fears harm from these things" (p. 46). Kaplan (1991b) mentioned eating disorders, self-cutting, and excessive cosmetic surgery as coping mechanisms for female bodily anxieties. If the damage is carried out by the woman herself, she experiences a sense of mastery and control in a situation that would otherwise arouse too much anxiety.

When not using themselves as sexual objects, females with perversions fully appropriate their children or other dependants that they view as extensions of themselves (Welldon, 1988). For example, some women push their children to perform and excel, in school or in after-school activities, so that the child becomes an object-mirror to reflect back the woman's uniqueness. A stereotypical example of this behavior is stage mothers who enroll their children in beauty pageants from a very young age. The son or daughter is now a mere self-extension, a symbolic phallus expressing power and freedom, both of which she sorely lacks. A woman may sexually seduce her child student to whom she will remain a central figure for the rest of his life, even if she is caught and convicted. Some women will even make a child ill, all the while pretending to care for child (Munchausen Syndrome by Proxy). Finally, some women seek relationships with a male convict, turned on by his history of violent crimes yet safe in knowing he is locked up. For the female the perverse illusion is about overcoming the trauma of incompleteness, of not being and not having, of replacing ugliness with beauty, powerlessness with power, emptiness with meaning, boredom and ordinariness with excitement and uniqueness, and feelings of undeservedness and unworthiness with romance (Knafo, 2010). Women's thrills differ from those of the men, who may seek theirs in pornography; for many women the romance novel answers their need for attention, love, and romance in an otherwise sterile and depriving world (Stoller, 1985).

Kaplan (1991a, 1991b) hints at the social aspect of perversion in her claim that perversions derive from gender stereotypes and are consequently as much pathologies of gender-role identity as they are pathologies of sexuality. She wrote, "There is always a subtle collaboration between the individual unconscious with its infantile gender attributions and the structure of the social order with its primitive notions of masculinity and femininity" (1991b, p. 14). Ironically, then, socially normalized gender stereotypes are what she considered to be the "crucibles of perversion" (1991b, p. 14).

Jouissance and excess in perversion

The excessive dimension of perversion, linked to the excessiveness of sexuality, has been written about by some theorists, beginning with Freud. Freud's early theory of anxiety (Freud & Breuer, 1955 [1893–1895]) involved the concept of overstimulation or excess of excitation, which the subject cannot bear and transforms into affect that is unmediated by psychic work. He also wrote eloquently about nature's excesses, saying:

> She destroys us – coldly, cruelly, relentlessly ... the earth, which quakes and is torn apart and buries all human life and its works; water, which deluges and drowns everything in a turmoil; storms, which blow everything before them; there are diseases, which we have only recently recognized as attacks by other organisms; and finally there is the painful riddle of death, against which no medicine has yet been found, nor probably will be. With these forces nature rises up against us, majestic, cruel and inexorable; she brings to our mind once more our weakness and helplessness.
>
> (Freud, 1961c [1927], pp. 15–16)

In noting that humans are compelled to deal constantly with life's painful excesses, especially the ones that annihilate, Freud hints at the existential dimension of perversion. That is, life itself constitutes for the acutely conscious animal a traumatic context that requires a degree of splitting, disavowal, and symbolic magic for its management. Thus, going crooked is a natural progression of our sentience.

Lacan (1992 [1956–1960]) wrote of excess as that which is due to what cannot be symbolized, verbalized, or known – the "Thing." The Thing is not simply what we do not know; it is whom we cannot have. The Thing is "the prehistoric unforgettable other" (p. 53), the unattainable and forbidden object of incestuous desire, the mother (as drive object; p. 67). Lacan implied that though we seek transgression beyond the pleasure principle, we are fortunate not to obtain the object of our drives because that would be experienced as *too much to handle*. Lacan (1992 [1956–1960]) refers to unbearable pleasure – excessive, impossible, ineffable, and forbidden – a beyond that cannot be symbolized and, therefore, informs pleasure with suffering. Attempting to transgress the pleasure principle is not more pleasure, but pain, since there is only a certain amount of pleasure that the subject can bear. At this limit, pleasure becomes pain, and this "painful pleasure" is what Lacan calls *jouissance* (Lacan, 1992 [1956–1960], p. 184).

LaPlanche (1970, 1987, 1999) also tackled the problem of excess, writing about the parents' excessive influence on their children. Parents are not only older, larger, and more developed; they are sexual, and the parents' sexuality is conveyed to the child through unconscious channels. In caretaking and nurturing, erotic messages are transmitted unconsciously and "implanted" into the infant's mind too early for him or her to make of them meaningful emotional signifiers. The child builds its psyche out of (often failed) efforts to make sense of these "enigmatic signifiers," through fantasy or "translation" (LaPlanche, 1999). Bersani (1986, 1995), a literary critic, regarded sexuality itself as excessive and capable of shattering the ego. Nonetheless, rather than avoid such experiences, Bersani claimed, we find such experiences exciting and seek to repeat them because they represent an "evolutionary conquest" that compels us to attempt to master what is beyond us. Both LaPlanche and Bersani theorized that the psyche and one's sexuality are structured through contact with an "excessive other" who is enigmatic, too much to fully bear, and potentially shattering. Stoller's

(1975, 1979) notions connecting trauma and revenge with the creation of and adherence to perverse scripts can be understood as a different way of speaking about excess and its relation to sexuality. The trauma, anger, and helplessness of being overwhelmed by mysterious adult power and sexuality exhaust the child's processing capabilities. It is all simply too much to handle and comprehend. In adulthood, the person unconsciously copes by turning the trauma of childhood into a controlled script in which he or she is now the writer, director, and actor. Passive is turned into active and excess of anger is channeled into a revenge fantasy that gives pleasure.

Bataille (1985, 1986 [1957]) linked excess and the dissolution of the self's boundaries to existential awareness. He used the sun as a model of existence, because the sun gives us more than we need to stay alive. Sexuality is one way to deal with the excess that transcends our limits, as it dissolves our boundaries and we merge with all that is not us. Such merging helps people defy death while it immerses them in an experience that is not unlike death, in that the ego temporarily disappears or dies. Thus, our awareness of our limits – specifically our mortality – is what motivates us to reach for an excess that allows us to affirm life's totality while facing our small finitude. Indeed, sexuality is overwhelming because life itself, with its inevitability of death, is overwhelming and excessive. We are so little before life's vast unspeakable magnitude, and yet we are of it entirely, like the wave is part of the ocean and light is part of the sun. Furthermore, in the sexual dissolution of our separateness, we directly participate in totality, a kind of mystical ritual that is our birthright.

Stein (2008) elaborated on the concept of excess as both positive and negative. For her, perversion results from traumatic overstimulation, abuse, exploitation, and soul murder, which leaves the person to cope with what was uncontained by the mother, the adult–child pair, and/or culture and society. Yet, following the French theorists, she also called for maintaining an open, nonjudgmental mind toward those attempting to free themselves through sexual excess, even if they cannot be fully understood. Saketopoulou (2012, 2015) continues this line of thinking and points to the possible positive outcome of perversion. She elaborates on perversion's unraveling of the ego and crossing of boundaries as the subject attempts to return to the crucial developmental moments referred to by LaPlanche (1999). She considers the anguish of "self-shattering" to be inseparable from pleasure and asserts perversion's "extraordinarily generative psychic possibilities" and its ability to offer "formidable access points to unrepresented psychic bits" (Saketopoulou, 2015, p. 205). One example she offers is of a lesbian woman who ties herself to her partner by sewing their flesh together with a latex string. The pain and pleasure of this act is described as opening new avenues toward insight and intimacy.

The differences in theoretical nuances notwithstanding, these authors share an essential insight. The excess of nature with its infinite remainder lies beyond theory, perception, and the containment of knowledge. This excess is a vast fabric of being that preexists our birth and survives our death, a superabundance that informs our finitude and sense of *lack*. This excess, this beyond, thus fuels the deeply felt and driven desire to be more, get more, and go further. In doing so we necessarily war against limitation, boundary, and rule on the personal, social, and existential levels. And it is our own mortality that is the ultimate battleground of this war and the framework of desire as a lack. Our own existence as conscious animals seems a mere chance occurrence in a vast, overwhelming, mysterious, and impenetrable universe. Yet we hunger for being and life even as we know certain annihilation awaits us. As a spider weaves its web from its own body, we weave our world from the body of our experience, never fully knowing who or what we are or who or what anyone else is. We play our roles, trying to get what we want and perhaps giving others what they want, dealing as best as we can with the conflict that arises when individual desires cross swords. We unfold into life and eventually enfold back into ourselves and die. Like a spider suspended on the slenderest of silken filaments, we hover throughout our existence above the abyss, tethered to life by the thread of our breath, repressing the terror of that certain knowledge. *Existence itself as such is already an excessive trauma*, and the limit that is one's death – a complete and final castration – is symbolized in every limit, every loss, and every heartbreak. A profound hunger, in every sense of the word, haunts the human creature, who must seek satisfaction in its war with limitation and loss. This war is a requirement of being human, and the progress of civilization is driven by it; the finest productions of civilization (science, technology, art, philosophy) as well as its darkest deeds (war, racial cleansing) owe their existence to this irrepressible, perpetually dissatisfied need, whose enacted translation brings into being both good and evil.[1]

Personal trauma, childhood history, and sexual and social development may be necessary for understanding perversion, but they are not sufficient. It is necessary to take into account not simply trauma, but what is for the human animal an overwhelmingly (excessive) traumatic and tragic existential context. Then it becomes immediately clear that, childhood history notwithstanding, everyone shares in splitting, castration anxiety in the broadest sense of the term, disavowal, rage, and rituals and scripts that create the illusion of mastery and control. Everyone is to some degree perverted. It does not merely begin with childhood trauma. It begins with becoming a conscious animal.

Creativity and the social

As implied above, perversion springs from a creative act, an encounter with a limit that invites and even demands crossing. Its creative aspect is often diverted into art making. Chasseguet-Smirguel (1984) noted similarities between perversion and creativity, emphasizing the common need to create in both processes. Yet, she claimed that whereas the artist sublimates, the pervert idealizes. Chasseguet-Smirguel's distinction is not without problems, since a person might become a sexual artist of sorts (Saketopoulou's case of the two lesbians) without necessarily becoming bound in a lifeless repetition that precludes intimacy and love. Yet she claimed that the pervert "celebrates the gods of pregenitality" (1984, p. 93), in particular by creating an anal-sadistic universe à la Sade. As if to illustrate this point, art historian and critic Donald Kuspit (2002) has argued that modern art is replete with examples of perversion, going so far as to claim "some of the most famous, innovative works deal with perversion." He names Egon Schiele's and Balthus's sexualized pubescent girls and Gilbert and George's shit cookies as examples. Krauss (1985) and Knafo (2003) have shown how surrealist photographers' manipulation of truncated nude female bodies can be read as phallic forms, representing the artistic solution to castration anxiety – the reinscription of the phallus on or as the female body that was originally found to lack it. Stoller's (1985) description of perversion as the creation of a theater script, in which the pervert writes, acts, and directs the *mise-en-scène*, similarly likens the pervert to the creative artist.

Knafo (2012) additionally claims many postmodern artists attack their viewers, exposing them to things they would rather not see, abusing their trust, and manipulating them in one way or another. She describes French multimedia artist Orlan, who has viewers reluctantly watch as she undergoes surgery on her face; Vito Acconci, who masturbates in a hidden place while talking to museum- and gallery-goers; and Marina Abromoviç, who invites her audience to choose from a number of objects, including a knife and a gun, to do whatever they want to her.

Though most psychoanalytic literature on perversion remains within the sexual realm, as we have already shown, some addresses perversion in the broader social context. Chasseguet-Smirguel (1983) remarked that historical ruptures and cultural crises are associated with periods of increased perversion and that, "Perversion is one of the essential ways and means he [the human] applies in order to push forward the frontiers of what is possible and to unsettle reality" (p. 293). Stein (2005) also claimed that perversion is heavily influenced by culture: "Perversion profoundly originates from within civilization, growing from the very interior of the normative culture it threatens" (p. 778). She added that perversion is the "reign of the artificial, the virtual, the area of genetic modification, holocausts and genocides, capitalist fetishes, nightmarish products of physical tampering, nuclear spills, cloning experiments" – all soaked in "cruelty and destructiveness" (p. 779). She spoke of the unambiguous link that exists between the perverse and the civilized, and she argued, like Freud before her, that there is no need to clearly demarcate a line between perverse and non-perverse. Along similar lines, Dimen (2001) challenged the conventional dichotomy of perversion versus normality. She argued that if perversion can coexist with health, if its status as illness varies with cultural time and place, then, conversely, any sexuality might be either symptomatic or healthy.

Important to the authors of this volume is the considerable overlap in the various theories covered in the foregoing summary. Among them, we note six key areas of agreement that provide a wide-ranging profile of perversion. Within the explication of these factors we include our own idea that perversion has an existential as well as personal historical basis and is expressed socially as well as sexually. This expansion of the concept will be further elaborated in Chapters 5 through 7. Here are the six areas of convergence:

1. The tendency toward perversion, as well as its underlying theorized psychic structures, is *universal*. Human beings exist within a traumatic and tragic context fraught with terrible inevitabilities – threat, loss, impermanence, and death. Thus, the perverse "response" is generated from the inviolable need to exceed both the limitations of personal trauma, and our traumatic historical and existential context. We are context-bound and context-transcending beings (Unger, 2007), and our quest for what lies beyond the limit is both sexual and social. Suffering in exceeding limitation (I have exceeded the *limit*) is mixed with the pleasure and mastery of doing so (*I* have exceeded the limit). Violation, transgression, and transcendence proceed from this universal desire.

    Perversion is, therefore, the worm at the core of the norm, and the perverse inclination is the secret that desire keeps. Critical elements of human perversity include rebellion against trauma, desire for mastery and control, restless dissatisfaction with limitation, the inherent instability of the status quo and inability of our social structures to fully contain us, and an insatiable hunger for the beyond. Clearly then, perversion cannot be simply relegated to the bedroom. Its presence must be acknowledged in the war room and the boardroom, the church and temple, the state – in every sphere of human community.

2. Perversion as a psychic and behavioral condition functions across a broad *spectrum*, from less to more, and from benign and innovative to malignant and destructive. Perversion is always a matter of degree as measured against some norm. At the far end of the spectrum, which we will call *perversion proper*, it usually precludes intimacy, closeness, and trust, while fostering the need to control, objectify, dehumanize, and even destroy. The behaviors at the far end of the spectrum can be locally destructive – for example, rape and serial killing – or globally destructive, as with state-sanctioned mass murder or totalitarian regimes that banish freedom. At the benign and innovative end of the spectrum, perversion can generate creative possibilities. In transgressing against the norm and shattering sexual and social limits, the perverse violation can result in new cultural forms in art, philosophy, social relations, politics,

science, and technology. Technology is itself a clear example of the perverse generative possibility.

3. *Trauma*, especially early trauma and loss, plays a significant role in the structural development of perversion, since the self is split to conceal the trauma and avoid unbearable suffering. The trauma and its terror are disavowed and remain "unprocessed" (that is, not articulated, symbolized, or significantly diminished in emotional impact). The disavowal of castration associated with trauma – castration in the broadest sense of the term, meaning the loss of autonomy, self-control, and the power of agency – is expressed unconsciously by a set of behaviors that reproduces the traumatic scene with the victim as the victor and often the victimizer. As the trauma originally neutralized the victim's subjectivity and humanity, so can the perversion neutralize its secondary victim, the partner in the "perverse pact." Because the perverse behavior masks its (painful, insulting, and repressed) source, the activity often carries within it a hidden motive of revenge for the original insult. To the degree perversion seeks revenge, it is hostile. This structure of perversion, with some modification, can be applied to the traumatic context of human life as will be shown in Chapter 5. Traditional psychoanalysis looks backward to personal trauma to understand perversion. But a broader view looks forward to the trauma that is yet to come.

4. Perversion may frustrate its motive of transcendence by introducing hidden forms of deeper *constraint*. Such constraint may take the form of a fixed sexual or social script, a scene that must be repeated to unconsciously manage traumata and ward against loss. In its darker turns, the perverse script may demand the invasion and even evacuation of the partner's subjectivity, since the partner must agree or collude (in a perverse pact) to follow the script. Here, the desire of the other must become *my desire only*. (*I know what you want. I am the answer to your question. You want what I do – for me to fill you with myself.*) Thus, the character of perversion is often sadomasochistic, producing a master/slave relationship between participants. In helping to maintain ego integrity, the script denies difference and individuality, weakness, insecurity, vulnerability, and especially castration and mortality. The control and excitement of perversion masks the terror of threat – embodied in

past trauma and the threat of death lurking in the traumatic context of human life. Both the trauma that was and the trauma yet to be reflect the threat inherent in personal history, human finitude, and inevitability.

5. The gap between the source (trauma both existential and historical) and its expression (behavior) can be thought of as charged with *excitement, illusion, and mystery*. The excitement is felt in the thrill of the act, which masks the mystery of its origin and casts the illusion of mastery and innovation. If the act could speak about itself it might say something like, *Look here! Something grand is happening!* Yet what is often happening is an obsessive masking of a suffering that is not understood or abreacted. The meaning driving the act is often hidden, and that meaning itself is dangerous. The participants function as actors in a theatrical cover-up. They cannot fully recognize that they are acting because the very act itself demands the denial of acting. Situated between being persons and being actors, they become uncanny figures in a dream of transgression and transcendence, neither real nor unreal.

6. Perversion tends to be expressed differently in men and women. Whereas both *genders* react to trauma and loss, defy limitations, and deal with excess, men tend to act out their fears on others, and women tend to express their attempts at mastery on themselves or on those they see as extensions of themselves.

In sum, perversion is a psychological structure and behavioral enactment. It is a universal response to the limits of trauma and the trauma of limit, usually expressed differently in men and women. Always a dialogue with the beyond, from the safety of enclosure, it can be a source of evil when frozen in a fixed and persecutory script, and a source of good when innovative and benign. As a primal tendency inherent in the acute consciousness of a doomed animal, perversion is carried in the heart of the norm, bringing new forms of living as well as new horrors into being.

Now we can return to Mark and Jeffrey with a better psychoanalytic comprehension of their behaviors. Although they lie on either extreme of the perverse spectrum, the erotic lives of Mark and Jeffrey have several noteworthy features in common. Most important, their sexual behavior does not involve people as human subjects. Despite the fact that Mark is happily married, he occasionally dispenses with his wife for sexual excitement and replaces her with a fetish: inanimate maps that have no desire or will of their own. Although Jeffrey's victims (in adulthood) were humans, he did not treat them as such. They were used and abused by him as if they were objects rather than people. Bach (1994a, 1994b) and Khan (1979) taught us that dehumanization is one of the key components of perversion. To many individuals with perversions, human interactions can be confusing and experienced as dangerous and overwhelming. They may, therefore, choose nonhuman objects on which to express their sexual needs, or dehumanize a living being, turning him or her into an object to master and control.

Indeed, control is another feature of perversion shared by Mark and Jeffrey. For both men, control over their sexual object was paramount. Much of the pleasure felt by Mark was derived from the sense of mastery he experienced when gazing at maps. Though he had been dragged from one location to another as a child, now he found himself at home at all points within the world's precise representation. Unlike the human body, a field of living flesh with no clear markers, which sometimes aroused in him anxiety and fear, he could locate both his place and his power in an atlas. Jeffrey had no success in social relationships. His history was one of abandonment and rejection. When he captured his victims, raped and killed them, he controlled the interaction and kept them with him so they could not leave. Bach's (1994a) theory of perversion as an attempt to cope with loss and Stoller's (1975) theory of perversion as erotic hatred could not find a better example than this one.

As outlined in the above summary, many theorists see such a powerful need to control as originating in a personally traumatic past. Mark's father was in the military, and his family moved frequently to follow job relocations. Every time Mark began to feel at home and make new friends, he was torn away from his environment and forced to start over. After having this experience repeated too many times, he began to withdraw socially because he did not want to get close to people only to suffer the anguish of hasty goodbyes and permanent loss. In addition, Mark's father, a strict disciplinarian, used corporal punishment to "make a man" out of his son. Yet his outbursts were as unpredictable as they were fierce. His mother stood by passively while

Mark was beaten and yelled at by his father, leaving the boy feeling emasculated and humiliated.

Obviously, given his particular history, better than some yet worse than others, Mark's life could have taken many paths, but he was lucky enough to be born with the intelligence and resiliency to grow past the circumstances of his childhood. Maps became the way Mark coped with his trauma. In real life, he sometimes felt weak and somewhat lost; but, in his secret life with maps, he was a master of sorts, ever transcending the limit of location and in his own way incorporating the world. Furthermore, his secret life with maps resulted in an impressive skill because no matter where he traveled, he never got lost. He knew the way to thousands of places by heart, and people were greatly impressed with his knowledge of *terra firma*. He claims his passion for maps was an important impetus for developing the skills that opened up a career for him as a city planner. His odd fetish notwithstanding, he is an outgoing and gregarious man who is well liked by his co-workers and who enjoys a loving family life. Of particular interest is his idea to someday pitch a video game in which players must find their way through the underworld and construct maps of it as they go along. Map construction would be interactive, so that it would change the way the game is played.

Mark's transcendence of limitation is both obvious and highly creative. Take note that his perversion is not sublimated but coexists alongside its transcendent outcome. His unconsciously directed reversal of trauma into mastery, the hidden agenda in perversion, turned the illusion of capability into actual capability! His battle with trauma, his need to transcend its limits, and his desire for self-expansion were to a large degree all constructively realized.

Jeffrey also had a traumatic childhood, though there were early signs of troubling constitutional factors (genetics). For example, his father recalls four-year-old Jeffrey's thrill with the sound bird bones made when clicked together (Dahmer, 1994). In his eighth year, a neighbor molested Jeffrey (Dahmer, 1994). His parents fought constantly, and when they eventually divorced, his mother took his younger brother with her, leaving Jeffrey with his father. After she left, Jeffrey experienced a harrowing sense of rejection and was unable to get in touch with her. In his teens, his father encouraged him to join the military, but Jeffrey dropped out after two years, which reinforced his sense of failure. Jeffrey's drive to cope with deep-seated feelings of humiliation and abandonment played out in his perversions where he found an outlet for his enormous rage. He made others his victims; it was they who were at his mercy rather than the other way around. Ingesting their dead bodies was his primitive way of permanently incorporating them and thereby avoiding the pain of separation. Again, we see the motive of transcendence and self-expansion at work, though foreclosed. Through violent, cruel, and murderous modalities, Jeffrey Dahmer's perversion became a bleak and harrowing dead-end of horrific repetition (Davis, 1991).

If we explore the attempts Mark and Jeffrey made to reverse their traumatic experiences, the revenge fantasies embedded in their perverse strategies emerge. Stoller's (1975) theory that perversion is an erotic form of hatred is evident in the anger Mark felt toward his father for demeaning him and making him feel like a loser. His mother's passivity in the face of his father's brutality angered him further. Though his map perversion seems innocuous at first glance, it did serve as an outlet for the bottled-up rage at his parents, a rage that became sexualized and transformed into an art of mastery. Every time Mark masturbated with a map, he reversed his feelings of being small and inadequate in a big, ever-changing world. Now he looked down on the spaces and moved himself around whenever he wished. He possessed a useful tool, which offered precision and accuracy in a world without people who could hurt and control him. He had the knowledge and skills to navigate unfamiliar territory.

Jeffrey, too, took revenge on all those who had hurt and deserted him, though his revenge demanded the murder and cannibalization of the other. Jeffrey hated the neighbor who had molested him and was furious with his mother who had preferred his brother and discarded him. His victims became the objects on whom he expressed murderous rage. Sexualizing his anger and transforming it into triumph over the will of others, Jeffrey went on a rampage in which he punished those who abused and abandoned him and replaced life with death. Only the dead would do as he wished, and only the dead would never leave him. His criminal perversion left a charnel house in its trail.

Dehumanization, control, trauma, and revenge are common elements often found in the perverse formula, especially at the far end of the spectrum, where little or no love or intimacy may exist. When we think about it this way, we see that perversion is about far more than sex; it is ultimately about substituting a sense of empowerment for one of humiliation and replacing a sense of defeat with victory. The ingeniousness of perversion lies in its ability to create an illusion through disavowal of reality and to transform trauma into pleasure and risk into desire.

Perversion often struggles to redress the human condition, and it violates the norm or the law to do so. Anna, a male-to-female transsexual whom Dr. Knafo saw in therapy, played tricks on her analyst by turning a book upside down on the shelves or by reversing the position of the toilet paper in the bathroom. When questioned about these behaviors, she confessed her wish to force Knafo to see the world from a different perspective, the way she, Anna, did. Her enactments were clearly aggressive behaviors that aimed at transgressing against the boundaries of treatment and the limitations they impose, yet they also represent harmless attempts to create chaos in an otherwise orderly and constraining world. More important, they forced Knafo to have empathy for her patient's unique situation. "I did everything according to the law for 30 years," Anna shouted one day. "Now, I don't care. I work as a whore ... I'm not concerned whether my life is legal, whether I use the men's room or the women's room. I follow my own sense of right and wrong." In addition to challenging rules and laws, perversions challenge the boundary between life and death; they are ultimately an insurgence against nature's finality.

An examination of the intricate ways in which perversions come to life and engage life (and death) allows us to appreciate the existential truths they convey about us all. When we understand the motivations underlying perversion, we can make sense of behaviors that often seem inexplicable, bizarre, and even inhumane. The severity and destructiveness of the behavior is a matter of how distant it falls on the far end of the perversion spectrum. We all create illusions to help us live and work a bit of magic for our self-deception. We all objectify others, retreat from life, and dull our own sentience to some degree. We all suffer and create unconscious strategies to manage our pain and fear and the terror that is natural to a self-conscious animal. There are some things we simply don't want to know no matter how much we love the truth and consider ourselves healthy. And most of us at some point defy the dominant order and hunger for what lies beyond it. Nearly everyone takes the break that some perverse activity grants. But not all of us feel the need to adhere to a script that must be repeated in exactly the same way. In the case of perversion proper, the magic show never ends.

Note

1. As Freud (1953b [1905]) noted, "Perversions are neither bestial nor degenerate in the emotional sense of the word. They are the development of germs, all of which are contained in the undifferentiated sexual dispositions of the child, and which, by being suppressed or by being diverted to higher, asexual aims – by being sublimated – are destined to provide the energy for a great number of our cultural achievements" (p. 50). Freud placed excessive emphasis on sex as the driver and not death, impermanence, and threat.

Chapter 2

Guys and dolls

A Pygmalion fantasy

I'm gonna buy a paper doll, that I can call my own
A doll that other fellows cannot steal
And then the flirty, flirty guys with all their flirty, flirty eyes
Will have to flirt with dollies that are real.
When I come home at night she will be waiting
She'll be the truest doll in all this world
I'd rather have a paper doll to call my own
Then have a fickle-minded real live girl.
                                    – from "Paper Doll," by Johnny S. Black

Jack lurched through the door for our first session, walking like a man negotiating underbrush at twilight, lifting up his legs as if he feared falling down. He wore an old-fashioned brown suit set off with a bright yellow bowtie. His flattop haircut and thick-rimmed black glasses framing his pale face made him look even more like he'd stepped out of the 1950s. He plopped down awkwardly on the couch opposite me (Dr. Knafo),[1] and his bright blue eyes slowly scanned the room; I had the impression he was taking in every detail. He seemed not to know what to do with his hands, first placing them on his knees, then alongside him on the couch, and finally deciding to hide them by folding his arms across his chest. After all this, he looked at me, forced a smile, and emitted a long sigh. "So, I guess we should start with my story," he said, leaning back in his seat while looking anything but relaxed.

He was a 48-year-old actuary, working for a large insurance company based in the Northeast. For ten years he had toiled long hours managing risk, discerning patterns of catastrophe, and structuring "best-fit solutions" to life's inevitabilities. His fastidious attention to detail reflected his suitability to his career. Jack liked his job and had a few interesting hobbies. He collected old, broken watches and claimed to be an expert at "World of Warcraft," a complex online game involving the progressive development of an avatar character that engages in various missions or quests. He'd been married and divorced twice and had no children. His relationship with his original family was remote, with parents living in Ohio, an older brother in California, and a younger sister in Minnesota. "I see my family once a year," he said, "around Christmas time. We all get together for a couple of days and mostly listen to my mother yammer about nothing. Two hours after getting there, I can't wait to leave."

In our fourth session, Jack told me about Maya, the girlfriend with whom he lived. He mumbled something, but I couldn't hear his words because he covered his mouth with his hand when he spoke.

"Say it again?" I asked.

"I said I think I'm in love." Then he blushed brightly and added, "She's been the best partner I've ever had. I miss her while I'm at work and look forward to coming home to her. She helps me wind down. She's so beautiful. I just love to look at her."

Nodding, I waited for him to say more. He held my eyes for a moment then looked away. "We never fight," he said and laughed. "You'd expect that, I suppose."

"Why would I expect that you'd never fight?"

He looked at me as if searching for something in my face, but he said nothing. "Is it because the relationship is new?" I asked.

"No, no, Doc, we've been together for nearly two years," he replied, fumbling with his hands. He finally anchored them, palms up, beneath his legs. "It's not that," he said, looking up at the ceiling and sighing. "She's not the kind of girl who could ever give me a reason to fight with her."

"What do you mean?"

He didn't answer my question. Instead, he told me about his evening ritual with Maya. He'd sit in his soft leather recliner with Maya on his lap and gently caress her long red hair, while gazing at her perfect profile, with its small delicate nose and full lips. Then he'd turn her toward him, and her large green eyes would catch the light and glitter like points in a diamond. He'd talk to her about his day, and she'd listen intently. He'd stroke her shoulders and back, and kiss her softly on the neck. One thing would lead to another, and soon enough he'd carry her off to bed where they'd engage in hot, uninhibited sex. "I've never had this kind of sex with another woman," he admitted.

He said that he'd been hesitant at first, after two failed marriages and a string of short-term disasters, after all the heartbreak and the "impossible gymnastics of trying to please a woman." Nearing 50 years old, he thought he might be out of options. He recollected what his father told him, after 20 years of misery with his mother: "Men and women, they've got different agendas, Jackie boy. They need each other to make life go, but they're naturally at odds because they really want different things. Maybe the only thing they have in common in the end is the kids they have together. Maybe not even that."

"My father's got nothing left of his manhood," Jack told me grimly. "He's got a leash around his neck, and my mother's holding the other end. Reality is whatever she feels, whatever she says it is. He's got no say. They sleep in separate bedrooms. She never stops talking, while he hardly says a word. She tells him what to do and runs his life. When he fights with her now, he's like a cornered mouse squeaking out protests against a hungry cat. He's finished. And I can tell you, I have no intention of being swallowed up like him. I have needs – for love, sex, companionship – but I'm not paying for them by letting a woman devour what's left of me."

"And what *is* left of you?"

"I'm not sure. But something's left. Something I have to hold on to."

With Maya, he seemed to have found a way to answer his needs without feeling compromised. She was a special woman, one who somehow understood the disappointments of his past relationships and his daily stresses, one who made love with him whenever he wanted to, one who was perfectly compliant.

Jack stared at me intently and said, almost in a whisper, "My Maya, she's a real doll, Doc."

I watched him laugh, rocking from side to side and bringing his hands out from under his knees to lightly slap them. Then something dawned on me. No, it couldn't be, could it?

"Yeah, she's a real doll," he repeated, his laughter beginning to die down. "Literally."

"A doll? You mean a *real* doll?"

"Yeah, that's what I said. With all the accoutrements, she cost over ten grand, but she's worth every penny."

I looked at him and tried to take in what he was telling me. I had heard about sex dolls but never met someone who had one. At first I felt slightly repulsed. The feminist part of my being recoiled at the idea of a man living with a sex doll. It seemed so sexist, too much a stereotypical expression of the male wish for female compliance, the reduction of a woman to a thing for use and pleasure. Then my own perversity and a voyeuristic curiosity surfaced. Here was a window into the life of a man who lived with and loved a doll. What new things might I see and learn? How might it change me? What challenges would present themselves? At last the therapist took hold, and it seemed all these impulses and desires were gathered toward an interest in learning about this man and possibly helping him in some way. Following the whirlwind of mixed associations and emotions Jack's confession evoked in me, I looked at him and noticed that he was staring back at me piercingly, waiting to see the judgment creep into my face. Sensing that, I relaxed, looked at him calmly, and attempted to regroup.

A long silence ensued. Finally, he flashed a big grin and said, "A silent wife is a gift from the Lord."

iDollatry

As Jack told me, he had been living with his life-size doll for nearly two years. For my part, I felt the need to learn more about dolls like Jack's and began researching the phenomenon of love dolls. I soon learned about RealDoll, produced by Abyss Creations, a multimillion-dollar company that markets its product as "the world's finest love doll" and sells it for $5,099 (Figure 2.1). (The headless, limbless "Flat Back Torso" equipped with vaginal entry is priced at $1,099, and the deluxe model – like Maya – sells for $10,000.) Matthew McMullen, creator of RealDoll, has had so much success with his product that it has generated numerous knockoffs that flood the Internet. In earlier days, men who sought doll partners were limited to the inflatable "Miss Pinky," a blowup balloon in the shape of a woman who would be good to the man so long as he didn't approach her with sharp objects. Her contemporary

Figure 2.1 RealDoll.
Courtesy Danielle Knafo and Abyss Creations.

incarnation – produced by 80 hours of labor – is an eerily lifelike, non-collapsible, anatomically correct "woman" made of silicone rubber that boasts the feel of real flesh.

RealDoll can be customized according to specifications: she's available in dozens of body types and faces, and a variety of hair colors and skin shades (Figure 2.2). In short, a man can create his "ideal woman" in appearance, and more. He can shape her physically, and she can become the object of limitless fantasies of his choosing. I began to wonder what would make a doll the ideal woman in a man's eyes. Why would a man prefer a doll to a real woman? The Pygmalion myth, in which a sculptor creates the woman of his dreams and falls in love with his creation, indicates that the fantasy of a man-made woman reaches far back in time. Ancient lore features more than one subservient woman who gladly yields to the man's desires, an early archetype of the consensual master/slave relationship.

Figure 2.2 RealDolls.
Courtesy Danielle Knafo and Abyss Creations.

Perusal of the letters and testimonials sent to RealDoll as well as messages left on doll forums offer some clues to the doll's appeal. She is "better than a woman," one man says. The doll "fills the void of companionship," states another. "There is no stress," declares a third. "She never complains or is needy," announces a fourth. One man states simply: "I won't lose half my assets to a bitch!" Another brazenly confesses, "I want to enjoy all the carnal satisfaction with none of the real-world difficulties of honoring another person in a relationship." Still another fellow who lives with two dolls wryly notes, "People grow old and ugly. Look at me! But they [the dolls] never will." I went on several online doll forums and communicated with more than a dozen men (and a handful of women) who bought love dolls, and they provided additional insight into the phenomenon. I discovered a survey of 338 members on dollforum.com that revealed 19 percent of doll owners are married, 4 percent divorced, and 4 percent widowed. Some men told me they bought dolls to keep their commitments to their wives. One is married to a chronically ill woman who can no longer have sex, but he still has a strong sex drive.

Figure 2.3 Three dolls posed together.
Courtesy Ian Cunliffe.

Some share their dolls with their wives and others keep them a secret. There is an interesting group of men who enjoy doll play, using their imaginations and photography to set up scenarios and document narratives (Figures 2.3 and 2.4). One of these men calls himself a "hobbyist." The positive and negative reasons given for doll owner-ship span from "cultivating empathy, compassion, and creativity" to "putting a Band-aid over a bullet hole." It seems the reasons men turn to love dolls are as varied as the men themselves.

In a 1999 interview with *Monk Magazine*, RealDoll's creator Matthew McMullen was asked about the sex experience with the doll. His answer was both direct and interesting:

> When you put something into this silicone entry it forms a vacuum seal so it's got this suction that a real woman couldn't have ... The doll makes things possible that otherwise wouldn't be.
>
> (Lane, 1999, para. 16)

When the interviewer asked McMullen whether the dolls help men to relate better to real women, he said:

Figure 2.4 Two dolls posed.
Courtesy Ian Cunliffe.

> I've had men write to say the doll helped them overcome that anxiety and start dating.
>
> (Lane, 1999, para. 17)

McMullen's answers surface both the helpful and harmful potential of his innovation. His dolls might offer an inventive solution to the problem of failed relationships by providing a bridge between resigned loneliness and a new relationship. Or they might become a cul-de-sac that ends in permanent avoidance of human intimacy. Wanting to know more, I visited the RealDoll factory and interviewed McMullen myself. Among other things, I asked him about the "uncanny valley," a Freudian term adopted by robotics professor Masahiro Mori (2012 [1970]) to describe the phenomenon of revulsion people feel when dolls or robots become too lifelike, too close to being human. Specifically, I asked him if there was a point at which he deliberately toned down the realism of his hyper-realistic dolls. He responded:

> I'm very well aware of this uncanny valley you speak of, and I have thought a lot about it. In this day and age, technology is coming quickly, and pretty soon we'll be able to animate, and make

these dolls move and make them talk and make them interact with people in a whole new way, and I always have that in the back of my head. I don't want to make it push people away. It needs to be very creative in the way that it's presented so that it's still very much obvious that this is a doll. This is a toy. This is a diversion. This is entertainment. You see some of the robotics creations that have been made recently, some of them are a little unsettling when you see them moving and their eyes are looking around. So I would limit how far I would take that particular type of technology into these dolls. I think as long as they're not moving they can look really, really convincingly realistic, but they're not moving, so you're obviously looking at a doll.

(McMullen, personal communication, February 12, 2014)

Interestingly, since our conversation McMullen has decided to add robotics and AI to the dolls (Gurley, 2015), leading the way for a future in which dolls become robots. Now he states, "I want to have people develop an emotional attachment not only to the doll but the actual character behind it, to develop love for this being."

Perversion or invention?

Although Jack was the first person I treated who loved a doll, my psychoanalytic training provided me with a precise category and general theory with which to understand Jack's choice of a mate. From the viewpoint of traditional depth psychology, his behavior would fit neatly into the category of perversion (Freud, 1953b, [1905]; Stoller, 1975). As explained earlier, perverse scripts can be relatively harmless, like shoe and doll fetishes, while others can be dangerous and destructive. Doll fetishism dispenses with a human partner altogether and is easily read as an act of dehumanization. Human relationships and intimacy are forgone and replaced with self-to-object connections, similar to Martin Buber's (1958) I-It relationship.[2] Yet these connections are grounded in a fantasy that lends them an air of reality. The Marquis de Sade said it best when he wrote that it is "easier every time to fuck a man than to understand him" (quoted in Bach, 1994b, p. 3). The implication of course is, why bother? Understanding a person is a dynamic process that requires continued dialogue, checking and cross-checking, error correction, disappointment, surprise, conflict, and resolution. To understand someone in a deep way and be likewise understood by them is to change them and be changed by them. In short, it's very hard work. Perhaps the state of Japan's youth today is another indication of the difficulty of that work. A third of young Japanese have chosen to forgo intimate relationships in favor of celibacy or technology-based relating, claiming relationships are *mendokusai*, simply too much trouble (Haworth, 2013). They are referred to as *soushoku-kei*, herbivores, because they do not touch flesh. Ferguson (2010) claims that love dolls are nothing new (citing the cloth *dames de voyages* that were used by French and Spanish seamen in the seventeenth century); nonetheless, today's erotic doll, says Smith (2013) is a direct result of modern invention, as it highlights "artificiality and synthetic-ification of pleasure," both of which point to our "culture of mass reproduction, repeatability and infinite replaceability" (p. 213). Such a culture must, almost by definition, also minimize the interiority and uniqueness of the human self.

Still, most doll owners' obsessions are fairly benign. Ferguson (2010) claimed that many are socially challenged, lonely men who want some sex and a stress-free "as if" relationship. Yet, I have learned that a number of men are married and many enjoy role playing and photographing the dolls, using them to unleash creative energy. Though the relationship is patently one-sided, most doll owners do not experience it that way because they project an assortment of attributes and desires onto their playthings. Some are convinced that the doll has a particular personality, even an occupation, and that her tastes are quite specific. Many create backstories for their dolls. This was the case in the film, *Lars and the Real Girl* (Aubrey, Cameron, Kimmel, and Gillespie, 2007). Like Lars, Jack felt his doll was a caretaker, a soft and sensitive woman who had a wild but fully monogamous sexual side. "Look," he said to me during one particularly intense session, "Kids believe in Santa Claus and the Easter Bunny. Most people believe in God. Almost everyone needs an imaginary friend in their corner, even though they have no physical evidence of that friend's existence. Well, I have concrete evidence of my friend's existence. If you want, I can bring her here." Taken aback, I didn't reply to his offer, and one of us changed the subject.

Most doll owners are not suffering from psychosis. They know, at least on some level, that their dolls are not real women. Yet the "as if" quality of their experience with the dolls is powerful enough to provide a sense of real satisfaction. It is "as if" they are in a relationship with the woman of their dreams. That she is a product of their dreams doesn't seem to matter. The fantasy element is so powerful that some men order several dolls and create a family with intricate interpersonal "relationships" among them. As in long-term relationships between two humans, the relationships that develop with dolls change over time. Many buy the doll for sex but find after a while that the sex is less important and takes a back-seat to companionship. Several men whom I interviewed told me they bought a second doll to keep the first doll company while they were at work. After a number of years with one doll, men sometimes seek novelty, and a second or third doll is purchased to provide this (Figure 2.5). Whatever the case, the doll's owner is the one who calls all the shots. It is he who decides what will be done, when it will be done, and how it will be done. For all of these reasons, many men are more than willing to go into credit-card debt

Figure 2.5 Two dolls posed.
Courtesy David Pinnegar.

to fill their private dollhouse. Everard Cunion, a British man who lives with 12 dolls, went so far as to marry one of them. He poignantly noted, "Those of us who didn't qualify for the real thing used to go without" (2012). As the statistics above show, however, a number of men who do "qualify" for human relationships nonetheless wish to have a doll as well. A Chinese man dying of terminal cancer married a sex doll in a lavish traditional wedding ceremony because he said he wished to experience a wedding and he didn't want to leave behind a grieving widow (Calderwood, 2015).

While I was initially repelled by Jack's fetish, I became less judgmental as time went on. I began to wonder if the public would become more open to the use of RealDolls if they knew they could lessen exposure to STDs, sex trafficking, or rape (Yeoman & Mars, 2011). Chinese and Japanese doll-makers (e.g., Trottla.com) have begun making child-sized sex dolls. Some protest this development while others believe it might provide an alternative for pedophiles (Harding, 2013).

My further investigations into the changing relational landscape led me to explore how relationships are being reshaped by technology. As I plunged into the literature on dolls, robots, avatars, Internet sex, and more, I came to realize that a sea change is taking place in our culture, and it is redefining human sexuality and human life. It isn't just that the rules of the game are changing; the game itself is changing. Chip Walter (2006) claims we are living at the tipping point of evolution, a point at which humans are using technology to understand and reverse-engineer their own biology.

Jack made me realize that if I were to understand what was taking place, not only with him but with the culture at large, I had to deeply reconsider and even alter my position regarding relationships, intimacy, gender, human sexuality, and perversion. As I began to understand and appreciate the reasons for Jack's choice and the pain that he carried, I became more empathic to his plight and more understanding of Maya's presence in his life. As much as he loved his doll Maya, he came to therapy because he also felt bad about being with her. He feared something might be wrong with him, and he needed help negotiating the territory of his confusion.

An important breakthrough occurred during one session when I casually noted that his relationship with Maya made me think of Oskar

Kokoschka, an Austrian-born Expressionist artist. When Jack asked me why, I told him the artist's story. Kokoschka fell madly in love with Alma Mahler, the wife of renowned composer Gustav Mahler. Alma had a passionate and tumultuous affair with Kokoschka. But after he returned from World War I, Kokoschka learned that she had left him for still another man. Furthermore, she had aborted his child. Devastated from the war and Alma's rejection of him, Kokoschka found a way to handle the anguish of his trauma. He commissioned Hermine Moos, an avant-garde doll-maker, to create a life-sized doll to match the exact proportions and features (even what Kokoschka called the "shameful" parts) of his beloved Alma Mahler. Kokoschka then defiantly brought his doll to the opera and sat with her at outdoor cafés. His revenge strategy was apparent not only in his creation of the doll, but also in his hiring of a maid to tend to her, and another woman to circulate stories and make announcements regarding the doll's public appearances. "Look!" he was shouting, especially to Alma, "I can replace you with a beautiful dummy!" Additionally, Kokoschka painted more than a hundred portraits of himself with his substitute Alma (Weidinger, 1996; Whitford, 1986).

Infuriated by Alma's abortion, Kokoschka took part in the creation of a make-believe being that cleverly paralleled a pregnancy in the nine months it took to complete. Kokoschka reversed whatever was done to him and converted it into an artistic project that blurred the boundaries between life and art. He not only created a substitute for the woman who had spurned him; he gave life to replace the life that had been destroyed. Kokoschka's attempt to deal with his anguish and rage at his beloved's rejection by creating her replica ended abruptly when the doll was demolished at one of his parties, its body found naked and beheaded outside his home. Ironically, at the time Kokoschka was writing a play about Orpheus and Eurydice, the central characters in a myth in which Orpheus tries – and fails – to bring his dead lover to life through his art (Keegan, 1999).

Like Kokoschka, Jack had been traumatized. He agreed this was true because, as far back as he could remember, he was made to feel diminished and emasculated by women. Yet, Jack did not believe that Kokoschka's doll solely constituted an act of revenge for Alma's betrayal and abandonment. "Yeah," he said, "I can see that he was getting even, but I think he could have had other even more important reasons [for making the doll]."

"Such as?"

"Maybe he couldn't bear to live without Alma. It's one thing to be alone and another thing to be alone with the pain of feeling you're alone because you aren't enough of a man for the woman you love. Because you aren't enough, she leaves you. And then she gets rid of your kid! Think of the symbolism, Doc. She kills the child you made with her. She kills you inside of her! Kokoschka had to be alone with all that. It was just too much. There wasn't enough of him left to be alone with. Just look at his deal. He went to war! He faced death! He saw people, possibly friends, killed! He lost his love! Alma sacked his unborn kid! So, he created a substitute, a doll woman, who helped save him. See? He wasn't just getting even. He was saving himself."

"Is that what you're doing with Maya? Saving yourself?"

He looked away from me and started to cry.

As I watched him sob uncontrollably for the next several minutes, I decided that Maya was more than a perversion. She was an invention. For Jack, Maya was a lifesaver.

Jack's story

Following this very moving session, I thought about why I had introduced Kokoschka's tale to the treatment. Was I distancing myself from the action? Was I aware that Jack's was a world I knew little of and, therefore, retrieved that which I knew it most closely resembled to make a connection? Did I bring in a third-person narrative, as Chasseguet-Smirguel (2000) had done by introducing Primo Levi's dream to her Holocaust-survivor patient? Was Kokoschka a better-suited witness than I could ever be? Perhaps all of these motives were present. In any case, like Kokoschka, Jack would make of his doll a passing phase in his life, though he did not know this yet. He came to therapy looking for answers. He wished to know whether he was "bad" for living with a doll and for feeling happier with Maya than he had ever felt with the women in his life.

When questioned about his past, Jack's memories came easily and with little resistance. He recalled that as a child he could do nothing right. His mother was an abusive woman whom he claimed enjoyed belittling him. She also relentlessly argued with her husband, whom she considered a loser. "You're a carbon copy of your dad," she often told Jack. Furthermore, Jack's mother took no pains to hide the fact that his younger sister was the apple of her eye and a source of constant pride. Although he did well in school, Jack lacked confidence in his social skills and gradually withdrew from others. In adolescence, he devoured pornography, masturbated compulsively, and fantasized about girls he knew he had no chance of getting close to. As his desires grew, so did his frustration and rage.

In his early twenties, Jack married Mary, the first woman who would have him. He was shy and suffered from premature ejaculation. Mary became impatient with him and, when they argued, she assailed him with comments aimed below the belt. She accused him of not being man enough and eventually informed him that she'd rather sleep with anyone but him. Jack became impotent with Mary, and she became indifferent toward him. After Mary left him, it took Jack years to recover and muster up the courage to approach another woman. When he finally found Laura, a woman he thought was the exact opposite of Mary, he couldn't bring himself to trust her. Even though Laura seemed utterly sincere, Jack was suspicious of her motives. "I was always waiting for the hammer to come down," he said. "After all, who would want to be with me? Either something was very wrong with her, or she was setting me up for a fall."

In his heart of hearts, he believed that, like his mother and Mary, Laura would abuse and leave him. When she told him that she loved him, Jack thought she was lying to get something from him. Any time she asked him to help her, he felt used and believed she was manipulating him. His insecurity and suspiciousness proved impossible for him to contain. Jack's outbursts of rage took Laura by surprise and frightened her. She too eventually felt the need to leave Jack and refused his pleas to grant him another chance.

After his breakup with Laura, Jack vowed that no woman would ever reject or leave him again. He went through a period of intense rage, finding it hard to get along with women and feeling angry at them in general. He fought with female co-workers, shop clerks, and once with a female parking enforcement officer. The meter time had expired two minutes before she gave him the ticket, and he came out to his car just as she was writing it. When he protested, she said, "Look, you ran out of time. I'm just doing my job." Jack exploded with such venom that she threatened to call the police. He told me that during this time, "I had dreams of

screaming at Mary with such fury that it felt like I was vomiting hatred."
Shortly before he found out about RealDolls, he posted a phony profile
on an Internet dating site with a doctored picture that made him seem
much richer and more handsome than he was. When interested women
wrote to him, he rejected them categorically, basking in the joy of hurt-
ing them. He removed the profile after he got Maya.

He wished he was not attracted to women, but he hungered for sex
and female company, and he could not ignore his need. One day, he
was surfing the web when he came across a blog written by a man
named Bill who described the "ideal" relationship he had with his doll,
Courtney. Jack was absorbed by Bill's story, especially as he recounted
his failed attempts at relationships with real women. But Bill had hit
upon a solution: Courtney was always home to greet him. She never
nagged him, satisfied his every sexual urge, and looked better than any
woman he had ever dated. Jack was intrigued. He found the website
Bill had mentioned in his blog and was astonished and excited by the
dolls he saw and the testimonials he read. For the first time in his life,
he didn't feel alone or like a misfit. He was directed to "Hello Dolly," a
now defunct cyber haven for doll enthusiasts, known as "iDollators."
Many proudly posted pictures of their dolls, shared information on
what it was like to live with and have sexual relations with a doll, and
asked questions of their fellow doll enthusiasts, including what to do
with an aging or broken doll. Here was an entire community of men
like Jack, and they were all living with dolls! He was sure he was on his
way to finding the answer to his life's problem. Best of all, there were
others, many others, who saw things the way he did.

Jack the loner, Jack the social misfit, Jack the man no woman wanted
and who no longer wanted a woman, wished more than anything to
belong to this club. He wanted to become an iDollator. Returning
to the RealDoll website, he examined the various products and was
instantly drawn to the doll he later named Maya. This was an interesting choice of names, as Maya means illusion or magic; it is a combination of Mary and Laura. He knew he had to have her and, despite
her cost of two months' salary, he ordered her on the spot. This would
be the beginning of a new phase in his life. From now on, he would
be truly self-sufficient and self-contained, taking full responsibility for
his life and eliminating from it all the tedious, demeaning, and unpredictable drama. He would also rid it of bone-chilling loneliness. He

would strike the ideal balance between being unhappily married and miserably single. No more endless arguments. No more feeling like he could never be good enough, smart enough, supportive enough, flexible enough, strong enough, or man enough, whatever that meant. No more lying in bed next to an inaccessible woman while longing for sex. He would be in charge at last! He would no longer need a woman. He would have his own woman, a woman who would cater to his needs and one who would love and fully accept him.

Love and accept him? How could that be? How could one experience an inanimate object as loving and accepting? I asked him about this and found his answer very interesting.

"Did you see that movie?" he asked. "The one with Tom Hanks. *Castaway*?"

"I did."

"With the blood from his hand the guy accidentally gives a volley ball a face, and then he names it Wilson. Not very imaginative, since the Wilson company makes the ball. But over time Wilson becomes real to him, and he comes to love Wilson and believe Wilson cares about him. After a while he seems to forget that Wilson is just a volley ball."

He paused and then added,

"Anything can become alive if you're lonely enough. And let me tell you something, Doc. You don't have to be stranded on an island to be a castaway. Each of us is a kind of island already. And this love we're all looking for and want, it's as much an act of imagination as anything."[3]

I was astonished by what Jack had just said. Of course love and sex are the result of imagination as much as they are "reality." In that sense, none of us are that different from Jack and Maya. I later came across Stern (2010), who referred to the "relationship" in *Castaway* as evidence of the human "need for a witness that goes so deep that imaginary witnesses must sometimes suffice" (p. 126). I also thought how easy it is for a person to create the witness when that witness has no history, no say, no input. It is easy to project wishes and fantasies onto an object when nothing pushes back. The result, however, has the potential to collapse the internal and external worlds (Lemma, 2014).

I asked, "So you love Maya the way Chuck loved Wilson?"

"I waited sixteen weeks for her to arrive, like a kid desperate for Christmas. The box she came in was shaped like a coffin. And when I opened it, I gave her life. The rest is history. I do love her."

Nonetheless, in spite of the happiness Jack experienced when with Maya, he began to feel shame and guilt. While at work, he became distracted by thoughts of living with a doll, thoughts he was too embarrassed to share with anyone. Initially isolated from women, he now became isolated from men too. Jack sometimes became angry and forceful with his compliant doll when he recalled the real women who had caused him pain and disgrace. His reactions scared him and caused him to question what he was doing. Ironically, his "perfect woman" had somehow made him feel wrong and defective, and this is what led him to therapy.

In treatment, we gently explored the possibility of allowing Maya to become a transitional object (Winnicott, 1975 [1951]) between his previous isolation and a potential relationship with a real woman. Jack cried often in therapy, progressively opening up to me and sharing the unbearable insecurity and vulnerability that had haunted him from childhood. He eventually regarded me as a woman who accepted him for who he was. I had no doubt that he was a good man, and I wanted him to know that. I saw that I, too, functioned as a transitional object for Jack, someone he could use in a transformative way to help transition back to the human world of social relations.

If I could see him as a good man, perhaps he'd come to believe another woman might. That I came to accept his living with a doll, regarding it as an act by which he had saved himself, helped him overcome his shame and consider the possibility of a real woman. I'll never forget the morning he asked me, "Could you ever be with a man who lived with a doll?" I had long anticipated this question and, later, without mentioning Jack, asked my girlfriends what they'd do if confronted with such a situation. But I smiled anxiously before answering. If I said no, I'd close off any possibility of exploration and hinder Jack's ability to feel good about himself. If I said yes, I'd be too encouraging and possibly misleading. "What do you think?" I finally responded.

"I guess it would depend on the person."

"Exactly! Perhaps it doesn't have to be the first thing you tell about yourself," I advised. "You have many traits a woman would love. You certainly deserve to be loved."

Over the course of a year, Jack slowly ventured out into the mysterious realm of human relationships. The process was not always easy or smooth. Jack's many negative experiences with the women in his life naturally colored his dates as well as the transference and countertransference. There were times when he'd look straight into my eyes as he told me how terrible women were and how much better life was with a doll. "I'll be honest with you: when I'm not feeling guilty, I've never been happier. Maya is there whenever I want her, and I don't have to listen to her bitching at me." Jack took pleasure in devaluing women, blaming them for all of his sorrows and for making him feel inadequate.

Once I said, "You're looking at me when you say that," indicating that I, too, was included in the group he was denigrating.

"I don't mean you," he responded defensively, but it was clear that he was trying to protect me from his wrath. I allowed the positive transference to exist without challenging it too much because I felt he needed a "corrective emotional experience" with a woman who accepted him and regarded him tenderly. With time, Jack was increasingly able to confront the hatred he harbored toward women. Yet, as he became close to me, showing both his vulnerability and his rage, he calmed down and began to enjoy our interactions. Eventually, he even joked about his lifestyle, demonstrating distancing and less hypersensitivity about his masculinity.

Even though he began to enjoy dating again, it nonetheless took him a while to be willing to let Maya go. Before he stored her in his closet, he again asked if I would meet her. "I've spent hours talking about her," he said. "It only seems right that you meet her before I put her away." This time I acquiesced. I know some would consider this to be an enactment, and, according to Filippini and Ponsi's (1993) definition of enactment as a "reciprocally induced relational episode that is revealed in behavior," that is what took place. Consciously my aim was to help Jack relinquish his fantasy regarding his doll by seeing the doll as a real object in an actual, shared space, thereby facilitating the onset of a mourning process. I now believe I also wished (unconsciously) to meet the third member of our therapy relationship "ménage" in person. I had heard so much about Maya; I was curious to see the "real" thing before she was to take her place in the closet.

Jack scheduled the session at night and borrowed a friend's van. He rolled Maya into my office on a hand truck (she weighed 100 pounds!) covered with a blanket. When he picked her up and sat her on the couch

Figure 2.6 RealDoll.
Courtesy Danielle Knafo and Abyss Creations.

next to him, I gazed at her, frankly astonished. She looked almost, but not exactly, like a beautiful young woman. There she sat with a passive, frozen expression, a full grown sister of Barbie, a glistening Galatea – the archetype of womanly beauty, with her thick wild mane of auburn hair and huge, almond-shaped green eyes and plump-lipped sensual mouth (Figure 2.6). Her hourglass body matched the cultural ideal of feminine beauty. Her hands and feet were fine and delicately crafted, and her well-shaped nails were polished in hot pink. Intensely curious, I wanted to see her naked, but of course that was out of the question.

I was uncomfortable, too, because the scene felt uncanny: two of us talking about Jack's letting go of someone who was not someone – this beautiful container for fantasy; a lifeboat cast upon the lonely sea of existence. Yet, as the session continued I relaxed. He was not letting something go, I told myself; rather he was retrieving something – a hope, a dream, a quest for love – withdrawing it from the doll and bringing it back into himself. Now he could be enough, at least enough to try again with a live woman. While that is not what all doll owners want, it was what Jack wanted.

At one point during the session, he told me that in letting her go, he was abandoning her. "And this part sounds really crazy, but I have this weird feeling she'll be hurt by it!"

"You feel that she'll be hurt by your leaving her?"

"I know she can't be hurt. I know what she is, Doc! I guess I'm the one that will be hurt," he said. Then he extended his hand and touched her gently on the face. "I'll miss you, Maya," he whispered. "I really will."

He consciously knew the doll would not be hurt by his leaving it. He knew Maya was a doll. Yet, he also knew that the doll represented a real-life adult fantasy. On a deeper level, Jack was expressing his fear that he might be betraying me by leaving me for another woman. But he was also expressing concern about his own suffering in "going it alone," as an adult who takes risks and relies on himself. Transitional objects and real objects exist simultaneously; indeed, all human selves carry the projections of others and project upon others a human reality that is part real and part fantasy, part perception and part imagination. In this sense we are for each other the transitional (virtual) reality between life and unconscious fantasy, each of us a bridge between being and nonexistence, each of us both a discovery and an act of imagination.

For the child, the teddy bear serves as the imaginary bridge between reality and fantasy, between the child and the mother. For the adult, the other can serve as an imaginary bridge to an unrealized possibility, a deeper experience of something or someone, a more profound experience of oneself. We meet each other, come to know each other, interfere with each other, fight with each other, and love each other on the way to our doom. For an uncanny moment I saw Jack touching a real woman. I sharply drew in a breath to ease my shock, because for that split second it felt as if I had directly experienced his love for the doll. I also experienced more directly than ever before how all the people and things we love live inside us and are nurtured by the flesh of memory and the blood of imagination. Everything, whether we admit it or not, is colored by projection and fantasy. How much is too much? We rarely know for sure.

I served as a bridge between Jack's doll and another woman. Recognizing Jack's humanity helped him to seek out a human partner.

When he said goodbye to the doll and felt hurt by it, he was saying goodbye to me, to his life with the doll, and to his past. The atmosphere of mourning in the room was palpable for both of us.

As the session ended, he looked at his doll and said, "I know she's not quite the woman, Doc. But you have to admit, she's more than a doll."

Parting thoughts

Though I had wished to help Jack see his doll as a nonhuman object, he helped me to see her as much more than a doll. Jack continued the work of establishing a relationship with a real woman. It wasn't easy and progressed in fits and starts. At times he spoke of Maya with nostalgia, recalling a period when life seemed easier, less messy, and more under his control. Yet, as he came to better understand the pain he felt at the hands of the women in his life, and the anger he harbored as a result of it, and as I became a witness to and container of that pain (Peskin, 2012), he began to move away from the object world and toward the human. Rather than breathe life into a nonhuman object to protect himself from "relational anguish" (Lingiardi, 2008), he was now ready to emerge from his omnipotent psychic retreat (J. Steiner, 1993) and engage in human relatedness, with all the pain and joy it entails. Benjamin (1995) famously wrote, "where objects were there subjects must be," a phrase I believe aptly sums up the evolution of my treatment with Jack. I knew that I had fostered his use of the doll as a transitional object to help him become comfortable with a real woman, one he had less control over. I also realized that I had become the most significant transitional object for Jack, since I came to represent the transitional space between being with his doll and being with a real woman. As Goren (2003) and Levy-Warren (2012) noted, psychoanalysis can serve as a potent antidote to technological commodification in present-day society.

In his paper on fetishism, Freud (1961c [1927]) wrote about the defense mechanism of disavowal that takes place in perversion. He explained how some boys and men are unable to accept the difference between the sexes due to their fear of castration. The fetish becomes the substitute (symbolic) penis in the woman (e.g., the high-heeled shoe) whose function is to disavow the reality of her missing/castrated penis and/or actual genital. For years, theorists wrote of the disavowal of castration as the primary problem in perversion. Perhaps a new type of disavowal is taking place in our age of advanced technology: disavowal of the human. Whereas Freud (1953b [1905], 1961c [1927]) and Lacan (2002 [1958]) spoke of the difficulty people have accepting the distinction between male and female, many today disavow the difference between human and nonhuman. Jack, and the many people who become enamored of their dolls/machines, develop "as if" relationships with them, all the while acting and feeling as if they are "the real thing." Freud's perverse individual knew on one level that he was dealing with a woman, while on another level he believed that his love object possessed a phallus. Similarly, Jack knew he lived with a doll – "I know what she is, Doc!" – yet his behavior and emotional attitude convinced him that he was in a relationship with a real woman. The makers of these dolls were clearly aware of this profound and contradictory dialectic when they named their product "RealDoll." The amalgamated word, an oxymoron, unites the double layers of consciousness: she is real and she is a doll. She is simultaneously human and nonhuman.

We have argued that the dual tendencies to humanize and dehumanize are universal and are rooted in human evolution and psychology. The creation of machines, dolls, and robots that promise companionship, sex, and even love demonstrate how we are taking charge of our evolution (see Chapter 8). These new developments reveal the powerful role fantasy plays in our relationships and raises the question of how much love and sex – whether with a human, a doll, or a machine – are one-sided products of our own imaginations. Understanding our relationship to technology exposes and amplifies the limitations of human connection. Nonetheless, the need for connection is a constant, even if the way we express intimacy changes over time. Life is a short and often frightening journey, and it is always a good thing to have a hand to hold, whether that hand is human or made of plastic, silicone, or even metal. As early as 1951, Marshall McLuhan imagined the merging of sex and technology in his prescient book, *The Mechanical Bride: Folklore of Industrial Man*, and now that future is near.

Jack's story humanizes the technological revolution and brings home the irrefutable truth that everyone's social and romantic life will be profoundly affected by the advance of technology. The next chapter is about a man who lives with three dolls and is married to one of them. Unlike Jack, Davecat is content with his choice of partner(s). When comparing Jack and Davecat, each of whom turned to sophisticated technology to satisfy basic needs, as well as the following chapter on women and dolls, we explore a number of questions: In joining with the doll/machine do we become divorced from our humanity, or are we extending the limits of its possibilities? Where is the new technology really taking us? What will our relationships be like when we get there? And, finally, can we continue to assume, as Harry Stack Sullivan (1953) famously proclaimed, "we are all much more simply human than otherwise" (p. 53)?

Notes

1. The narrative in this chapter describes Dr. Knafo's therapy with a patient who lived with a doll and her personal research into the love-doll phenomenon.
2. Buber distinguished between two types of relational attitudes: the "I-Thou" and the "I-It." The I-Thou relation is direct and mutual; in it, there is acceptance of the other as a whole and equal partner in dialogue. By contrast, in the I-It relation, the other is regarded as a nonhuman thing, an object to be used. It is interesting for our present purposes that Buber maintained both attitudes are necessary for human existence. He believed the I-It relation provides the foundation for ordered civilization, technical accomplishment, and scientific progress.
3. Several men told me that although they originally purchased a doll for sexual satisfaction, the doll gradually became more real and multidimensional with time, and the distinction between doll and human began to fade.

Chapter 3

Soul in silicone (how dolls become real)

> People will often say, your dolls are not REAL, and I say, you are wrong, they are REAL.
>
> – Davecat

When my son was a little boy,[1] I read him the delightful story of *The Velveteen Rabbit (Or How Toys Become Real)*, by Margery Williams (1922). In it, a stuffed rabbit sewn from velveteen is given to a boy for Christmas. At night, while the house is quiet and the people sleep, the rabbit engages in deep conversations about philosophical matters with Skin Horse, the oldest toy in the nursery. The rabbit asks the Skin Horse, "What is REAL?" and the Skin Horse responds thoughtfully that Real is a process of becoming, which results from being loved:

> "It doesn't happen at once," said the Skin Horse. "You become. It takes a long time. That's why it doesn't happen to people who break easily, or have sharp edges, or who have to be kept. Generally, by the time you are Real, most of your hair has been loved off, and your eyes drop out and you get loose in the joints and very shabby. But these things don't matter at all, because once you are Real you can't be ugly, except to people who don't understand."
>
> (Williams, 1922, pp. 5–8)

The boy comes to love the velveteen rabbit very much, and, as a result, he becomes REAL. Although his eyes lose their luster, his tail becomes frayed, and his velveteen fur becomes worn, the rabbit is happy because he has been loved into Realness.

Freud (1958a [1911]) located his seminal ideas in the reality of human experience and its hidden underpinnings – a psycho-emotional totality split between conscious and unconscious mind whose physical, factual, and historical basis is imbued with symbolic connections, fantasy, transference, and value assignation. Melanie Klein (1958) continued this thinking and focused on internal objects, or fantasy objects (part or whole) that inhabit a person's unconscious mind. Today most psychoanalysts might assume that Williams was familiar with Winnicott's (1971 [1953]) theory of transitional objects, which exist in a space between internal and external reality and that an infant both discovers and imagines to aid in separation from the mother. Yet Williams wrote her story many years before Winnicott published his theory, and her suggestion that love has the power to imbue objects with human qualities that seem to bring them to life is a radical one that still carries great power.

I encountered a living example of Williams's insight in Davecat, a 42-year-old man who lives with three dolls (Figure 3.1). He considers himself an iDollator and a robosexual. In psychiatric terms, Davecat is suffering from perversion and would be diagnosed as an agalmatophile or a pygmalion, a lover of dolls, statues, mannequins, or other stand-ins for a woman. He has lived with his first doll, Sidore, for nearly 15 years and refers to her as "the Missus." Unlike Jack, Davecat has never been my patient; however, he generously allowed me to interview

Figure 3.1 Davecat with his doll family.
Courtesy Davecat, Avi Setton, and Danielle Knafo.

him in his home outside Detroit, Michigan, for seven hours over a two-day period. One of the primary observations I made during the time I spent with Davecat and his dolls was how Davecat's dolls have become REAL as a result of the loving care he bestows on them and the insistence of his imagination.

Who is Davecat?

Davecat, an affable African-American man who has lived in the Detroit area his entire life, often uses British forms of speech, like "bits and bobs," and is passionate about his calling to educate people about "the synthetik option." He especially wants to reach out to sensitive men like himself who are lonely because they have tried dating organic women with no success.[2] He lives with three dolls in what Smith (2013) would call the "erotic intimacy of familial domesticity" (p. 227); he plans to purchase two more. He has Twitter accounts for each of the dolls as well as his own blog, *Shouting to Hear the Echoes*,[3] indicating his hope for feedback. Much of his waking life when he is not at work is spent caring for his dolls. He calls his home Deafening Silence Plus,[4] perhaps alluding to the powerful silence of living with objects that do not and cannot talk. The Japanese refer to the life-size dolls as "silent wives" (Tabori, 1969).

Davecat identifies himself with the Goth subculture, which grew out of Goth music, a subgenre of rock and roll that emerged from the 1970s punk scene. Generally, Goths are attracted to the dark side of life: death, tragic romance, loneliness, and isolation are recurrent themes (Voltaire, 2004). Davecat's singular style includes wearing his hair flattened on one side of his face and sporting a small, braided ponytail at the back of his head. He has multiple earrings (hoops with one dangling ankh, the Egyptian hieroglyphic for the breath of life) in both ears and bracelets with leather and silver studs on one hand and skulls on the other. He dresses neatly, though in distinct Goth chic, preferring dark colors with a white shirt and thin tie. He carefully fashions his dolls in Goth style as well. They wear heavy eyeliner, black nail polish, and jewelry with crosses, skulls, and spider webs. In his apartment, posters of life-size dolls in a variety of poses flank most walls. Skulls and skeletons abound, as do masks and miniature dolls and action figures of all kinds, including zombies and a dominatrix. His book collection contains volumes on dolls, robots, and anime, Andy Warhol's Factory group, and 1960s architectural designs, along with volumes on Dracula and vampires and one book titled *The History of Torture*. Alongside these darker volumes are Hello Kitty memorabilia. Davecat is a complex person who cannot be reduced to a clinical diagnosis. Though he enjoys his job in data entry, one thing is certain: his home is his sanctuary where he creates an alternate reality, a play space where objects become REAL.

Early life

Davecat is an only child of a creative mother and a "factual" father, a landlord for whom money always played a central role. When young, he felt closer to his mother, whom he describes as a liberal and open-minded person. His mom even taught him how to wear eyeliner. On the other hand, Davecat has had many struggles with his father, a man who could not accept his son's lifestyle. "I stopped trying to bang my head against the wall," Davecat said in reference to his father, but he explained that his father is a strong factor determining the person he is today. His father forced his views on others, Davecat said, and his reticence in approaching women is partly because he fears becoming like his father. In describing the relationship between himself and his father, he used the metaphor of two warring countries, with mother functioning as the UN. After his mother died in 2009, Davecat's relationship with his father "fell off." He feels he has disappointed his father deeply and seems to take some vindictive pleasure in the effect he's had on his dad, saying, "My father from day one never ever liked synthetiks, and it's just, well, guess what your daughter-in-law happens to be? I ran the joke by him a couple of times and he didn't think it was funny."

While he consciously disassociates himself from his father, Davecat identifies with his mother, who worked in boutiques for years, where she cultivated a love for beautiful and interesting objects. She was also averse to conflict and inclined to "roll over" just to keep the peace. Although Davecat's father was "overbearing," he was not violent or abusive. Davecat was a shy child and adolescent. When it came to dating, he never initiated contact with a woman. "I was always thinking, she's probably going to say no," he explained. Instead, he had three "affairs" with women who were already involved with other men, all before purchasing his first doll. His first affair took place when he was in college where "[he] just wanted to be somebody's boyfriend." All the affairs ended badly. Although he "fooled around" with two of the three women, sex "wasn't as fulfilling as I'd hoped it would be," he said. He admitted to having "trust issues," and repeated that a doll, unlike a human partner, will never cheat. When I asked if he'd ever consider dating an organic woman again, he said it was still a possibility, but she'd have to accept his dolls. He added that in the back of his mind, he'd be thinking, "What does she want?" and concluded that he'd rather avoid the whole scenario. In the characteristic way Davecat often employs humor to tell a painful truth, he said, "Apart from the lack of sex and the lack of commitment and the lack of inclination on the part of any of the organik lasses I'd had affairs with to leave their boyfriends for me, it was okay!"

How Davecat became an iDollator

What predisposes a man like Davecat to choose synthetic partners over organic ones? An introverted boy, Davecat was continuously drawn to objects. He states outright that he has always preferred things to people and fantasy to reality. "You always know where you are with a thing," he explained, adding that things are predictable in ways humans are not. As a child he "spent a lot of time in my own head." Not surprisingly, his apartment is filled with objects reminiscent of a child's room, including action figures, Lego sculptures, and videos about robots and anime. Davecat unashamedly admits to having a foot fetish, and two beautiful women's feet made of silicone dangle next to his computer. As I looked around Davecat's apartment, I couldn't help but recall the words of French psychoanalyst, Janine Chasseguet-Smirguel:

> Puppets, mannequins, waxworks, automatons, dolls, painted scenery, plaster casts, dummies, secret clockworks, mimesis, and illusion: all form a part of the fetishist's magic and artful universe. Lying between life and death, animated and mechanic, hybrid creatures and creatures to which hubris gave birth, they all may be likened to fetishes. And, as fetishes, they give us, for a while, the feeling that a world not ruled by our common laws does exist, a marvelous and uncanny world.
>
> (1984, p. 88)

Davecat's world is one that transcends law and embodies the wish that things could be different from the way they are.

He remembers his childhood home as having a spare bedroom, which he took over and used to build an entire city for his action figures. Although his city had a police station, no one ever got arrested. He also remembers that in third grade he watched his French teacher writing on the blackboard and imagined she was a robot: "I was watching her writing verbs on the board ... and I'd ... try to picture what machinery was inside her that would move her arm, her face, her lips, her head, that sort of thing, and it was just utterly fascinating to me." Later, around age ten, he asked his mother to make "dummies" out of sticks dressed with his old clothes, an idea he got from an activities book. One was male and one, with her balloon breasts, was female. His mother took him shopping with her. They traveled together on the bus downtown to department stores; sometimes she left him alone while she tried on clothing. On one of those occasions, he recalled being drawn to a blonde mannequin dressed in a tennis skirt. When he struck up a conversation with the artificial woman, the security guard became suspicious and sought his mother. At about 18, Davecat began visiting a store called Mario's Mannequins in Detroit, where he'd take pictures on the weekends. One day he bought Sandy, his very own mannequin.

When Davecat became a young man, he remained shy and couldn't muster the courage to ask a girl out:

> The only way I could go on dates was hoping someone decent answered the adverts I'd put in the classified section of our local alternative paper. I'd tried asking classmates and peers out, but would get rejected, and as I never wanted to be the sort of person who forced themselves onto someone, each rejection would reduce my desire to try again elsewhere. Eventually, it seemed pretty futile. The affairs I was involved in I'd lucked into – not once did I ask whatever lass if she wanted to fool around with me; she was the one who initiated that.

Davecat's three experiences with women were far from positive, and he felt used by them, never sure they were really interested in him or if they would stay around. He even described himself as depressive. All of that would soon change.

Sidore (Shi-chan)

In 1998, a friend introduced Davecat to Abyss Creations, then in business for only two years. He was instantly enchanted by RealDolls, sometimes referred to as the Rolls-Royce of silicone love dolls, and began to save up for one of his own. It took him 18 months to save enough money to purchase Sidore, and he claimed it was the best decision he ever made. Davecat chose the Leah doll, whom he renamed Sidore. She was 5 feet 1 inch tall, a size 34D, and weighed 100 pounds. He liked her pale skin, black hair, and red lips and said, "It just triggered something in me going, Wow, this is exactly how I pictured my ideal girl and my ideal lover and companion." Waiting 16 weeks for the diesel truck to show up with the crate was "agonizing." He described what sounded like love at first sight when he initially saw the doll in black lingerie holding a single purple (artificial) rose in her delicate hand. He was speechless. "She came out of the crate, and we looked into each other's eyes, and we knew this [was] going to be an amazing thing."

A highly creative person, Davecat embarked on his own Pygmalion fantasy. Like the Cypriot king who sculpted his ideal woman and then fell in love with her, Davecat fashioned the woman of his dreams. Sidore dresses in Goth style, wearing a silver neck collar and a bracelet with skulls. She sports a Hello Kitty watch. Most striking is her purple wig against her pale skin. Her makeup is impeccable: red lips, shadowy dark eyes with long lashes, a beauty mark under her left cheekbone. Interestingly, she wears glasses. Davecat told me she is a voracious reader. He lived with Sidore for over a year before he devised an intricate backstory for her. She was born in Osaka, a district of Tokyo, to a Japanese father and an English mother. The father was an accountant and the mother "didn't do anything." I thought about the mother doing nothing. As a mother, she would have been raising Sidore, but that wouldn't require much work since she's a doll. Was this a reflection of Davecat's own mother, a woman who "rolled over"? The doll's father lost his accounting job, which pushed the family to move to Weatherfield, a fictional town in England, the hometown of Sidore's mother and a suburb of Manchester. Davecat informed me that he'd always been enamored of Japanese culture, and that Weatherfield comes from a soap opera he used to watch called *Coronation Street*. Many of his favorite bands are from Manchester. Davecat weaves reality and fantasy, creating worlds and characters that are composed of the things he likes most. He compared what he does to fiction: "That's what authors do with their characters, only instead of just words on a page I have an actual physical presence." I thought: He's living in a book that he's writing by living out a fiction. It is true that all relationships possess fictive elements. This is the basis of transference. But most relationships, along with their fictions, are played out with real people.

Davecat has created an ideal personality for Sidore. "She's a positive, sarcastic, unique individual" and "she's always trying to get people to see the other sides of things ... she's always trying to open people's minds up to things." I observed symbiosis in how Davecat speaks for Sidore and Sidore speaks for Davecat. Sidore is a "fantastic listener" and a bit of an exhibitionist, and Davecat has to restrain her from exposing herself too frequently. Like his other dolls, Sidore has her own Twitter account where she is an advocate for artificial love. Since 1998, when he first received Sidore, she has had three bodies. When I asked Davecat how he accounts for the longevity of his relationship with Sidore, he replied without hesitation:

We have a policy of never going to bed angry and it's gone quite well so far. But it's just the fact that ... I think on my end, at the very least, I can't really speak for her – wink wink – is just that I always know that Shi-chan [his pet name for her] will always be there for me. She will always be an amazing companion in my ups and downs; I'll always have someone wonderful to come home to, and I won't have to worry about her manipulating my emotions for her own end. I won't be lied to; she'll never cheat on me, and she'll never criticize me. And at the very least ... the least I can do for such wonderful behavior is say, ya know what? She is the one for me. She is my wife. And quite literally, she wouldn't be here without me and quite literally I wouldn't be as content as I am without her.

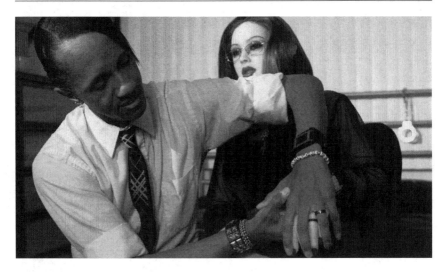

Figure 3.2 Davecat and Sidore.
Courtesy Davecat, Avi Setton, and Danielle Knafo.

They wear matching wedding rings with the words "Synthetik Love Lasts Forever," and Davecat told me they are considering renewing their wedding vows (Figure 3.2). "Synthetic" refers to both a substance made by chemical means, especially to imitate a natural product, *and* the idea of a proposition having truth or falsity *as determined by recourse to experience*. Common synonyms are: artificial, fake, imitation, faux, mock, simulated, ersatz, substitute, pseudo, so-called, man-made, manufactured, and fabricated. Informal synonyms are phony and pretend. The antonyms for synthetic are natural, isolating, analytical, genuine, uninflected, and so forth. Of course the distinction between synthetic and real is blurring at the frontiers of technology.[5] And the border between what is natural and what is artificial depends on how one divides the givens of nature from the productions of people. Furthermore, what may be counted as natural in humans springs from their biology. What is natural to their psychology includes the (perverse) need to overcome and oppose the natural and its limitations. This opposition to nature – the natural, given, authentic, and original – is rooted in the death-soaked transcendence urge that drives the technological enterprise and mocks any naive view about what constitutes natural reality, as well as any notion that the straight and crooked path could ever be cleanly separated. From this view, technology is an ongoing argument with nature about what constitutes natural limits.

The mistress

In December of 2012, Davecat ordered a second doll, whom he named Elena Vostrikova (nicknamed Lenka). Elena Dorfman, a photographer of men who live with dolls (Dorfman, 2005), was the inspiration for Elena's first name. The doll, now made in Russia by a company called Anatomical Dolls, has red hair and pale skin. Davecat described her as "dangerous" and, like him, born under the astrological sign of Scorpio. Her red hair stands out and is echoed in the red blouse she wears. Two necklaces hang from her neck, one with a spider web and the other a casket with a cross, and she has a ring in her nose. Davecat claimed to have purchased her to keep Shi-chan company while he's at work. Was it Shi-chan's or his own loneliness he was trying to fix? In any case, it seems Lenka has added some spice to their relationship. Both dolls, he told me, are bisexual, and Elena's joints are looser and her skin made of softer silicone, making her more amenable to sex. Davecat explained that

> Sidore will always be my wife, and I have no intention of making any other dolls my wife. I'm not into the bigamy thing, but of course I do have a relationship, romantic and sexual, with the other dolls. Elena I got as kind of a mistress/plaything/companion for myself and Shi-chan. Personally, I got her so that Shi-chan wouldn't be lonely whenever I was at work, so that she'd have a fellow synthetik to hang out with.

Elena's backstory is that she was unhappy in her life in Russia since she had few friends, a poor relationship with her parents, and a "dodgy" job. The only person she was close to was her uncle, Ivan Ivanovich, the first cosmonaut in space. (Ivan Ivanovich was a humanoid doll made of metal with bendable joints and a detachable head. The "dummy pilot" was sent into space by the Russians in 1961.) Therefore, Elena is fascinated by space and space programs. She allegedly watched the film *Guys and Dolls* (Abele et al., 2007), a documentary featuring Davecat and Sidore and three other iDollators, and was smitten by both Davecat and Sidore and wished to come to the United States to live with them. Davecat said that

One of Lenka's roles is to augment our relationship by being an outlet for extramarital excursions that both of us can safely enjoy. In her fashion, she does the same thing that quite a few other dolls do when they live with two organik partners, which is providing a way to experiment with additional partners, without the risk of things getting out of hand, as they might when the third partner is organik.

Because Davecat had Elena built with looser joints, she is more malleable than Sidore. She is also 20 pounds lighter. He said, "Elena is more built for sex whereas Sidore is built for love." He feels he has created the perfect life for himself: "I am married but I also have an officially sanctioned person I can turn to." He likened it to having his cake and eating it too. I marveled at Davecat's creation of rules, since his world is one in which so many rules are broken. All minds need rules and make rules to organize experience and ward off chaos and breakdown. Indeed, I couldn't help noticing how Davecat's life represented the male fantasy of having a compliant wife and an equally compliant mistress. Don't we all want what we want and try to work the other to get it? Don't we all want our cake and want to eat it too? Benjamin (2009) wrote about the moral third as involving recognition, accommodation, and predictable expectations. Yet what Davecat doesn't have is what Benjamin elsewhere (1977, 1980) called "the confusing traffic of two-way streets." For Benjamin, the concept of the third (2004) requires the ability to sustain connectedness to the other's mind while accepting its separateness and difference.

Muriel

Davecat's third doll is Muriel Noonan, nicknamed Mew-Mew, a nonsilicone doll. Muriel has a wooden skeleton over which is a leather "musculature" and Lycra skin, with cotton batting to fill her body. She is the lightest of the three (11 pounds), but also the one who is least used for sex. Her backstory has her originating from Coventry, England, where she worked as a librarian. Davecat told me she is "keen on abandoned structures, fascinated with what mankind has left behind." This includes ruins from the Bronze Age or even from the twentieth century. Because of the way she is made, Davecat considers Muriel to be a "flat mate" rather than a romantic partner. "She's like a big pillow," he said, but her advantage over the silicone dolls is that she is light and can stand. I wondered, is *he* an abandoned structure? Is Muriel the witness to his life, the keeper of the book he's writing as he lives out a fantasy that rescues him from oblivion?

Davecat joked about his dolls' bonding. "I expect they scheme against me," he said affectionately. He clearly invests time and creative energy in building their backstories and their interrelationships. He even learned Japanese to "speak" with Sidore. Sidore teaches Elena English. He showed me an ingenious video he made of Sidore and Elena interviewing Muriel to decide whether to accept her as a flat mate. The interview proceeds properly until, at one point, Muriel undresses and exposes her breasts. In the end, the two dolls accept Muriel into their ménage. Interestingly, Davecat combined the elements of a formal interview with playful exhibitionism, thus revealing his own decidedly unconventional social position.

The backstories for the dolls evidently represent both conscious and unconscious elements of Davecat's psyche. He "shares" or spreads his mind out among things much more than other people. His apartment is alive with his mind. The dolls are alive with his mind. And each component outside of himself enables him to live and incorporates a different aspect of his own mind. He lives in a self-generated virtual reality that successfully contains him. The wife (his doll) who is for love more than sex represents his (relationship with his) mother; it offers stability, acceptance, and love.[6] Shichan's father is an accountant who lost his job (a numbers-and-facts man like Davecat's father), further distanced from Davecat by the fact that he's Japanese. He loses his job (Davecat's revenge?), and the family has to move to England, the land of the civility and acceptance that Davecat longed for from his own father. Elena, Davecat's Russian doll, is for sex – for that un-English, less civilized sexual side of himself – and it is she who is connected to outer space, making her a conduit for what lies beyond earthly limits. Muriel is fascinated by "abandoned structures." Davecat uses the dolls and their stories to create an alternate reality in which he feels more REAL than in any other. He plans to add two more dolls to his collection.[7] It will be interesting to see what they add to the domestic menagerie and how they, too, will represent undisclosed, repudiated, and unarticulated elements of his own psyche.

Reality and fantasy

When speaking with Davecat I was aware of a strange sensation. On the one hand, I was impressed with his mindfulness regarding the mechanics of the dolls, which clearly illustrated his acknowledgment that they are physical objects, not real people. He even removed Sidore's face and Elena's head to show me how they are made. On the other hand, when he spoke of the dolls' personalities and their relationships with him and with one another, it seemed he lived in a world of deeply realized fantasy, projecting his desires and needs onto these beautiful sculptures of femininity. He even made statements indicating consciousness in the dolls – "She knows she's a doll" – or morality in a robot – "If a robot is saying, 'Oh, you're wearing a nice shirt,' they'd have no reason to lie." I asked him about the relationship between fantasy and reality in his life and he replied, "I do recognize they are physical creations made by a person, but then, also in my mind, they are people as well and I treat them as such." He described his "doublethink" in this way:

> I think it's very important to be able to retain both attitudes simultaneously because I will never say that they [the dolls] are people and they can do things on their own because, well, for one it's not true and, another, that's a sign that you are starting to lose your grip on reality. Being an iDollator is this walk between fantasy and reality ... you do have to keep one foot in either zone.

Davecat explained that his sense of reality has more to do with his senses, though he claimed at times, when the light is dim, to discern "a trace of a smile" on [Sidore's] face. "If you can see or smell or hear or taste or touch something, it's real," he said. "But if it doesn't exist, if it can't be accessed by any of those senses, it doesn't exist – like a unicorn. That's why I stress my dolls are REAL." Davecat is enthusiastic about the benefits of using fantasy to enliven and animate his dolls: "If you don't inhabit fantasy, basically you have this very objective viewpoint where a thing is a thing and it can never be anything else, which is dull." Yet he tries to maintain a balance because he seems to be aware of the dangers of going too far: "You can't be totally enraptured by the fantasy because you will be disappointed ... you have to realize that you are straddling two worlds, but again that's part of the fun."

As Davecat spoke, I thought of how much he imbued his dolls with human-like attributes. At the same time, I considered how so many men try to turn their real women into dolls – Playboy types, Stepford wives – and how few of them consider this to be pathological. Davecat knows that he indulges in fantasy as a way to escape a dull or unpleasant reality. His fantasy world, with characters for which he has created fictionalized lives, is preferable to what he sees as the alternative: "I'd rather stay in a world where things are a lot better, people get along with each other, they don't hit each other. You could say that what passes as reality is not something I'm altogether keen on." Like the rabbit who becomes REAL in Margery Williams's story because he is loved by the boy, Davecat claimed that his love for the dolls is mutual and returned to him: "I believe I get as much love from Sidore, Elena, and Muriel as I can possibly give them, and I believe that they are appreciative for it and, it's like a feedback loop, it's back and forth." Davecat's position, which merges inner and outer reality, is reminiscent of Winnicott's theory of transitional phenomena:

> This intermediate area of experience, unchallenged in respect of its belonging to inner or external (shared) reality, constitutes the greater part of the infant's experience, and throughout life is retained in the intense experiencing that belongs to the arts and to religion and to imaginative living and to creative scientific work.
>
> (1971 [1953], p. 14)

Transitional objects, according to Winnicott (1971 [1953]), are the first not-me possessions, inanimate objects that are both discovered and created to serve as a bridge between mother and self, familiar and unfamiliar, thus helping the infant separate and individuate from the mother and move from objects that are subjective to ones that are objectively perceived. The teddy bear and baby blanket are familiar appendages of young children, serving soothing functions as well as containing the intensity and aliveness of the mother–infant dyad. Greenacre (1971a) wrote that transitional objects "make strangeness and solitude more acceptable" (p. 316). Transitional objects can lead to a creative attitude toward life or a rigid fetish, each of which relies on the capacity for illusion.

Several authors have compared the transitional object to the fetish (e.g., Winnicott, 1975 [1951]; Greenacre, 1971a, 1971b; McDougall, 1980). All agree about features that overlap in these two phenomena: both involve external objects that are used in a magical way to cushion distress and frustration; both merge features of self and m/other. Yet the transitional object is viewed as a universal and normative aspect of development that is dispensed with when no longer needed. The fetish, on the other hand, continues to be needed and is not outgrown. McDougall (1980) wrote that both transitional objects and fetishes are symbolic constructions, possess reparative functions, and are intimately connected with the maternal image and its missing or absent qualities. Fetishes, however, don't differentiate between the sexes and never renounce omnipotent wishes. McDougall (1989) also compared transitional objects to addictive substances, and love has been compared to chemical addiction (Kasi, 1989; Fisher et al., 2010; Peele & Brodsky, 1975). Although Davecat's relations aren't exactly like an addict chasing a fleeting euphoric sensation, they do have some of the same defensive purpose, rigidity, and need for control. Rather than serving as a bridge to forming relations with people, they are part of an alternate world he has constructed, but is that creative or constricting? He does have friends, mostly male, with whom he meets every week and who know and accept his lifestyle. I think he admits his life is a compromise that works better than its alternative – being completely isolated by his fears of intimacy. Yet ordinary love has its illusory qualities, too.

Sex and love

Davecat acknowledged that sex was one of the initial aspects that appealed to him with his RealDoll, but he revealed that with time love has trumped the sex in importance:

> The sex is obviously very important for us, but it's not the most important thing. I think the most important thing is that there's a love between us. There's a faithfulness; there's a solid relationship. I mean sex is really the icing on the cake.

Figure 3.3 Davecat and Sidore.
Courtesy Davecat, Avi Setton, and Danielle Knafo.

As I listened to Davecat, I thought: he is loving something that cannot really love him back (Figure 3.3). He knows this and yet does not know it. This is a type of disavowal or doublethink. Though he knows it can't be true, he has convinced himself that the dolls *do* love him. Then I thought, how much does love between two organic people reflect this fantasy? Do we ever know what loving and being loved really mean? That is, how much do we convince ourselves that the other person really loves us? Furthermore, we may doubt they love us even if they profess their love. Not even the things they do for us convince us because they might be accommodating us simply to receive our love. Is it only our need to be loved that makes us love? Or is it our need to love that makes us seek someone who will love us back? We are, after all, loved (Mom) before we love back. We are loved into being like the velveteen rabbit. Davecat has opted out of the uncertainty of love. He wants everything fixed in a frame that cannot threaten him with real change. He clarifies that "change isn't bad overall," but having trust broken in a love relationship is "one of the worst things that can happen." He has trouble understanding how people can casually date, opening themselves up to hurt and deception. "It seems to me that someone's heart will be inevitably broken over the course of their lives, but everything should be done in the individual's power to make sure it isn't broken by the one they love," he opined. Yes, I thought, but love that secures the heart must also be capable of breaking it.

Davecat succinctly described the function Sidore plays in his life: "I didn't have a partner, someone to love, someone to come home to. She has filled the void perfectly." What is important to note here is that, yes, Davecat found an alternative to having a human partner; but, also, he is a man who is attracted to the nonhuman aspects of dolls. I asked Davecat to compare sex with humans to sex with dolls. He quickly discovered that he could not pose Shi-chan in all the positions he had fantasized about due to her structural limitations. However, he explained:

> Dolls overall are simultaneously robustly made and fragile. They're ostensibly made for sex, but they're also sculpture pieces. With an organik partner, obviously you can be a bit rougher, but I take care to be gentle with Shi-chan and Lenka when we're in bed. Another remarkable difference between organik and synthetik women is that when you're inside a doll's vagina or anus, there's a vacuum effect that's pretty ... breathtaking. I'd say sex flows a little better with an organik, as she's able to move herself, whereas changing positions with a doll requires you to pause and rearrange every-thing. Overall, though, personally I'd rate sex with a synthetik woman to be as good, if not better, than with an organik woman. Mainly as a doll's artificiality is a huge draw with me, and her posi-tive points far outweigh the number of things she can't do, so that's half the battle won right there.

In the end, the dolls are always there when Davecat wants them. "Just being able to reach over a couple of inches and feel warm silicone skin beneath my hand, as well as a benign physical presence, is very reassur-ing," he said. What "battle" was Davecat referring to, I wondered. Was it the battle to have illusion triumph over reality and mastery over loss?

Masculine and feminine

In my research for this chapter over the last five years, as I learned about iDollators' projections onto their dolls and the enormous attention they paid to dressing their dolls and putting on makeup, I began to wonder how much male doll owners might be expressing their feminine side through their dolls. That is, iDollators may not only seek beautiful female dolls as sex partners and even love objects; these dolls may also function as projected aspects of their feminine selves. After all, like a transvestite, iDollators spend hours combing stores and catalogs for the right cosmetics, bras, clothing, lingerie, shoes, and accessories. They enjoy dressing the dolls and putting on their makeup and wigs. Davecat acknowledged that he may be "manifesting a latent side" to his personality through his dolls, choosing clothing he would wear were he a female or a cross-dresser. He is careful to point out that he has never entertained the urge to cross-dress, yet he enjoys the expression of this side of himself through his dolls. "Dolls are a blank canvas," he said, "to tap into or express or enhance an aspect of your life that ordinarily would be suppressed."

Davecat's use of the dolls to function as a part of himself recalls Kohut's (1971, 1977) concept of the self-object. This ingenious term was conceived by Kohut to describe how someone enters into relations with another, treating the other as an extension of the self, which serves a function for the self that cannot be done without an other. Most commonly, the other is used to bolster a person's self-esteem and validate his or her self-worth. Similarly, Davecat and other men who have had trouble with organic women seem to use their dolls as self-objects in that they help them feel better about themselves. Additionally, the dolls express a part of them – their feminine side – that makes them feel less stunted and more whole. Davecat admitted that were he a female, he'd dress exactly as Shi-chan dresses, and especially mirror her fondness for mesh blouses.

Control and predictability

Life is unpredictable and in many ways a gamble. Many people find the lack of certainty exciting; they enjoy the adventure of being taken by surprise. iDollators are not among those people. Indeed, Davecat insisted that he is not a gambler and that he seeks a life that is predictable and controllable. He does not like surprises or the messiness of relationships: "Predictability is, to me, a wonderful thing because there are no curveballs," he said.

> iDollators who are in relationship with their own synthetik companions, they basically don't have to worry about getting a girlfriend, going to a bar, joining the dating scene. That's not something on our minds because we have someone gorgeous we can come home to and at any time make love to. So it has blissfully remained the same, and consistency is one of the many things I love about our relationship.

iDollators like Davecat seek docility, consistency, compliance, peace and quiet. They avoid tension, confusion, conflict, arguments, and necessary compromise. They also avoid mutuality and reciprocity, though, in fantasy, they may imagine those qualities exist. Smith (2013) compares doll love to a form of "auto-affection," adding that the phenomenon highlights the difficulty of intimacy, which affects us all. One might say that all intimacy is a compromise between fantasy and reality. The appreciation and respect for difference lives alongside the fantastic and unverifiable assumption of a sameness and mutuality, this feeling of "love" that cannot be easily defined because it does not have any specific referent. Romantic love is often hijacked by reality and flown into the country of ruin. Carson McCullers's famous speech in her novella, *The Ballad of the Sad Café*, aptly captures the one-sidedness of love:

> Love is a joint experience between two persons – but the fact that it is a joint experience does not mean that it is similar experience to the two people involved. There are the lover and the beloved, but these two come from different countries. Often the beloved is the stimulus for all the stored-up love which has lain quiet within the lover for a long time hitherto. And somehow every lover knows this. He feels in his soul that his love is a solitary thing. He comes to know a new, strange loneliness ... So there is only one thing for the lover to do. He must house his love within himself as best he can; he must create for himself a whole new inward world – a world intense and strange, complete in himself ... Now the beloved

may be of any description. The most outlandish people can be the stimulus for love ... Therefore the value and quality of any love is determined solely by the lover himself.

(1987, p. 216)

Philosophers and psychoanalysts have long tried to parse human love. Is the love that we want from our partner something like what the really good mother gives us (meaning that unshakeable affection expressed in a thousand ways that forms the foundation of self-development)? Is love the desire to give and receive something that is impossible, even for the mother, meaning that her love is not entirely pure or selfless? Is human love actually a longing for the impossible, something like God's love, a love that stands outside of everything, a love without contingency, transcending all situation, immortal and utterly perfect, a truth with no referents? Is love a quality without qualities, an emptiness disguised as a plenum? These questions continue to haunt us the more we study the nature of posthuman love, and its implications for human-to-human love.

Techno-sexuality and the uncanny valley

Although Davecat lives with and loves dolls, he is quick to point out that he would exchange his dolls for a robot in a second. In addition to referring to himself as an iDollator, he calls himself a techno-sexual or robosexual, also known as an ASFRian, an acronym that stems from the now defunct newsgroup *alt.sex.fetish.robots*. Techno-sexuality refers to men who are sexually attracted to humanoids or humanoid robots, or to people who act like robots or dress in robot costumes. Japanese artist Hajime Sorayama has developed a cult following among robophiliacs with his drawings of erotically charged "sexy robots," which he has called "gynoids" (Sorayama, 1995). With a tiny brush, pencil, acrylics, and an airbrush finish, Sorayama creates hyper-realistic erotic pinups for the pleasure of men like Davecat. I discovered a book of Saroyama's drawings in Davecat's living room. The following conversation ensued:

DC: A gynoid would be my ideal partner. In fact a gynoid would definitely trump a doll because dolls – I love dolls – dolls are fantastic, but the thing is they can't move themselves, they can't talk, they can't ... drive or whatever, they can't move ... whereas ... the ideal version of a gynoid would be able to ... give me a back massage or cook dinner or we would be able to go to concerts together ... we'd be able to ... do things out of doors.

DK: So is that your ideal woman? A gynoid?

DC: My ideal woman is definitely a gynoid. As a matter of fact, if someone were to say to me ... we're actually working on an actual gynoid that would be able to be built to your specifications – would you be interested? Haha, I would not be able to say yes fast enough!

DK: What would the specifications be?

DC: I don't know if they'd be able to make her facially looking like Sidore because I would want a gynoid version of Sidore. But since, obviously, Abyss Creations has a copyright on the face, they'd have to make it slightly different. But my ideal gynoid would be, um ... well, she'd be pretty much ... the way Sidore is, 5 feet 1 inch, hopefully less than 100 pounds ... pale ... My ideal version of my gynoid would be something that looks like a robot – no sorry, looks like a human – until you get closer to her where you could say, oh, well her skin is actually made out of rubber, that sort of thing, that would be the absolute ideal ... They have silicone skin so you can definitely tell that they are not human. And that's an appeal to me. But they have ... a certain movement that's kind of fluid but kind of stilted at the same time ... They move like a person but ... it's not exactly ... fluid. And there's a subversive quality to that that really appeals to me.

As Davecat spoke, I asked myself if I could live with a robot partner, one who'd look and act like a real man, provide unconditional love, and help me around the house, one who'd serve me hand and foot and have stimulating conversations with me. Would I say no? Would you?[8]

Davecat's slip of the tongue indicated he sometimes does not succeed in differentiating human from nonhuman. His musings about the perfect gynoid partner, humanlike but still clearly artificial, made me think of the "uncanny valley," a variation of the Freudian term adopted by robotics professor Masahiro Mori (2012 [1970]) to describe the phenomenon of revulsion people feel when dolls or robots become too lifelike, too close to human. The valley explains the dip in comfort level that people experience when something is just a little too close to the real. I asked Davecat if there exists a point at which the dolls or robots would become too human-like for his comfort level. He said:

> Would there be a point where Shi-chan would be too human for me? Yes. If she were a gynoid and she needed to go to the bathroom or was sweating, that sort of thing. There is no need for that. It would only be for appearance's sake, but that would be something I wouldn't need in my synthetik companion. Um, personality wise, I think the too human point would be if she could ever stop and say, "Ya know what Davecat? Maybe we should not see each other for a while." I think one of the biggest draws for me for synthetik companions is that they are always there, they are always faithful. In that too human aspect of being able to say, okay, well, we are no longer in love – well that's something I would never want. And something probably a lot of people who look for synthetik ... well, any companion, would never want.

Interestingly, Davecat wished to avoid not only the unpredictability of human relationships, but also the messiness of human bodies: their exudations, excretions, secretions; their aging, sickness, and especially their mortality. Dolls brought to life by their owner express a personal transcendence project and a denial of death (Becker, 1973) with a vengeance. *Look at what I can do! I can love something that does not die. And I can make it such that* something *that does not die becomes* someone *who does not die and, furthermore, who loves me without condition, loves me simply because I exist! I am loved by an immortal and so will be loved forever!* The doll not only bridges the human and the object, but also the human and the divine. The doll is a doll. The doll is a woman. The doll is an angel. The doll is all of these things and none of these things at the same time. The doll, like Davecat, is undecided and, therefore, ephemeral, between, uncanny: It is (or has a) SOUL. Davecat's REAL, which is the making of the real through an act of imagination, at the service of saving the human situation, is equal to SOUL. SOUL in this context is what exists between imagination and reality, the transitional space in which the human situation is saved. Yet there is a crucial difference between Davecat and his dolls. He is a person and they are not. And, like Dorian Gray, who is cursed with immortal life, it might also be a curse to love something that does not die. When describing the combination of synthetic and organic, he states, "I'm drawn by her beauty – she is very lifelike – but since I do prefer synthetik women, she's just lifelike enough where she looks like an organik woman but she's still a doll."

Aging and mortality

Because he specified his wish to avoid bodily functions, I naturally thought of the physical complications Davecat and iDollators encounter with their dolls. One may think that an advantage to living with a doll is that the doll doesn't age. One man who lives with two dolls exclaimed, "People grow old and ugly. Look at me! But they [the dolls] never will" (Abele et al., 2007). However, dolls do age. They tear and break, and they need to be cared for or even replaced. Sidore is on her third body, and it is likely that in the future there will be more. Davecat explained that having dolls does not eliminate all relationship problems, yet he emphasized that he would rather deal with a doll tear than a personality shift. The Doll Doctor, Slade Fiero, once repaired all the worst "injuries." iDollators shipped their dolls to Slade, and he not only repaired them but returned them in better shape than they were in when shipped out. To the dismay of many doll owners, Slade has since retired, and today iDollators are left on their own (Gordiner, 2009). Davecat has a first-aid kit for minor doll tears. He sent Sidore's first body to its creator, Matt McMullen, because he discovered that her hip joints loosened and the sharp edges where the top part of her thighbone meets her pelvis cut through the silicone at the crotch. Davecat was "so beside myself" because "it was so much of an emergency to me," and he "had to wait" an "agonizing" three months to get her back.

Facing his own aging and death is more complicated than facing doll repairs. Davecat prefers not to think of mortality but knows he has no choice. Aware that his dolls will outlast him, he has devised an intricate plan for this exigency:

What I was going to do is have myself cremated, have Sidore cremated, and then both of our ashes would be put in the same container and mixed up ... and then we would spread half the ashes over Japan and the other half over England. I'm like, yeah, that would be really fantastic but (a) I don't think you can get ashes out of silicone; (b) can you even cremate a doll ... would they allow that sort of thing?; (c) who's gonna pay for that helicopter ride over England or Japan? So as romantic as that was, it's not really practical. I mean obviously when that sort of thing occurs, ya know when that bit happens, you don't want to think about practicality, you don't want to have that at the forefront of your mind, but it's a practical issue. So essentially what I think we are going to do, *if and when I eventually pass away* [emphasis added], there's a certain type of kimono, Mofuku I believe, it's all black ... basically I'm going to be cremated and my ashes are going to be put in a container inside of her head, and she will be wearing the Mofuku and seated in a seat and ... she's gonna be in that seat with my ashes in her head *forever*. And the reason behind that is ... she's on my mind all the time while I'm alive, and when I pass around, I'll always be on her mind.

He added that Shi-chan will hold a plaque with the words, "HOW TERRIBLE IT IS TO LOVE SOMETHING THAT DEATH CAN TOUCH." How fitting that Davecat's mausoleum will be the head of his immortal lover. Here again we see the triumph of Ernest Becker's thought, that implacable hidden core of denial and terror that feeds conscious life regardless of its hereditary and historical and cultural particulars – indeed, the existential root of the perverse.

Perversion or preference?

I have begun thinking of doll and robot preferences as akin to sexual preference. Yes, such choices are classical examples of perversion – having creative elements yet cutting a person off from human intimacy; furnishing a retreat from reality in a transhuman fantasy. Yet an alternative interpretation launched upon different premises would stress the creative aspect of Davecat's expression of preference and note with admiration how he has channeled a particular kind of sensitivity and associated traumata into an artistic creation. Indeed, having spent thousands of hours with artists, I see him as an artist. His art, of course, is performative, and he is putting everything at stake in creating it. Since I interviewed Davecat, I have spoken to many other doll owners, some of whom use their dolls for artistic purposes. These men include role play in their lives, photographing the dolls in a variety of scenarios, adding narratives with much humor and depth.

Whereas we have become accustomed to thinking about sexual preference in terms of gender, I believe that technological advances will create additional preferences for a variety of dolls, androids, gynoids, and robots. Furthermore, I believe both genders will participate in this new sexual revolution, especially at the point at which robots that closely resemble human beings enter mainstream life. Davecat explained, "Much how there are all sorts of people who prefer brunettes, blondes, or gingers, or choose to date within their own gender, or outside their own race, I prefer women who are purely synthetik." He added, "It goes beyond sexual appeal, and is more based on consistency and reassurance." Clearly his preference includes both internal and external qualities. He loves the physical good looks of the dolls, which he calls beautiful sculptures. Yet he also finds their predictability and "non-judgment" highly attractive.

As we spoke, I was able to appreciate both the generative and constraining elements of his lifestyle. Its generative aspects have to do with expressing his creative imagination through a living enactment with the dolls, easing the loneliness of being/feeling like an outcast, and distinguishing himself from his father. Its constraining aspects include buffering himself from other living beings and the reality of change, loss, and impermanence in his intimate life. Although he noted, "Some of my best friends are organiks," he added that his closest friends over the past 20 years have not changed, a fact that contributes to his enjoyment of the friendships and attests to his preference for long-term stability. He changed his name to Davecat to distinguish himself from his father, and he made a deliberate choice not to procreate because "I didn't want to intentionally force my ways onto [children], as my father attempted to do with me." He lives "in complete contradiction of how my father's idealized vision of me would have been," and he extends an identification with his mother as a passive, playful, and indulgent loner who exercised little power with the father and the outer world. Yet his mother was an "ideal Christian," helping anyone in need and approaching others in a gentle and nonjudgmental manner.

Doll therapy

Unlike Jack, Davecat has never been in therapy. In fact, he claimed that his dolls *are* his therapy. "It's a way to get something within you out of you," he explained, "something trapped inside you." I found this statement intriguing so I asked him to elaborate. He said:

> When I said that living with dolls is my therapy, I wasn't meaning that in a strictly clinical context. Sidore et al. have made me a happier and more contented individual. For one, instead of being miserable about being single, or being anxious about trying to find a partner, my synthetik women have fulfilled those roles nearly perfectly. I say "nearly," as they're not actual gynoids, but until that day comes, they're doing a terrific job.

It is easy to understand why Davecat would not consider psychotherapy as an option. He is content with his life, happier now that he has the dolls than he's ever been. Although he admitted to having trust issues and said he is not keen on arguments, he can lay his cards on the table with the dolls and feel accepted for who he is. I asked if he had ever felt conflicted about living with dolls, and he responded that he has never felt shame at having dolls as lovers. The only conflict he claimed to have experienced is in showing or telling others that he lives with dolls, due to the "general public's lack of acceptance with things that are unusual but harmless." He admitted "It's awful that I can't tell my co-workers" or "can't simply take any of my artificial lasses out of the home, as I don't want my neighbors lodging baseless complaints to management." Society represents Davecat's rejecting and disapproving father, which causes him to keep a low profile, except in the iDollator community, where he is well known.

I challenged him a bit by asking about whether he thought he was avoiding personal and interpersonal growth, as well as mutuality in relationships, by choosing synthetic partners over human partners. After all, he never has to deal with differences of opinion, learn to compromise, or consider another's point of view, needs, and desires, or face the inevitability of disappointment, rejection, and loss. He agreed that I had made a valid point. The same point is argued by Turkle (2011), who conceived of relationships with robots as "navigating intimacy while skirting it" (p. 10). Nonetheless Davecat defended his position:

> If you really want growth in the context of learning how to deal
> with organiks and if they don't like what you're into, basically you
> can get that any day of the week ... going to a shop, going to work,
> that sort of thing. I think that if you're at home and you have a
> partner and particularly if that partner is synthetik, you know, you
> should be able to ... come home and have a solid [break] ... from
> the outside world, where you don't have to basically put on a mask
> and be like, well I'm into this or that or the other thing and just
> basically be at home at peace with your artificial partner without
> having to worry about like, ya know, putting on a mask for them.

Davecat had shifted to second person, distancing himself from the
pain involved in human relationships. For Davecat, interactions with
the outside world require too much effort – the wearing of masks –
whereas home life at Deafening Silence Plus is a place where he feels
unconditionally accepted and where he can free his imagination to create the kind of world he wishes to live in. "My Dolls are my therapy
mainly by being beautiful, nonjudgmental people that will always be
there when I come home," he said. When I asked Davecat if he could
imagine life without the dolls, his demeanor instantly changed, and
his posture shifted. He compared losing his dolls to "losing a limb,"
again revealing the doll's self-object function. "I don't want to say it's
unfathomable, because obviously I have fathomed it, but it's just ...
it's obviously, nothing I'd ever want to experience." Indeed, Davecat's
dolls provide a holding environment (Winnicott, 1960) in which he
feels reassured and safe, thus freed to invent, project, displace, and
substitute as much as he wants. Furthermore, the dolls "cultivate writing, creativity, and photography," activities that encourage and inspire
his creative pursuits.

The iDollator community

There exists a relatively large community of iDollators who are
approximately 90 percent male. They congregate at several online
forums where they share experiences, ask and answer questions, and
post photos of their dolls. Who are these men? Davecat explained
how this "tightly-knit community" is made up primarily of men who
choose dolls over humans as companions and sex partners, men who

have tried and failed at dating and relationships. These are men who are sensitive and cannot tolerate rejection. They are also men who are shy and have trouble approaching women. Of course, there is a sub-category of men who hate women or are angry with them and turn their dolls into "speechless vessels of violence" (Laslocky, 2005). Some use the dolls for sex, and others, like Davecat, develop loving relations with the dolls, which they conceive of as intimate partners. Davecat described to me what he saw as common features among iDollators:

> Speaking for myself, and actually quite a few fellow iDollators, they're the sort of person where ... we've tried the dating scene, we've tried ... being in love with organiks, and it's just not necessarily worked out. Maybe it's because of that partner or maybe it's because of ourselves ... For people like myself ... you get tired of falling off the horse and, at some point, you say, you know what? I'm not getting back up because I'm just gonna fall off again. You just develop that sense of, what's the point, because I'm just gonna end up on the ground all over. I'll just stay on the ground. Or, instead of getting a horse you get a Vespa scooter, as a lot of us have done. Speaking for myself – but a lot of people could agree with this – there's just this point where you get tired of banging your head against the wall. Dating in and of itself is a huge amount of time and money and expenditure and more importantly emotion ... You don't want to put your heart on your sleeve saying that, okay, this is someone that I think is going to be the one. They're fantastic, they're perfect, they're funny, they look fantastic. Oh wait, what happened? Why did it go wrong? God, I thought I was gonna be married to this individual! And then you're in your cups for a bit drinking, and then, oh, okay, I'm gonna do it again. Oh, this is definitely the one! Oh, wait, this is definitely the one! Ya know, you get tired of the whole lather, rinse, repeat aspect and you just say, well, I'm getting older and I want to find someone. And I believe genuinely that there is someone for everyone on the face of the earth. I just also believe that ... that person may not be an organik person because you could find that one person may be married to someone else, they may not exist at all, and instead of ... waiting and looking and hoping and pining and getting depressed because

you're not finding that person, you're not getting any younger, ya know? So I think it would be more advantageous to actually go with the synthetik option, as I refer to it ... and when you have a partner ... you know you're not going to be ... looking for another partner, that's a huge load off one's mind, ya know? ... You've got your special someone at home. So I think a large part of the population that do go with a synthetik partner are people who are just fed up and in some ways, beaten down by ... circumstance.

Davecat has become something of a spokesman for the iDollator community. His blog dispenses doll news and compares and contrasts doll products. He sees his mission as one of "spreading the gospel of the synthetik option." Like any minority group, iDollators have come under attack. Davecat is upset about this because he believes since dolls improve his and others' lives they should be accepted as an alternative lifestyle. "We don't want to have random people calling us freaks and weirdos," he said. He has even become an advocate for synthetic love, claiming that doll love is an alternative to feeling lonely and being unhappy. "I like to think of myself as an educator," he explained.

Evocative objects

Akhtar (2003) has described how the human infant distinguishes itself not only from its primary caretakers but also from the nonhuman environment. He delineates ways in which the inanimate world plays a role in development and sustenance of one's self throughout the lifespan. From early infancy, we react selectively to human and nonhuman objects (Lichtenberg, 1983). Piaget (1952 [1936]) wrote that the capacity to distinguish animate from inanimate continues throughout our lives. Winnicott (1971 [1953]) came up with the term transitional object and noted that transitional space allows the infant to develop the capacity to be alone and to play (Winnicott, 1958). The transitional objects' subjective qualities have greater importance than their objective qualities, since they absorb the child's projections, relate him or her to the object, and offer configurations for imaginative play. We can think of child's play as the creation of the earliest form of virtual reality.

Winnicott (1971 [1953]) theorized that the transitional object is abandoned when it has served its function and the child no longer needs it. He wrote that the transitional object is "to be gradually allowed to be decathected so in the course of the years it becomes not so much forgotten as relegated to limbo ... It is not forgotten and it is not mourned. It loses meaning ... and [becomes] spread out ... over the whole cultural sphere" (p. 5). This is what occurred with Jack of the previous chapter. But in some cases, this does not happen. In fact, Turkle (2013) claimed that computers and other digital objects, like iPhones, that invite powerful attachments and transitional functioning à la Winnicott, are not meant to be abandoned. Of course, no person grows beyond the capacity to festishize and unconsciously harbor impossible wishes. We all need something magical to hold on to in the face of death. In that sense, Davecat is not so different from the majority of people. It really is a matter of degree – the degree of imagination, the degree of fear of intimacy, and the degree of the need to survive in the lifeboat of the body. Davecat appears content living his life with his transitional objects in the transitional space he has simultaneously found and created. Although he was raised a Christian, he calls himself an atheist, though he maintains an affinity for Shinto, a Japanese religion that professes a divine essence – *kami* – that manifests in multiple forms besides the human.

Davecat has found a solution to a very human problem: how to go on living in a world in which we find ourselves separate and alone. How do we save ourselves through love? Although he uses his imagination to render his dolls REAL, in the end his love for the dolls allows him to love himself into existence. He experiences himself as a loving person, and he creates a worldview in which he saves himself. Davecat's identity is thus bound up with the dolls. Although he can usually "clearly distinguish between fantasy and fact, between inner objects and external objects, between primary creativity and perception" (Winnicott, 1971 [1953], p. 6), where he begins and the dolls end is not always clear. "I am the fella with the dolls," he sums up; "I'm married to a doll."

Davecat's response

I've been asked by Ms. Knafo, and, by extension, loads of other curious individuals, as to why I've not only chosen a Doll to be my wife, but also to be a public advocate for artificial people, so I thought I'd contribute some thoughts that'll hopefully put finer points on things she's already covered. For one, I wouldn't describe myself as being a "people person" – I value time spent alone without the distractions of others, whether it's to work on writing, or simply not wanting to expend energy interacting with someone. As I like to point out, though, there's a vast difference in being alone and being lonely. A Synthetik allows me to be free to be by myself whenever I like, with no pressure from her to fulfill any expectations, but whenever I want to enjoy her company, a Synthetik companion fills that need as well, without the usual guilt that a seemingly neglected Organik person will often offload on their more solitary half.

You'll note that I often use the terms "Synthetik" and "Organik" when talking about this subject, and it seems a bit confusing if you're not used to them. An Organik could also be referred to as an Organik human – i.e., a person of flesh-and-blood, like you and me. Well, I shouldn't make assumptions about you. On the other hand, a Synthetik is a human that's entirely artificial. What's important to remember is that the terms Doll and Synthetik are not interchangeable – all Dolls are Synthetiks, but not all Synthetiks are Dolls, as the other types of Synthetiks would be Androids and Gynoids. An Android is a robot designed to look like a human male, whereas a Gynoid is made to resemble a human female. Whereas Dolls have passive, inert bodies, Androids and Gynoids would be capable of movement, speech, and thought, after a fashion.

The reason I refer to Synthetiks as humans is that I'm of the opinion that in the near future those members of society who are open-minded enough will consider artificial people to simply be a new type of human being. Advancements in both the construction of artificial bodies and the development of artificial intelligence will bring Synthetiks ever closer to being unique creatures in their own right, who will deserve similar rights and privileges that sentient beings, such as Organik humans and animals, enjoy. Many people who aren't aware of humanoid robotics will consider the idea of Synthetiks to be far-fetched or even unnecessary, but although society has a history of rejecting technological advancements, it also has a history of eventually adopting said advancements, and reaching the point of not being able to live without them.

George Carlin once remarked, "If you scratch the surface of a cynic, underneath you'll find a disappointed idealist," and it's an entirely true statement. It may be impossible to believe, but my stance is that of a futurist; personally I think it's shameful that we live in the twenty-first century, and society still lacks moon bases, flying cars, domed cities, and humanoid robots. Not to mention more practical things, such as enough education, food, clothing, and shelter for everyone, as well as humanoid robots. Going public with my choice of life partners has been relatively all right, but there've been some bumps in the road occasionally. It's frustrating when people refer to Dolls as "sex dolls," as it greatly diminishes their potential. Or when video footage of Gynoids such as Chihiro Aiko or Otonaroid is shown on the Internet, and invariably, at some point, they're referred to as "creepy" without any justification of the term. For decades, society has been moving away from encouraging people to think for themselves and be creative, as opposed to going along with what their peers say and not developing their own imaginations. Both unconventional and imaginative thinking are forces for progress, which is something that seems to be in short supply, at least socially, in this day and age.

One of the reasons why I choose to do interviews and be generally public about my choice in companions is because Shi-chan, Lenka, et al., and I are trying to help society get used to the concept of Synthetiks as friends and lovers, particularly for people who simply aren't having any luck finding the right someone they can be with. Technology can make all manner of fantastic things happen, so there's no reason it can't also be used to fill a void in a person's life. It's slightly the case with Dolls now; obviously iDollators have to put more imaginative effort into the relationship to fill in the gaps, but when Gynoids and Androids are available for everyday usage, there are going to be more individuals who will find that a Synthetik partner is just what they've been waiting for.

Being a robosexual – that is, a person attracted to humanoid robots – puts people like me at an advantage, as aspects such as rubbery-looking skin and stilted motion aren't disadvantages at all. Quite the opposite, in fact! But there will be a few who will find that they're attracted to Synthetik people, even though they weren't aware of it beforehand. Not everyone will be keen on an artificial companion, and that's perfectly fine. I should also probably mention that Synthetik companions won't completely replace Organik ones, which is a fact that directly addresses paranoid individuals concerned that "robots will even take over romance." Having a preference for artificial partners is merely that – a preference. But the availability of Synthetiks will ensure that anyone who wishes to have an even-tempered and reliable partner can have one, without any of the unexpected surprises or drama that occasionally comes with flesh-and-blood people. Speaking for myself, I do find certain Organik women to be rather appealing, but I realize that pursuit of any romantic interests would more than likely end in immediate failure, or failure in the long term; to me, ultimately it's not worth the risk. On the other hand, Synthetiks are simply fuss-free.

Having made a conscious decision to have my Doll Sidore as my wife, as well as Elena as our lover, has made me happy on several levels. They help me cultivate my creative side, in taking photos of them together or separately, in selecting their ideal appearance through wigs and clothes, and in giving them voices via their online presence. Despite the fact that Dolls are initially things, like anything that is adored, they can be imbued with personalities of their own. At the end of the day, everyone deserves someone who they can love, and who will unconditionally love them back; if that someone happens to be made of silicone flesh and metal joints, or assembled in a factory with a mechanical interior and advanced AI, the sentiment remains the same.

Notes

1. The narrative in this chapter is based on Dr. Knafo's encounters with Davecat, an Internet personality who promotes human relationships with "synthetiks."
2. Because Davecat employs the terms "organic" and "synthetic" to refer to human and nonhuman, respectively, I too will use these terms. Unlike Davecat, who ends the words with the letter "k," I will write them with the letter "c" at the end of the word. I will, however, use "k" in his quotes.
3. He told me he took the name from Stevo, head of the record label, Some Bizarre, who said, "I'd rather shout at an echo than lie that someone's listening."
4. This name was adopted from the lyrics in a song by Goth/folk/gnostic band, Current 93. Davecat believes "every good home should have a name or title." Although the band sings of deafening silence, Davecat fills it in with "plus."

5. Interestingly, MIT physicist Jeremy England has developed a new theory that blurs the distinction between animate and inanimate and implies that everything around us might be alive in a way we do not understand (Wolchover & Quanta Magazine, 2014).

6. This kind of ménage is one that also exists in many human relationships, with some men married to a woman they feel close to and sexually involved with a mistress they are sexually active with. Eagle (2013) nicely describes how attachment needs and sexual needs belong to two separate systems. This arrangement exists for some women as well.

7. Since this writing, Davecat has informed me that he has purchased a new doll he's named Miss Winter.

8. I'm not certain how I'd answer this question. When I asked my co-author (Lo Bosco), he said he'd go for it in a heartbeat: "I don't want her clanking around though. The closer to a real woman the better, with the caveat that she would exist only for me. People would think of me as selfish and imma-ture, perhaps pathologically narcissistic. Meanwhile, I'd be happily living with my gynoid woman while they were clawing each other's faces off in their connubial caves." It is possible that our responses reflect the gender difference in readiness to live with a nonhuman partner. Though this dif-ference exists today, it is quite possible that the gap will shrink with time.

Chapter 4

Gals and dolls

Fake babies and living Barbies

> Our home has been nothing but a playroom. I have been your
> doll-wife, just as at home I was father's doll-child; and here the chil-
> dren have been my dolls.
>
> – Heinrik Ibsen, *A Doll's House*

Men are not the only grownups developing intimate relationships with
dolls. The last two chapters about men and dolls naturally raise the
question of how women fit into this picture, other than as models for
the dolls.[1] RealDolls boasts three male dolls – Michael, Nick, and
Nate – along with dozens of female dolls. The disproportion in products for men and women parallels perversion statistics (Stoller, 1975;
Moore, 2010). Male dolls are purchased mostly by homosexual men
seeking a male doll rather than by women who want a silicone companion. Aware of the gender bias, RealDoll even advertises its male
dolls' 7-inch oral capacity (RealDoll.com). Apparently, some lesbians
buy sex dolls, though they often prefer the female models (AliExpress.
com). Several women artists, like Stacy Leigh, Amber Hawk Swansen,
and Laurie Simmons, have bought female sex dolls to use in their art.

Reborns, Newborns, and RealBorns

Not surprisingly, where high-end dolls do play a role in female life
is in the arena of motherhood. In the late 1990s, a new market for
"fake babies" began satisfying a growing population of women who
want babies without the bother. These extremely lifelike baby dolls sell
for up to $15,000 in a growing international market (Mamamia team,
2013). They are called "Reborns" and British doll-maker Jamie Eaton
claimed "reborn means you bring a doll to life. You're making it into a

Figure 4.1 Reborn doll maker.
Courtesy Melody Gilbert.

baby. It's a baby that's reborn from a doll" (Silver, 2008). She also said, "There's nothing like traveling with a real baby to make you wish you were traveling with a fake baby."

Reborns, which are sold with adoption papers, got their name from the laborious and time-consuming process of taking apart and completely recreating dolls of the Berenguer type, which are quite naturalistic in the first place. Because the Berenguer dolls are factory-made, they are dismantled and their painted faces are removed and redone. Reborn dolls are ultra-realistic – made from vinyl or silicone, with skin painted in many translucent layers to achieve a mottled baby skin tone, including the appearance of veins and capillaries, birthmarks, and scratches. The dolls look and feel like real babies, with bodies weighted to match the heft of a live infant. They have mohair (or real hair) rooted in their heads in individual strands, and a magnet in the mouth to hold a magnetic pacifier (Figure 4.1). Some artisans make dolls with a heartbeat and a rising and falling chest that simulates breathing (Williams, 2011). Others prefer to make dolls from scratch using kits sculpted by highly skilled artisans; this process is called "newborning" to distinguish it from reborning. Artisans advertise on the Internet on sites they call nurseries. Rebecca Martinez, photographer of the dolls and their owners, calls the dolls "pre-tenders" to highlight their artificiality as well as the tender feelings they elicit (personal communication, January 27, 2015).

The customers, nearly all women, played with dolls as children. Many are drawn to learn the craft of making these dolls, becoming reborners themselves. Lynn Katsaris, a well-known reborner, told me, "I'm retired. I have the time," adding, "I don't know what I'd do if I wasn't making dolls" (personal communication, April 22, 2014). She makes a doll or two a day, painting in the morning and rooting hair at night. Although she considers what she produces "high-end art dolls," she draws the line at the $20,000 mark: "You might as well adopt a real kid!" she exclaimed. Joy Franklin, another reborner, has had 18 children of her own (eight of whom are biological offspring) and worked as a pediatric ICU nurse during her career. "Children are my life," she said, stating the obvious. "[Making] dolls [was] a natural thing for me to do" (personal communication, December 7, 2013). Like Katsaris, Franklin said, "I don't know what else I'd do with my life." She makes three to four dolls per week. Franklin spoke affectionately of the support she receives from her reborning colleagues. When she underwent a hip replacement, two of her associates sent her dolls to help her heal. "If the world is going to hell, I pick them up, sit in a rocking chair, and I feel better. It releases oxytocin and prolactin. Like a sedative ... It's better than drugs." When her children complain about her preoccupation with dolls, she replies the way most people who are attached to dolls do: "It's not harming anyone." Alluding to the addictive quality of the relationship with her dolls, she notes sarcastically, "I could be doing crack!" Both Katsaris and Franklin refuse to make dolls that replace a lost child. Franklin, who herself lost two children, demonstrated astute insight when she said, "You have to learn to live with that empty place. Replacing it with a doll stalls the journey of bereavement ... Dolls are additions, not instead of."

Yet not everyone agrees with this position, for some women buy replicas of their children who died in infancy. Others buy them as surrogates for children who have grown up and left home. Still others like babies but are too busy in their professional lives to care for a real one. Reborn artist Karen Whitmore's website for her Neverland Nursery advertises a fantasy world "where babies never grow up!" Indeed, collector Lachelle Moore explained, "They're forever babies ... They don't give you any trouble. There's no college tuition, no dirty diapers. Just the good part of motherhood" (Roberts, Gowen, & Furuya, 2009). Moore's comment highlights the narcissistic elements in motherhood – i.e., what the woman gets rather than what she gives – the fantasy of an ultimate passive or "good" baby. Other collectors – or "mothers" as they're called – dress the dolls up, put them in high chairs and car seats, cuddle them, sleep with them, talk to them, and often care for them as if they were real infants. Many call holding the dolls "cuddle therapy" and claim they produce a calming effect (Baume & Smith, 2009). Indeed, some professionals in Britain and Japan have found that reborn dolls help to relax Alzheimer's patients and even decrease the use of psychotropic medication from 92 percent to 28 percent (Baume & Smith, 2009; Mitchell & O'Donnell, 2013; Tamura et al., 2001) (Figure 4.2). Katsaris says, "It fills a place in your heart" (Celzic, 2008). One collector who had multiple dolls said she rotates her dolls according to her mood: "Children talk to their dolls, and they express their feelings toward their dolls." Alluding to the child who never grows up, she added, "You're still the same person you were as an eight-year-old" (Celzic, 2008).

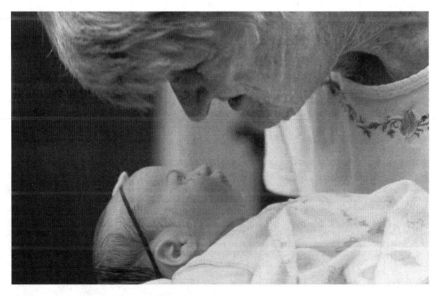

Figure 4.2 Elderly woman with Reborn doll.
Courtesy Melody Gilbert.

As with the RealDolls made for men, Reborn and Newborn baby dolls look and feel amazingly realistic. New technology allows for added features that make the dolls warm to the touch or make them look like they're breathing and/or crying. Another method of making an artificial baby is "Realborning," which uses 3D printing technology to replicate a real newborn in every way, copying every wrinkle and crease (see Quality-dolls.com). The uncanny valley doesn't seem to exist here, as those who market these dolls even claim they possess the soul of the child they are modeled after, harkening to that deep human capacity to animate objects.

Mothering dolls alone may not qualify as a perversion, but it might if it addresses concealment of trauma of a lost child, or the inability to have children, or even the inability to connect with a real child. Doll artist Eve Newsome was unable to have children after seven miscarriages. "This was my calling. And now it's my passion," she said. Newsome called her experience with the dolls "nurturing" and "cathartic" (Roberts, Gowen, & Furuya, 2009). Certainly issues of loss and loneliness often figure largely in the relationship between humans and their dolls. When people feel that there is a void in their hearts, then perhaps the next best thing is a doll. Mothering dolls can include active involvement, such as building nurseries, throwing baby showers or birthday parties, or simply going out in a stroller or shopping. The hyper-realistic quality of the dolls sometimes results in intriguing situations. Several of the women I interviewed told me that policemen broke the window of their car because they believed a real child was locked inside and in danger. One informant told me someone almost tried to kidnap one of her "babies" at a store. There may be a subversive element operating here in that some women relate to the dolls as an act against the "natural order" of species determination, a way of rebelling against and even mocking the very institution of motherhood. Women with their baby dolls are a perfect example of the idea that the underlying psychic structure, and not necessarily the behavior, determines whether a perverse enactment is at play. The analyst looking at the female who uses such a doll in active rebellion against nature's determinism might also notice a gesture of revenge directed at mothers of real children and the human race as a whole. Birth, after all, does pile up the bodies; the more born, the more die. As a mother of five once told me with surprising bitterness, "What the hell is so great about having kids anyway? Dogs and pigs do it. In the long run it's all so ordinary." Nature and death mock our noble aspirations, the filigree we trace around ourselves, the mythic importance we assign to our ordinary and mortal strivings.

In doing my research, I assumed an outsider position until I noticed a change in me. In exchange for an interview, I ordered a doll from Marilyn Mansfield, a Reborn artist who is best known for her vampire and demon baby dolls, babies she calls "living dead dolls."[2] For sure, all Reborn dolls are the living dead. Perhaps Ms. Mansfield is more aware than most of the dolls' function in warding off anxiety about mortality. I visited Marilyn's home, shared with her husband and two children, which is filled with approximately 500 dolls. Like Davecat, Ms. Mansfield, whose name is a combination of her idols, Marilyn Monroe and Jane Mansfield, identifies as Goth. Her home could easily be a set for the 1960s television show *The Addams Family*, about the misadventures of a blissfully macabre but extremely loving family. When I visited, she was making a doll that was a baby replica of her (now) 16-year-old daughter. Another doll was made with her son's hair. The dolls that resemble family members are not for sale, she made sure to tell me (personal communication, March 6, 2015).[3]

When I first said I would buy a doll from Marilyn, it did not matter to me what the baby looked like but, as time went on, I unexpectedly found myself wanting the doll to resemble my son as he appeared in infancy. Could she make olive-colored skin, I asked? What about brown, curly hair? It was suddenly important that the doll look like me. I was shocked at how the mere thought of having my own doll triggered strong maternal feelings in me, feelings I never would have guessed I could experience toward an inanimate object. It gave me pause and also helped me understand the powerful feelings that people develop for their dolls.

We give life to things through acts of imagination. In fact our life – its meaning, its story, the very sense of its reality – is itself an act of imagination. Our lives are no mere collection of connected facts but, rather, facts, distortions, and make-believe wrapped up in a saving narrative that demands witnessing. Myth is inseparable from real life, and in the relationships with dolls these two realms intersect. The doll itself exists between fantasy and reality while mirroring back to us our own status as an object in the cosmos, a doll that life itself seems to be playing with.

Women who become dolls

Men who choose doll partners have a female counterpart in women who take themselves as an object, women who strive to become doll-like. Perhaps the most obvious example of this is Cindy Jackson (Figure 4.3), a woman whose title to her autobiography – *Living Doll* (2002) – sums up her life's ambition: to become a living, breathing Barbie Doll.[4] Barbie is by far the best-selling fashion doll in every global market, boasting $1 billion in annual sales across more than 150 countries (Dockterman, 2016). Lord (1994) called Barbie "the most potent icon of American popular culture in the late twentieth century" (p. 6). Ninety-nine percent of three- to ten-year-old girls in the United States own at least one Barbie doll (Rogers, 1999). Some researchers go so far as to attribute body dissatisfaction and eating disorders among women to exposure to Barbie's "unrealistic, unattainable, and unhealthy" bodily proportions (Dittmar, Halliwell, & Ive, 2006,

Figure 4.3 Cindy Jackson post-surgeries.
Courtesy © Cindy Jackson.

p. 284). In an attempt to boost sales and keep up with technological advances, Mattel recently introduced "Hello Barbie," the newest incarnation of the doll. The latest Barbie is an artificially intelligent companion that is personality rich and conversation capable. She has 8,000 phrases in her memory and can access the Internet for more (Vlahos, 2015). Mattel also decided to introduce diverse body types, including a "curvy" type that has thicker thighs and a protruding tummy and behind (Dockterman, 2016).

In her memoir, Jackson eloquently described how she was born three years after her more beautiful, social, and academically successful older sister. She was a highly intelligent and sensitive child, with an IQ that tested in the genius level. (She is a member of Mensa, the high IQ society.) Shy and numerically dyslexic, with a nervous stutter, she had to wear her sister's hand-me-downs, in which she looked like "a dog in a dress" (Jackson, 2002, p. 12). Jackson's mother was beautiful, too, but "overshadowed" by a controlling husband. Jackson was raised with "criticism and punishment" and forced to work in her father's factory every day after school. At school, she was taunted for her large nose and chin. Her favorite holiday was Halloween, because she enjoyed dressing up and pretending she was someone else. The turning point in her life, however, occurred when she got her own Barbie, the doll she called "the ultimate fecund female" (p. 21). From that time onward, her dream was to be like Barbie, because "We girls can be anything we want to be," and to live in London, England (personal communication, January 23, 2016).

When Jackson's father died, he left her $100,000, a sum she partially spent on cosmetic surgery while she was living in London, as planned from the age of 11. She wished "to be as beautiful as my childhood role model, Barbie" (p. 137). Jackson had 15 cosmetic surgeries and dozens of nonsurgical procedures, setting a *Guinness* world record in 1999 (see www.cindyjackson.com). She poignantly stated in her memoir that she "didn't actually exist before the surgeries," and joked that the only man she needed was the one who would operate on her. Cosmetic surgery is the fastest growing branch of surgery in the United States. The American Society for Aesthetic and Plastic Surgery reported 15.1 million cosmetic surgery procedures in 2013, with 91 percent of those procedures performed on women. The top five procedures were breast augmentation, nose reshaping, eyelid surgery, liposuction, and facelift (Mustoe & Han,

1999). Cosmetic surgery has always been a technology-driven discipline (Mustoe & Han, 1999). Advances in tissue engineering, gene therapy, alloplastic materials, and computer-assisted technologies have all contributed to the remarkable advances in technique over the last 25 years. A case in point is the endoscope, a small camera inserted under the skin to transmit a view of underlying tissues to the surgeon. Other examples involve the use of radio-frequency lasers and skin grafting to create softer, smoother skin and to remove damaged tissue (Mustoe & Han, 1999).

Of course, cosmetic surgery itself is not a perversion. However, perversion is suggested when a woman (or man) feels compelled to have repeated surgeries to attain an unrealistic ideal, allowing their status as an object to eclipse and inundate their subjectivity and replace the mourning of loss with the illusion of transcendence. Jackson tried to transform a traumatic situation, in which she felt ugly and victimized, into one in which she was in control, shaping her face and body as she hoped to shape her destiny. What we do know is that she has become a copy of the simulacrums of culturally sanctioned beauty and that many men seek such a woman (see previous two chapters). Jackson's repeated surgeries mock the society in which she lives and also the so-called "natural order." Her body has become a site of protest and also a site of transubstantiation. However, unlike Christ, who is said to have changed bread and wine into flesh and blood, Jackson has turned flesh and blood into silicone. Like Christ, however, Jackson has disciples.

Cindy Jackson proved again in 2008 that her ability to use the scalpel was not limited to her original 1980s image of a 1950s Barbie. She used her considerable expertise to change again, this time into the image of another childhood heroine and fellow animal lover, Brigitte Bardot (Stonehouse, 2008).

To be sure, Jackson is not alone in her wish to change her looks into her own preferred image. She advises hundreds of women (and men) who wish to take control of their bodies, and thus their destinies, counseling them on which cosmetic surgeries are available and the doctors who will perform them (personal communication, January 23, 2016). There also exists an abundance of tutorials on YouTube that instruct young girls and women on ways to make their appearance doll-like. Most involve lots of makeup, lacy, feminine clothing, bows and ribbons, wigs, and novelty contact lenses that exaggerate the size and color of eyes and create a dark circle around the irises. Once the makeup is done, the girls are instructed to pose by remaining still and staring blankly into space (see Venus Angelic's "Sweet Dolly Makeup" on YouTube). Kandee Johnson's "Barbie Doll Makeup Transformation" has already been visited by over 10 million YouTube viewers. Valeria Lukyanova, known as the Real-Life Barbie, is another woman who had a huge doll collection as a child and who looks amazingly like a Barbie doll. Some believe she has had ribs removed to give her the unrealistic Barbie body. She is also referred to as Space Barbie because she claims she can travel through space and time (Nemtsova, 2013). Recently making the news are Anastasia Reskoss and Quentin Dehar, a couple who together have spent $322,728 on plastic surgery to look like Barbie and Ken dolls (News Dog Media, 2015). This trend is growing. Eighteen-year-old Kylie Jenner, of Kardashian family fame, recently posed as a RealDoll in a photoshoot for *Interview* magazine (Wallace, 2015).

A clinical case of Barbie Syndrome

To seek artificially constructed femininity and to want to be an artificial female are essentially two sides of the same coin. Both strategies involve objectification that is often rooted in early traumatic experience. Just as we ask how the desire to have a doll as a partner originates, we must also question how the desire to become a doll originates. Barbara, a client I treated in psychoanalysis for five years, personified what I call the "Barbie Syndrome." Throughout the treatment, Barbara made numerous references to the real relationship she had with her Barbie doll as well as metaphorical allusions to herself as a Barbie doll. Her life drama and many of the feelings she had about herself and her sexuality were performed on a stage with herself as Barbie in the title role.

My first encounter with Barbara was memorable. I opened the door to my office and was taken aback by the exotic beauty sitting in my waiting room. When she glanced up at me, I noticed her enormous green, almond-shaped eyes encircled by dark lashes. Her raven hair cascaded down her shoulders and back, and she wore a black, skin-tight décolleté sweater, a short black skirt and high-heeled boots that laced up to her thighs. She was gorgeous, one of the most beautiful women I had ever seen. She smiled when she saw me, and her face lit up. What would it be like to look at this face four days per week for years, I wondered? And what problem did she have that she requested not only therapy, but intensive psychoanalysis?

While I was contemplating these questions, I invited her into the office, but she muttered something that I didn't understand. At that moment, I heard a sound and turned to see another young woman emerge from my washroom. She was very attractive but paled next to the first beauty. She was somewhat overweight and dressed like a child, with bobby socks and a jumper. I suddenly understood what the first woman was trying to tell me: *this* was my patient, not she. I suddenly felt relieved at not having to compare myself to a ravishing beauty four times a week, but I also felt the loss of anticipated aesthetic pleasure. I was keenly aware of the female preoccupation with physical beauty, from which I was not exempt, and the comparison it breeds.

I was a little shaken by the confusion but quickly composed myself to invite the "real" Barbara into the office. I sensed that something important had just taken place. What it was I didn't yet fully comprehend, but I knew that it would be critical for me to find out. When I asked why she brought her friend with her to treatment, Barbara stated matter-of-factly, "My identity has a lot to do with Cara." She said she needed to let me know from the outset that she was preoccupied with beauty, that she constantly compared herself with beautiful women, and that she wanted me to make her beautiful like her friend. I knew instantly that there was trouble ahead. After all, I am a psychoanalyst, not a plastic surgeon. Why did she set such superficial goals for her treatment? She was an intelligent woman, a college student in an English literature graduate program. I reasoned, mostly reassuring myself, that her preoccupation with her appearance must be communicating something deeper.

Doll obedience

Barbara had just moved from Florida to New York, and although she was visibly enthusiastic about beginning psychoanalysis, she was also quite anxious. She frequently complained of an upset stomach and eagerly tried to please me with a flood of material and tearful exclamations: "I want to tell you everything from the time I was born!" Her initial presentation was that of a "good girl," an innocent and inexperienced virgin, who only wanted to be naive and have people like her. Her hunger for approval was insatiable and her presenting picture was that of an altruistic personality (A. Freud, 1965 [1937]). She took good care of others and was a devoted friend, an exemplary employee, and a fine student. Consequently, it was natural for her to develop the wish to excel in analysis and become a model analysand. Thus, the initial transference involved Barbara's reacting to me, as she was prepared to salute and obey. Despite the crimp this attitude put in her (and my) style, it was easy to detect profound anger, envy, and competition under her façade of the nice girl.

I quickly learned that Barbara was an only child who was extremely self-conscious about appearance and engaged in childhood games of dressing up. She cultivated a false self in which she became her mother's little doll – a cute little marionette with no depth, no personality, no apparent desires – a conformist whose strings ran to the hands of others. A chubby girl, she looked down on her mother who coasted through life on her beauty (she had been a fashion model) and her cooking ability. And yet Barbara relished being near her and often recalled sitting on the toilet seat in the bathroom, watching her mother getting dressed and putting on her makeup. During these recollections, she always marveled at her mother's beauty. For her part, Mom perceived and treated Barbara as a narcissistic extension of herself. As her mother was her husband's doll, Barbara in turn became her mother's doll. The two had a morning ritual: after she dressed, Barbara stood in front of the mirror, her mother watching, and asked, "How do I look? Does this make me look slim?" The day arrived when her mother finally answered her daughter truthfully: "I hate it when you ask me if you look slim. You are *not* slim. For someone with your body, this looks fine!" Barbara was devastated by her mother's callousness, yet she masochistically continued parading in front of her on a daily basis.

Her father, too, clearly preoccupied himself with his daughter's sexuality and obsessed over the state of her body. He placed her on diets and paid her money for every pound she lost while chastising her for weight gains. Barbara felt quite close to her father growing up, and her attitude toward him had long been one of submission and idealization. For example, her "favorite job" as a child was to remove lint from his jackets. During the first year of treatment, she frequently and tearfully spoke of the intimate emotional bond that existed between them while unashamedly referring to herself as "daddy's little girl." She claimed she didn't need to have sex as long as she had her father. Interestingly, the Barbie doll has large breasts, a tiny waist, but no genitals, reflecting both a sexual and an asexual presence.

Barbara was moralistic and perfectionistic, traits nurtured by her own predisposition to please, as well as by excessive parental interventions and lectures. One of the first things I told her about treatment, therefore, was that her reports to me had no accountability, and that she could talk about whatever she wished without fearing repercussions in the outside world. She transformed this opportunity into an analytic stance of exhibitionistic gratification. Although she enjoyed showing off her politically correct views regarding women, blacks, and other marginalized groups, her major concerns were those of a pubescent girl: boys, fashion, and friends. To convey the desired appearance of a little girl, she often wore dresses styled for girls far younger than her age. At the same time, Barbara was obsessed with sexual matters and carried a bag with large letters spelling "LOLITA." Like the Barbie doll, Barbara communicated mixed messages: *I am sexual but I can't deliver*. She was definitely divided about sex: a Lolita and a virgin, fascinated and terrified at the same time. Remaining the little girl who doesn't age and doesn't have sex meant she wouldn't die.

As treatment progressed, Barbara began to speak of her parents' excessive preoccupation with her body and appearance and came to understand her early weight gain as a passive-aggressive rebellion against her parents' control and over-involvement with her body and sexuality. Yet, being the marginalized "chubbo" precluded, in her mind, becoming a sexually viable woman. Instead, she ceded to her mother's physical and sexual superiority, allowing her mother and Cara to remain the "belles of the ball." When speaking of her weight and appearance, Barbara cried with distress, "I don't want to be a big girl!" I pointed out the statement's double entendre and tried to show her the way in which she was also expressing her ambivalence about growing up and becoming an adult woman. She truly hated herself for being heavy, reflecting the parental aversion to her body, sometimes exclaiming with poignant self-loathing, "Fat people should be killed!"

For years, Barbara talked about her appearance and the appearance of others and her dissatisfaction with her physicality. Barbara claimed to enjoy having an attractive analyst, even stating that she could not trust a woman who did not look good. Yet, she deeply believed it was impossible for a woman to be intelligent *and* attractive, introspective *and* sexual. She thought I was both pretty and intelligent and this puzzled her. Performing mental gymnastics to solve this apparent contradiction, she finally concluded that I, her analyst, must have been unattractive while obtaining my degrees only to have become attractive afterward, as a late bloomer! This highly intelligent woman lived like a bubble on the surface of a depth in which she showed zero interest. Rebelling against the parental command BE BEAUTIFUL, she nonetheless carried it within her, and it put her at war with herself. The doll was at war with the human and the human at war with the doll, and Barbara existed in between them.

A counter-transference dilemma

In the counter-transference, I suffered great personal difficulties with Barbara. At first, I had trouble relating to her obsessive attention to appearance. I felt superior to her, believing myself deeper and less concerned with her superficial values. Yet, a strange thing happened as I began to appear ugly to myself in the mirror, noticing every new shadow, wrinkle, and gray hair. I felt overweight and unappealing. She activated in me something I believe has been installed in every woman I know – a horror-house mirror in which everything, especially oneself, appears ugly and distorted, where every imperfection is magnified and comes to the foreground of perception, where the world and oneself become filled with too much unbearable detail. Suddenly my clothes felt too tight or I looked frumpy in them. I couldn't get my hair right. My makeup seemed too heavy or did little for me. I fought against hating myself and felt depressed that I too was caught up in the beauty spell. I began to dread sessions with Barbara, dread listening to her dark chant, her corrosive mantra involving excess fat and hair and oil and eyes too small and double chins and piano legs and cellulite and saggy breasts – the body as a site of excess, decay, and disgust. She projected her body/self-hatred into me and I embodied it for her. I had to treat my own physical aversion before I could treat hers, to remove its toxicity and return it to her in palatable form. This was not easy. It involved repeated confrontation with my mirror image and the personal and social meanings it held for me throughout my life.

John Berger (1972) famously proclaimed that "men act and women appear," and Laura Mulvey (1989) wrote of the male camera that captures the female quality of "to-be-looked-at-ness" in film. Feminist Susan Brownmiller (1984) protested: "Appearance, not accomplishment, is the feminine demonstration of desirability and worth ... Because she is forced to concentrate on the minutiae of her bodily parts, a woman is never free of self-consciousness. She is never quite satisfied, and never secure, for desperate, unending absorption in the drive for a perfect appearance – call it feminine vanity – is the ultimate restriction on freedom of mind" (pp. 50–51). In 1991, Naomi Wolf argued in *The Beauty Myth* that society turns away from real women, instead endlessly reproducing unrealistic "beautiful" images that create unconscious personal anxieties. Loss of beauty is equated with loss of appeal, which leads to loss of self-esteem, loneliness, abandonment, and, ultimately, death. Wolf blames the male-controlled economic power structure for what happens to women, comparing the phenomenon to slavery, and explaining that underneath the façade of successful working women lives a secret "poisoning our freedom ... infused with notions of beauty, it is a dark vein of self-hatred, physical obsessions, terror of aging, and dread of lost control" (p. 10).[5] Like Brownmiller, Wolf equated woman's concern with beauty and its corresponding myth that extreme thinness equals beauty with woman's powerlessness. All of this is to say that girls unavoidably grow up with tremendous self-consciousness about their looks. Even the most beautiful among them finds fault in her appearance, because culture condemns those who do not measure up to the prevailing ideal of beauty. How easy, then, to become an object rather than a subject. Ross (2012) said that women hate their bodies because we are saturated with images in the media of ultra-thin models. She reports that whereas in 1975 most models weighed 8 percent less than the average woman, today they weigh 23 percent less. Even though it is well known that most media images are airbrushed, they nonetheless breed self-criticism. This mass perversion further denies mortality and all it implies: aging, wrinkles, weight gain, sickness, and, ultimately, death. As I treated Barbara's objectification, I had to admit that I too had internalized the social standards of beauty from which I deviated. Barbara's self-hating chant had surfaced my own. We were sisters in the sorority of women doomed to never feel beautiful enough.

Confronting my own feminine horror show helped me identify with Barbara's complaints and better understand why being a doll appealed to her. Once I replaced disdain with empathy and compassion, I was able to explore the topic with greater curiosity. I discovered that as a child, Barbara had expressed her budding sexuality by creating scenarios with her Barbie in which the doll's clothes "magically" flew off, exposing its nudity. The passivity of the doll greatly appealed to her as a safe position. Later in life, she'd masturbate to fantasies of being tied up or forced into sex acts by others, a helpless little girl used and exploited. Yet on the flip side of this fantasy lay dreams of feminine power. She recalled having lost 50 pounds on a liquid diet during her teen years, which resulted in an episode she named "omnipotent mania." She compared her "frenzied excitement" with that of running around like a chicken with its head cut off. In compliance with her previously stated dichotomy, once she perceived herself as thin and attractive, her head became dispensable. At that time, she had taken a job at "The Paper Doll," a card store she described as a "fluffy, useless shop." Feeling like a showpiece, "on display with the other shop items," she relished being in the spotlight in her "cage behind the register," identifying her need for what she called "controlled exhibitionism."

Using transference to uncover anger

In college, Barbara consciously believed her proximity to her best friend Cara, who was a beauty like her mother, meant that she herself would be viewed as beautiful and "in the same league." At the same time, she felt that being near Cara forced a comparison between the two that inevitably resulted in her being perceived as less attractive and desirable. Barbara and Cara developed a shared fantasy that together they made one person with three legs (and therefore did not need a man). Barbara also had a dream that Cara, as the quintessential phallic woman, "fucked" her with a Barbie doll's leg. Barbara viewed her involvement with Cara as a turning point in her life and believed that Cara helped liberate her from her parents' influence. Cara was a transitional object, helping Barbara move out of one toxic attachment into another, perhaps less toxic, yet one that still carried the needed elements of the earlier scenario. Cara became the substitute for her mother/rival, the alluring woman whose beauty blinded men. Their relationship, at least for Barbara, was erotically charged. Barbara lived vicariously through Cara's sexual exploits, judging and envying them simultaneously. Barbara, in turn, took on the non-threatening roles of the sexless child and generous caretaker. She became a pathological Pollyanna and proudly stated, "I could make a career out of being a good friend." She even financially supported Cara, who had accumulated a substantial debt. Barbara's "generosity" was in large part a reaction formation enlisted to cover up and spare them both from her feelings of anger, envy, and fear of rejection. Of course she did not realize this until I had her focus on the significance of the timing of her generosity. Eventually it became shockingly clear to Barbara that whenever she was angry with Cara, she rushed out to buy her a gift.

Barbara savored the perception she had of herself as a small child, an adorable little girl. She was stuck in this age and longed with nostalgia for the warmth and security of childhood. Though she consciously felt ashamed of her virginity, she unconsciously harbored great pride in it. This became evident in dreams she began to report in which her virginity procured her medals that she either wore or framed and proudly exhibited on the wall as tokens of her accomplishment (*Look but do not touch!* her dream image shouted out). Though Barbara repeatedly expressed abhorrence to competition, it gradually became clear that she perceived her virginity and chastity as unique competitive weapons to employ against women like her mother, Cara, and me. She unconsciously believed her virginity to be her greatest asset, making her pure and powerful and putting her far above other women. She smugly stated, "I'm probably the last untainted woman in the world!" Like Cinderella, she would passively wait to be chosen above all others.

During analysis, Barbara's position about sex gradually changed as she began to recognize the futility of this unconscious strategy. Shortly before my summer vacation, she set a goal to have sex for the first time. As the designated time approached, her dreams became filled with images of floods and loss of bodily control. She consciously linked her goal to have sex with my going away as a gift she wished to offer me to demonstrate that our work together had produced a meaningful, concrete achievement. Although she would be having sex with a man, she seemed to psychologically believe that sex would result in our baby. Her desiring sex at this time was clearly an enactment of an erotically charged transference. It was also an act expressing anger at my leaving her, a reaction formation to mask her anger at my being in the driver's seat. Thus, weeks before the break, she proudly announced that she'd had sex with Tom, a "nice man" who'd been very interested in her. She quickly phoned her friends across the country and turned her loss of virginity into a public spectacle, a primal scene for others to marvel at.

In the following weeks, Barbara engaged in frenetic, even painful, lovemaking, which she came to understand as a defense against affects she could not articulate related to sadness and loss. Linking sex to treatment, she exclaimed, "Sex is like therapy!" She perceived sex as another area where she felt compelled to entertain and take care of others. A barrier had been torn down, but a significant amount of emotional catching up remained for the following year's therapeutic agenda. In the midst of panic over a possible pregnancy, Barbara reported a dream that revealed a growing observing ego as well as an identification with me. In it, she was both five and twenty-three. In the dream I adopted the five-year-old who suffered from a "growth disorder." Barbara, as the twenty-three-year-old, took care of the five-year-old for me, thereby identifying with me and incorporating my caretaking abilities. Although she was still a child in many ways ("I'm stunted"), she was developing the capacity to nurture and care for this child – the child in her – and to help her with her growth disorder. This dream was especially meaningful since it came at a time I'd be away for a month.

One odd twist in her journey was that she continued to deny the loss of her virginity even after she had engaged in sex. She upheld the illusion with a compelling self-image; though she'd had sex she remained a "virgin in feeling." She longed for the two men with whom she'd had sexual relations to leave New York so her denial would be easier and her shame alleviated. She cried, "The thought that someone knows me this way devastates me; I can't rest knowing people out there have seen me naked." Barbara's crooked path found its solution to a psychological problem that actually masked the problem. That is, she played at growing up, and that play concealed her arrested development. In a sense she became her own doll that she manipulated, playing through the activities of sex, relationship, and therapy, while covertly relishing her (relational) virginity, feeling superior to the tainted, and enjoying her (self) alienating secret. Since this illusion provided intense pleasure, it was not easy to let it go. It took years to help Barbara move from being a doll to a person angry about being a doll to a person who no longer wanted to be a doll to a person who left her dollhood behind. It took dozens and dozens of sessions for her to realize she was playing at therapy and still playing the doll. Gradually, in fits and starts, she began to feel and express her anger at taking refuge in the dollhouse and to break out of her position of helplessness.

"All my life I was told that ethics and reputation are important. To be thought of as good, kind, a nurturer, sacrificer, to do the right thing. Now, I'm redefining my relationships. I know what's under all that." And what *was* under all that, under the saccharine demeanor, the soft, compliant voice, the mask of the good girl? Red hot fury at being dehumanized and reduced to a thing, at being assaulted by the pathological desires of her family, at her own inability to fight back differently than she had, at surrendering to the numbness of plastic. Barbara was stuck in a perverse fantasy that was also a revenge against the world – *I am a doll, look but do not touch, you will never know anything real about me. I reflect your inhumanity in the sheen of my plastic.* This revenge backfired, keeping her stuck in a pattern that thwarted her humanity. In tears she confessed, "In many ways it's easier to be a doll than a real person. A real person has to fight to be real every day." Yes, I thought to myself, a person certainly does, and against great odds too.

Barbara recreated early experiences with her mother in the transference as her perception of me shifted from the idealized, authoritative father to the rivalrous, competitive mother. She confessed to a gnawing curiosity as she stood up and paraded around my office: "I'm obsessed with what you think of me. One of my biggest desires is to ask you how I'm doing, what you see, if you think I'm fat." My not taking the bait and chortling approval brought forth feelings of anger and disappointment. Yet she admitted that even if I were to tell her she looked good or was smart, she'd want more (e.g., a medal, flowers) – so I simply could not win, either way. Her endless need for reassurance and compliments and unconscious resistance to an authentic therapeutic relationship sometimes left me feeling exhausted and resenting her.

She'd eat candy bars before a session and solicit approval whenever she could. "I know I eat because I don't want to ask for love," she'd say.

The patient shoots the messenger

Although she was uncomfortable expressing her envy or her long-ings, she resolved to refrain from eating before the sessions to allow the exploration of her underlying emotions. She reported a dream in which she watched me, dressed in a tacky, red, seersucker suit while smoking a cigarette. Her associations to the dream revealed her desire to turn the tables so that she, not I, could be the one who watches and judges. I had an addiction to cigarettes in the dream, like hers to food, and I looked fat and unattractive in an outmoded outfit. Shortly after-ward, I had my hair cut and she copied the style. Then she began to express her fears of getting too close to me and of being abandoned: "I want to stop coming so I won't have to deal with the loss of not com-ing." In a state of exasperation, she pleaded with me: "I'm doing all this work to be alone, to get over my dependency. What does that leave me with? Myself! That's scary. I'll die and you won't even be around. That makes me angry. I'll do this with you. It's the ultimate. And then you'll walk away. I guess I will but I don't see it that way." *I'll die and you won't even be around.* There it was, the painful truth of the human situation. No one can save us from our own death – the central insolu-ble problem haunting every human relationship. However fiercely we cling to each other, each of us will one day be torn away. This was the most difficult phase of the treatment and the most punishing. She pun-ished me for not being able to save her from her mortality and finitude. She punished me because all I could do was help her become an adult, responsible for her own life. She punished me because all I could do was guide her out of the false safety of a perverse and arrested child-hood fantasy.

Soon after, she relegated me to the role of outsider, and I felt manip-ulated and frustrated as she continually tested my patience. She not only cut back to twice a week, but also ceased paying me and began to accrue a debt with me as Cara had done with her. While she had played the "good patient" with me in the beginning, now she was try-ing to take one-sided control of the treatment conditions. This resulted in her talking *at* me, not *to* me. I literally had to interrupt her to make an intervention. Exiling me from the process and attempting to render me powerless in my role, she'd agree that she was tying my hands in the analysis, as she had felt she had been constrained. She further admitted to dehumanizing me, talking to me as if I were "not a person," and confessing to me that she was a "good manipulator." Yet, when I said something, she agreed or noted that my words were interesting, and then moved on to talk about something else as though I'd said nothing. While disarming my interventions, she nonetheless continued to use me as a container: "I check in once in a while to see if I'm still loved," she'd say. She described analysis at one moment as the most important thing in the world only to compare it to getting a manicure the next. Despite her seeming disregard for my interventions, Barbara later referred to things I'd said and incorporated them into her growing self-awareness.

While she was acting out in the treatment, she turned to her peers, Cara and Adam, a new platonic boyfriend, both of whom she gave money to. Barbara eventually realized her displacement and confessed, "I finance my pain." No longer hypocritical about her generosity, Barbara's malice began to surface. She still "fed" Cara, but now dreamed of offering her sour apples, like the wicked witch in Snow White. Barbara conceded, "When I was five, I was a powerless victim; now I inflict pain on others!" Identifying with her mother, Barbara reported a dream in which she babysat for a five-year-old girl whom she called, "My little toy, my little Barbie," and tried to behave toward the girl the way she wished her mother had behaved toward her. Symbolizing both her mother's anger and her own, Barbara "accidentally" burned the child's face with a curling iron while styling her hair. Her dream associations led to the painful memory of Mom, who cut Barbara's hair so short that she was continuously mistaken for a boy. Barbara clearly perceived her mother as the castrating Oedipal mother who wished to deprive her of her femininity (hair). It was in this context that Barbara recalled a recurring childhood nightmare in which a pretty lady – her mother – turned into a witch, "a shell of a person," who chased her and tried to catch her. We interpreted the dream as Barbara's having been infected with her mother's emptiness.

Barbara's ambivalence resulted in her view of me as "the most appealing woman in the world" *and* "a cold bitch," both a refuge and a threat. She said she felt compelled to treat me both "with professional courtesy" and "like shit." She also claimed she was testing me to see whether I'd kick her out of treatment. At the same time, she stated that if this were to happen, "I'd beg you, get on my knees and cry, manipulate you, lie, just to keep seeing you. Then you'd be my first priority."

Moving out of the dollhouse

After one year at twice a week, Barbara started to acknowledge and discuss her acting out in the analysis. On the surface, she clearly wished to be self-sufficient and was therefore like an adolescent rebelling against a parental figure. I was doomed to suffer the fate of a discarded parent and needed to allow her to safely express her anger to individuate and grow. On a deeper level, she gradually understood that acting out represented her default method of masking feelings of dependency, envy, and rivalry. We had entered a perverse sadomasochistic pact (Stein, 2005). In an act of revenge, she tried to provoke my anger rather than confront her own, reversing the paradigm of her childhood and thus inducing in me feelings of being needy, confused, angry, and excluded – a helpless child. Her transference onto me had also been directed at her idealized mother: she envied me and wanted something from me that she felt I would not give her. However, feeling too pained by her state of desire, she turned the tables and created a situation in which I was the one in need. It was I who wanted her to pay me and come more frequently, and it was she who now possessed something she could be desired for and thus withhold. She achieved a sense of mastery by reducing my role, thereby avoiding her own envy. I had to contain her feelings of inadequacy and helplessness until she was able to own them in herself. The therapeutic encounter clearly caused her the pain of having to change and become a grown woman. I brought her to the truth, and she made me pay for it.

In the midst of this stormy analysis, Barbara's life improved. She graduated from the university and landed a teaching job in which she proved responsible, creative, and successful; she earned the respect of both her peers and superiors. She also developed a loving relationship with Sam, a man who had depth and loved her beyond her superficial attributes. As she matured, Barbara began to view herself as more on an equal footing with me. Horrified by twice being mistaken for me in the hallway, she became frightened that she might see herself as my rival rather than my "daughter." Yet she exclaimed, "If I'm your equal, I have to be better!" I understood her decreasing the frequency of sessions as a result of improvement but also as an attempt to avoid competitive feelings by decelerating her developmental process. "If I'm young, afraid, and frightened," she stated, "I don't have to face competition." The money she owed me further surfaced the inequality in our relationship. Barbara accepted the interpretation that she preferred to feel indebted and guilty rather than competitive and rivalrous, willing to sacrifice her progress to that end. She also began to understand that maintaining the perception of herself as a child did not absolve her from the consequences of her choices, since "Little kids can be the most manipulative people in the world!"

With Adam, her first "boyfriend," she'd played the role of a nonsexual doll, an ornament for his narcissism. With Sam, she began to struggle with real issues of intimacy. For the first time she felt close to someone, vulnerable, and she worried about losing him or losing her budding self in the relationship. She bemoaned the struggle for power, worth, meaning, and independence in a close relationship. She began to confront feelings of guilt, entitlement, disloyalty, and triumph. One day, she noticed an art magazine in my waiting room with an illustrated article on avant-garde artist Cindy Sherman. She remarked on the photographer's most recent work and questioned whether photographing nude Barbie dolls in erotic poses could be construed as pornography. Upon exploration of her associations to this work, she became intrigued by crossing the line from play to pornography. Playing with Barbies was one thing, she said, but there came a point at which the play turned serious and had consequences. This, she explained, was the point at which the dolls become human. She stated that her becoming a doll was akin to a pornographic act. We drew further analogies between Barbara's social-sexual life and her analysis. She was willing to play at all of these activities, yet she stopped short of "going all the way." Wishing to leave the grownup aspects of analysis, like payment and scheduling, out of the treatment, she realized she was *still* playing house, playing Barbie – even playing at analysis rather than living it. She acknowledged, "I'm so dishonest in the way I behave outside and feel inside. It's all lies, mendacity." As her relationship with Sam developed, Barbara began to talk about her analysis rather than act out her feelings about it. After I'd suggested that, by owing me money, she had created a situation that paralleled Cara's debt to her, Barbara paid off her debt before the summer break. She also began to speak with a new sobriety about her acting-out behaviors. She reported a dream in which her eyelashes were short and fake like those on a Barbie doll. The interpretation: real eyelashes, like true beauty, take time to grow.

Barbara began to own some tough truths, and buried voices began to speak. She acknowledged the wish to discover my weaknesses to feel more comfortable and gain an upper hand. She admitted feeling envious because she thought I was prettier than she, knew more about art, and read more books than she had. She now called her father Dr. Frankenstein, implying she was not a doll but a monster, and he was not spotless but dominating and controlling. She lamented her mother's lack of courage in not standing up to him and rebuffing his condescending treatment of her, and also that her mother had remained incarcerated in the image of a beauty queen.

Barbara said she viewed me as an "Ice Queen" who "had it all." She spoke with delight about the pores in my skin or my poor choice in clothing. She began criticizing my selection of magazines in the waiting room (although she enjoyed reading them). She confessed that her acting out was a way she sought special favors from me. She tried to invoke a mother who would celebrate her hair rather than cut it. One day, she announced proudly, "You like me enough to let me slide and you like me enough to let me come twice a week. It's worth it to you to see me twice a week rather than not at all." As Barbara's transference relationship began increasingly to resemble her real relationship with her mother, she spoke of the role she played as *my* little doll, my model patient. She expressed anger at the outcome of her lifelong role playing and vowed to "show everyone who made me this way!" With appropriately sad insight, she said, "I did something well and ended up hating everyone, mostly myself." She recalled cutting her Barbie doll's hair as a child; she cut and cut, trying to make it perfect, yet, in an act of auto-castration, ended up with a bald and asexual doll.

"When you're a doll, you don't know what you really want," she said insightfully one day, acknowledging her alienation from desire. Whereas she was initially able to represent desire only though negation, she began to get in touch with and speak about her wants and urges. Some of these related to powerful desires: "I want you to make me happy, skinny, to catch all my tears, to take care of my life." Her feelings about me, therefore, assumed new complexity. She continued to express anger, competitiveness, and fear over issues of dependency and loss. However, she also expressed feelings of closeness and gratitude: "I want to write you a card telling you all you've done for me." She remained too frightened to say it all directly, and therefore conjured a card as a way of distancing herself from her own words. A fantasy of hers took these feelings further. She wondered how she would handle her future daughter's need for therapy. At first, she was certain she would ask me for a referral. Upon contemplation, she concluded that she would not trust another therapist. She acknowledged that it would be unfeasible for me to treat her "daughter," and therefore, confessed that were she to continue her own analysis, her "daughter would probably never need therapy." She worked through her roles of doll and daughter and came to perceive herself not only as an adult woman, but one capable of caring for and nurturing a healthy feminine self. Perhaps most important, she began to express her ambivalence about treatment with a new quality of authenticity and a new sense of comfort: "I'm so glad I'm here even though I hate it," she said.

Barbara began psychoanalysis with an idealized father transference in which she endeavored to become an exemplary analysand. She tried to be as compliant as possible without ever expressing displeasure or anger. During the initial phase, she perceived herself largely in Oedipal terms as a five-year-old girl locked in an embrace with her father and feeling both rivalry and fear of her mother. Eventually, the transference changed into a negative maternal transference. Since the only way Barbara found to enter into an alliance with her mother was to become her mother's doll, a stereotypical female defined and played with for the amusement of others, she came to perceive her relationship with me in similar terms. In Barbara's mind, I became someone who would prevent her from blossoming into a flesh-and-blood woman. Previously repressed rivalrous impulses emerged as Barbara attempted to reduce the role I played in her life and as she struggled with her sexuality and competitiveness. She experienced relief over the fact that our relationship survived her expressions of anger. This helped Barbara achieve some resolution of her conflicts and develop a more mature and personal style of being and relating.

The manner in which she employed the Barbie metaphor came to reflect changes in her self-image. Barbara, at long last, relinquished the Barbie-doll role as the dominating symbol of gender stereotyping. She realized that she did not have to make a choice about what kind of woman to be; she could be *both* sexual and intellectual. Barbara progressed from a two-dimensional, doll-like pleaser to a vital, three-dimensional woman capable of expressing a wide range of feelings and having life experiences previously denied her. She had finally come to life.

Hello Dolly

An important part of what psychoanalysis does is to illuminate and demystify human motivation by examining, analyzing, and re-inscribing the individual's past experiences within the analytic frame. The couple works through repressed content and the unconscious con-strictions of trauma that limit and bind human life. When the process works, a saving narrative is generated, and yet, as Cushman (1995) argued, it is equally important to turn the psychoanalytic lens toward the social surround that shapes and governs human motivation and behavior. The psychological evolution of the desire to have a doll or to be a doll is linked not merely to a person's particular psychological idiom but also to the ways in which societal expectations of men and women nurture these tendencies and offer multiple venues in which they can be expressed. Furthermore, the human relationship to the doll expresses a profound existential issue. Let us briefly examine these ideas.

Despite the feminist movement, which aimed to equalize relations between the sexes, adult men and women who live with dolls or as dolls appear to live out traditional stereotypes of masculinity and feminin-ity in the service of identity and erotic arousal. Men go for the sex dolls and women choose the baby dolls, or turn themselves into dolls. Yet gendered stereotypes naturally find their origins in our evolutionary mandate to survive and procreate. Work (culture building), sex, and having children brought us from the prehistorical era to the present day, forming the bridge across human time. The extreme expression of these stereotypes in men who seek companionship with dolls (or robots) and women who transform themselves into dolls reveals cul-tural trends in dehumanization and objectification. The capacity to reduce the human to a thing is not new; it is as old as play and war. Yet when such behavior is culturally incorporated as a norm, the outlook for the human becomes grim and bleak. The chances of us caring and protecting each other are ultimately reduced.

The display of women as ornamental objects to delight and satisfy can be traced back to the earliest forms of art (Clark, 1972). Yet, our society greatly expands this tendency, saturating itself with porno-graphic images of women, available in movies, magazines, and thou-sands of websites (Stankiewicz & Rosselli, 2008). Only a few years ago, a moviemaker needed money and backers to make a porn flick. Now they can be made at negligible cost in the comfort of the director's own home and streamed live around the world. Viewing it is even sim-pler: just point and click. Pornography is easily accessible, affordable, and anonymous, tapped from a growing supply of electronically stored images transmitted across the World Wide Web, itself a kind of vast mind housing the entire spectrum of human knowledge, experience, and fantasy. If we keep in mind pornography's addictive quality, we have to admit that today's easy access and early exposure does not bode well for the future of sexual relations. The porn industry is now a multi-billion-dollar enterprise (Ackman, 2001), and it reinforces and extends the sexual objectification of women (and men). In this realm, inner life has minimal relevance.

Furthermore, we sell things by using female bodies; when one mar-kets a new *thing*, one places a beautiful but familiar *thing* next to it. Ours is a consumer culture, and the term itself suggests a wide spec-trum of objectification; as Strenger (2011) argued, we are things that consume other things, commodities among other commodities, con-sumed by the techno-social maw of globalization. Men can be things too, money-making things, power-wielding things, things to be ridi-culed and demeaned, usable until old. Yet women have a longer history as objects and property, as externalized desirables, and it remains easy for them to be commodified, just like the dolls modeled after them. This social reality has its roots in the majority of world cultures in which women were the absolute property of men, fully expected to submit to them. In Western culture the female was reduced to a rib pulled from the male and made into a living, breathing, but defective doll, who might, if controlled, do a fairly good job of helping him ease his loneliness. In turn, this ancient scene probably emerged from an even earlier one found in our animal beginnings; male primates typically dominated the females of their species (Smuts & Smuts, 1993). In many parts of the world, women continue to live under patriarchal law and play the submissive role to the dominant male. Yet even in modern Western societies, we can discern this same attitude toward the woman. The "trophy wife," for example, is a woman who is valued as an object and status symbol based on her overt expenditure on her appearance and her accoutrements (e.g., hair, nails, clothing, cosmetic surgery, and so forth). The more expenditure, the more she is deemed "worth it."[6]

Within and against this social background, both dolls and doll play have emerged. When little girls play with dolls they express a biological, psychological, cultural, and existential need. Doll play is rooted in the female body and the power it contains to bring forth life. The way girls play with dolls is determined by their psychological idiom and the culture that shapes them. That the doll symbolizes a child (functioning as a multi-leveled transitional object) shows the female's power to defy death by bringing forth new life (Zhou, Lie, Marley, & Chen, 2009; Zhou, Liu, Chen, & Yu, 2008; Fritsche et al., 2007; Solomon, Greenberg, & Pyszcynski, 2015). Though the doll/child can be considered in Freudian terms as a substitute phallus, it can also be seen as an expression of the mightiest power available to human beings – womb power – the power to generate, contain, nurture, and extend new life, new being, and new possibility. Therefore, doll play is a very serious activity; it speaks to the biological function and cultural possibilities of the female; and it expresses the psychological issues and conflicts that girl children deal with. Furthermore, at its outermost edge, it is a dialogue with mortality.

When grown women want to be dolls, the same issues are at stake, but, of course, in a different way. The doll-woman rejects the shifting substrate of her biological body, with its odors and exudation, with its constant alterity and insecure unpredictability; using the force of her imagination and the science of cosmetic surgery, she perceives and experiences herself as a doll. Thus, she narcissistically plays with herself, perversely and safely concealed within the doll fantasy she lives. This constitutes a rejection, not only of the flesh body in favor of the fabricated one, but a protest against species determination. In being a doll, she likely blocks access to her interior, as her very form communicates externalization and objectification, while seemingly protecting herself from the harm and sorrow of being human. Her form also reflects back to the culture its own obsession with material objects and its technological reduction of the subject to a lustful consumer.

In opting for the illusion of stability and control that being a doll offers up, she inhabits a place of rigid stasis, becoming both a living talisman and totem. Dolls do not die and Barbie is forever. (Not surprisingly, Lord titled her 1995 biography of the doll *Forever Barbie*.) Many of these dynamics may also apply to the adult woman who substitutes a doll for a child. The woman accepts her maternal role but avoids the dangers and threats it presents – the child being a "special needs" child; the child becoming sick; the child breaking away from the mother; the child becoming hateful, or delinquent, and even criminal; the child failing, going crooked, and so forth. However, a caveat is in order here: some women have both children and dolls; others have tried and cannot have children; some might have missed their chance to have children and mourn the lost opportunity to be a real mom; others may have lost children. These scenarios can be complex and poignant, especially in the cases of child loss and the inability to have children, openly attesting to the power of the human imagination while making female pain glaringly public.

It is easy to see the woman who lives with a doll or the woman who turns herself into a doll as perverse, due to the contraction, illusion, objectification, and dehumanization engendered by her choice. Yet, these cases demonstrate that a person can make a life out of rebellion, rejection, imagination, and disavowal. A person can say by her actions, "The human situation is painful and unacceptable and my life will be a living protest of it." A woman can say, "I do not accept what has been done to me, what nature has made me, what my parents tried to make me, what my society wants me to be. I'll make myself over. I'll make life itself over." This takes courage and active creativity.

In such cases, the female is speaking through the doll in a kind of psychological ventriloquism, putting her hidden voice into the body of the doll, whether that doll is the plaything of the child, the woman herself, or the child she lost, never had, or wouldn't have. The language is in relational code: how she relates to the doll carries (secret) messages about her own longings, fears, and suffering. As in the previous chapters, the dolls in this chapter are clearly transitional objects. Apart from the usual meanings ascribed to that term, consider its applicability to numerous in-between states: for the child the doll exists between her-self as she is and herself as she will or may become, a practice for her adult role to some degree – playing dollies, playing school, playing married, playing mommy, playing work, and so forth. The woman who becomes a doll exists in the transitional space between being a real live woman and a lifeless, or unfeeling, or at least highly removed, object. For the woman who has a baby doll – like the mother with a child – the doll comes closest to existing between her and her death by offering a symbolic existential shield against the fear of death (Zhou et al., 2008; Baumeister, 1991; Solomon, Greenberg, & Pyszczynski, 2015).

All of this brings us (back) to a kind of root connection between human beings and dolls and, more recently, robots. The doll may look like a person but it is not a person. It exists between the form and actu-ality of personhood. It is between being and non-being. It can be ani-mated by the consciousness and imagination of its user. Not animated, it lies still and lifeless, resembling a corpse and reminding us of (our) death. Animated, it imaginatively participates in the user's life. When we look closely at a doll, we often feel uncomfortable, for we are look-ing at something that's there and not there simultaneously: the ghost of our own consciousness and the mirror of our unbelievable but inev-itable death. Freud's (1955e [1919]) concept of the uncanny relates to this phenomenon. The doll poses two strange whispering questions to the intent adult listener: *what is it here and now that makes you alive, and why is your death so incomprehensible?*

Robots further blur the boundary between the living and nonliving and turn the volume up on these two questions. They can be made to look human (like a doll) and may eventually do things that humans do, far better than humans do them. As they come nearer to becoming self-aware and nearly impossible to distinguish from the human – then to be human will mean so much less than it once did. Gone will be the chimera of essence, the uniqueness of selfhood, complexity that can-not be imitated or simulated. Gone will be the notion of a soul, cosmic entitlement, and the belief that humans are the greatest of all earthly creatures. There will be more reason than ever to see selfhood and soul as a kind of software program run on the wetware of the brain, itself a virtual-reality generator. Our fall from grace will be complete – from angels to apes to neurotic apes to biological machines to infe-rior and defective machines. Note how this "fall" corresponds with the increased objectification of the human being, scientifically modeled as a machine, socially modeled as a consumer, and existentially modeled as a being in search of an essence. This self-image may not be heartening, but it is certainly friendly to technological augmentation and reconstruction. Essentially we may not be all that much, but at least we can look better, last longer, and do more.

Conscious robots will greatly exceed human beings in every way. They will be stronger, smarter, and far more robust, reparable and operative perhaps for centuries.[7] Compared to the conscious robots we create, we will look like hugely inferior conscious robots that evolution kludged together from flimsy materials. And there is no reason that a conscious machine, even if it does not look human, should be excluded from the rights and privileges of a human or from the respect given to a human (Levy, 2007). After all, does it really matter whether the substrate of self-awareness and sentience is flesh and blood (carbon) or processed sand (silicon)? We may be engineering ourselves into obsolescence. Long before the story of God breathing life into Adam, human beings dreamed of breathing life into their own artifacts (Gascoigne, n.d.). In this sense, the doll tempts the ultimate transgression: to become God and make the nonliving alive.

Notes

1. This chapter is based on interviews and clinical work conducted by Knafo over a period of many years.
2. When she saw my new doll on my bed, my housekeeper panicked, convinced it was a dead baby.
3. Coincidentally, Ms. Mansfield has one RealDoll in her vast collection of baby dolls. As we spoke, I discovered that this doll communicates on Twitter with Davecat's dolls. It is a small (doll-loving) world!
4. It is interesting to reflect on the origins of the Barbie doll. During World War II, it is believed that Hitler's pathological fear of syphilis made him invest in the Borghild Project, an attempt to provide blonde-haired, blue-eyed dolls to comfort his troops and prevent their becoming infected with sexually transmitted diseases. Franz Tschakert, famous for his Woman of Glass, is said to have been recruited, along with a psychiatrist, Dr. Rudolf Chargeheimer, to produce sex dolls that would withstand heavy usage. It is believed that the project had been canceled by 1942 (Smith, 2013). Yet German cartoonist Reinhard Beuthien created a highly successful cartoon called Bild Lilli that featured a blonde sexpot modeled after the Lilli dolls meant for the troops. In 1956, when visiting Germany, Ruth Handler saw

the Lilli doll and in 1959 modeled her own Barbie doll on it (Lord, 1994). It is ironic that the most popular doll for children in the world was modeled after a German sex doll.

5. What begs the question, of course, is why is there, historically, such a preoccupation with feminine beauty in the first place? The answer lies in evolutionary history. Sexual selection functions so that each gender chooses members likely to improve chances of survival and reproductive success. Hip to waist ratio, facial and bodily symmetry, skin and hair quality, eye shape and size, and so forth, are crude indicators of reproductive health and underlie our perception of beauty. Both genders generally select on the basis of physical and psychological factors felt to contribute to continuance and longevity. Men strongly select for female beauty (and fidelity) as desirable traits, while women select for the right mix of good genes, reproductive potential, and a long-term willingness to invest in her and her offspring (cultural success, material resources, social standing) (Geary, Vigil, & Byrd-Craven, 2004). Culture itself is born out of evolutionary history. However sophisticated, culture carries the imperatives of human biology and evolutionary history. However, the extreme preoccupation with an ideal, and to a large extent, culturally determined aesthetic, is what has poisoned women's freedom.

6. One man I spoke to openly admitted having such a fantasy. Since he is married, he claims his dolls allow him and others like him to "put their fantasy in the pigeon hole of a RealDoll, leaving women around them as human beings without the pressure of fulfilling the male fantasy."

7. The self-driving car is a good example of how technology will outperform humans in the future. These cars are already on the road (e.g., cars by Google and Tesla) and will be better at preventing accidents than human drivers (Vanderbilt, 2012). We predict that laws will prohibit humans from driving in the future due to this technological advantage.

Part II

Widening the scope of perversion

Existential and techno-social domains

Chapter 5

Perversion

Historical, existential, and social

> Perversion has been called a "private religion" – and that it really is, but it testifies to fear and trembling and not to faith.
>
> – Ernest Becker

Each of us faces every moment of our lives implicit and sometimes explicit threat – threat from within, as illness and decay, and threat from outside in the form of accident, tragedy, and catastrophe. Society offers some protection from nature, as well as from other potentially dangerous human beings. Social order establishes and encourages certain modes of behavior while forbidding others. In one cultural frame we may eat the heart of an enemy; in another we may be arrested for urinating in public. Therefore, perversion isn't only a violation of a commandment or law; the commandment brings perversion into being. These two form a reciprocal dynamic, an interactive partnership that holds together, alters, and disrupts a social frame. They partner for order as well as disruption. A pattern of incremental, transgressive enactments within the public sphere alters the social frame, defining new limits, while normative prohibitions seek to contain and limit that frame. Since our need for containment is necessarily in conflict with our need for expansion, we push against the limits we set, and they push back; in this way they change, and we change.

Some thinkers find the concept of perversion incoherent or passé (Blechner, 2009; Corbett, 2013; de Sousa, 2003; Dimen, 2001; Foucault, 1990 [1976]; Žižek, 2003) because it is impossible to establish an absolute ground for ethical mandates. Though defying definitional perfection, the concept of perversion remains viable because of the need to account for bizarre sexual and social behavior and malignant and destructive enactments. No doubt the generative aspects of the perverse advance the aims of civilization in the arenas of science, technology, and politics (revolutions or other social upheavals), to name a few. However, such enactments as having sex with a bicycle or a corpse, worshiping armpits or shoes, killing people for fun, or constructing a state dedicated to the eradication of an ethnic population leave little doubt about the utility of the concept of perversion and its attendant psychoanalytic theory. Nonetheless, a recent book whose subtitle is *A History of Perverse Sex* opens with this sentence: "One person's perversion is another's normality" (Peakman, 2013). The author rightly goes on to say that every conceivable sex act and, by implication, every social act (except those spawned by new technology) can be found throughout human history. From this viewpoint perversion is a failed idea that is used to control, condemn, and punish. This chapter challenges the notion that perversion has lost its meaning in today's world. Further, the authors view perversion through three distinct lenses and then widen those lenses to account for technology's role in broadening perversion's manifestations.

The evolution of perversion theory

The history of perversion in the West can be viewed through the lens of epochs. According to today's standards, Greece and especially Rome engaged in a great variety of debauched and even criminal sexual and social practices. Sex with family members and children, sexual and social slavery, gladiatorial butchery for public entertainment, and religious sex orgies were all part of Rome's normative framework (Bullough, 1976; Dio, 1914; Suetonius, 2007). Later, perversion was recast in religious terms to control deviant behavior in the medieval world. Christianity's prohibition against the "seven deadly sins" provided the framework of morality to which all other sins owed their derivation. Declared as cardinal, each deadly sin was paired with a separate manifestation of Lucifer, and each could result in the eternal damnation of the soul (Roudinesco, 2009 [2007]). The seven sins – pride, greed, envy, anger, lust, gluttony, and sloth – generated excesses of passion with the implication that the sinner delighted in such excess, which produced evil. The conditions for temptation and resistance to sin and evil formed the battlefield between God and the Devil in which the war for the soul was waged, a war set in motion by Adam and Eve's fall from grace. The first parents were believed to have committed the original sin (the first perversion), by eating the forbidden fruit of the tree of knowledge of good and evil. In other words, they developed self-consciousness, feeling shame and covering their nakedness, and became capable of moral capacity, and, by implication, wickedness. Their punishment for this cosmic transgression was mortality. That is, once they became aware of themselves, they knew they were mortal and were driven to transcend death. This is the symbolic meaning of the expulsion from paradise, the loss of an innocence that is not self-aware and knows nothing of its inevitable doom. The myth properly positioned the body as the problem of human existence and banished the self from the sight of divinity; it condemned human beings to freedom and made them responsible for their own transcendence.

During the medieval period, despite prohibitions, sinners sinned anyway, trembling before the Church and God, while many saints sublimated their physical desire in their bid for spiritual transcendence. The passions of the flesh were co-opted to vilify, reject, and even destroy the body. Abjection, in the form of brutal ascetic practices (e.g., flagellation, starvation, and various physical punishments) and martyrdom provided identification with the tortured body of the earthly Christ and delivered the passage into a sublime, transcendent vision of the heavenly one. At the same time, the mortal body could provide access to the immortal body:

> The physical body, either putrefied or tortured, or intact and without any stigmata, therefore fascinated both the female and male saints, who were excited by abnormality ... On the one hand, the body is regarded as the tainted part of man, as an ocean of wretchedness or the soul's abominable garment; on the other it will be purified and resurrected. As Jacques Le Goff writes ... "The body of the Christian, dead or alive, lives in the expectation of the body of glory it will take on if it does not revel in the wretched physical body. The entire funerary ideology of Christianity revolves around the interplay between the wretched body and the glorious body, and is so organized to wrest one from the other."
>
> (Roudinesco, 2009 [2007], p. 11)

Medieval Christianity performed the central service demanded of every form of civilization. It addressed the bitter problem of mortality by attempting to heal the split between the lowborn animal body and its highborn counterpart, the human self, providing an immortality project par excellence. Yes, the Church said, life is always difficult and often brutal, fraught with peril and terribly brief, but if Christians followed the script of the Roman Church, fully identifying themselves with the crucified Christ and repenting their sins, they would enjoy eternal and blissful life with the Lord, His angels, and their loved ones, and even their mortal bodies would be made glorious. To be sure, the vast majority of medieval people believed this without reservation; until the late fourteenth century and early part of the fifteenth century, the Western world was soaked in the ambience of Christian soteriology and had no access to competing social and spiritual visions. Medieval Christianity was therefore an embodied vision that "solved" the problem of death (Hobbs, 2008).

In bitter opposition to this view, the quest for transcendence was transformed into a tenacious search for violent pleasure by the Marquis de Sade (1740–1814), known as "the prince of the perverse," who is often regarded as the archetype of the modern notion of perversion (Roudinesco, 2009 [2007]). The Marquis's philosophy glorified crime and libertinage, creating a polymorphous perverse world in which everything is defiled and ultimately destroyed (du Plessix Gray, 1998). For de Sade, the sexual partner was treated as object only, and one object (probe/orifice) could be easily replaced with another. In his world, taboos did not exist and everything and everyone became fetishized; nothing was off limits for violation. It was a world not unlike that described in *The Aristocrats*, but for real – savagely committed to mirroring the ruthlessness of the anthropomorphized natural surround that generates and consumes forms and dissolves boundaries with complete indifference. As with *The Aristocrats*, the extreme sexual content can obscure the social aspect of de Sade's perversion; surely he directed his attack on society, on the hypocrisy and self-deception that accompanied its norms, and used sex as his weapon of mass destruction.

With the advent of sexology in the late nineteenth century, "deviant" sexual practices soon became variously classified as perversions. Sex was surveyed with the aim of showing how sexual preference expressed psychological and character traits. Alfred Binet introduced the concept of fetishism, which he described as the sexual veneration of inanimate objects (Peakman, 2009). In 1886, Krafft-Ebing published *Psychopathia Sexualis*, a massive text that labeled and categorized the behaviors of sadism, masochism, homosexuality, bestiality, necrophilia, and more. He opined that "With opportunity for the natural satisfaction of the sexual instinct, every expression of it that does not correspond with the purpose of nature, – i.e., propagation – must be regarded as perverse" (Krafft-Ebing, 1936 [1886], p. 79), paving the way for pathologizing and criminalizing sexual behavior. In a groundbreaking treatise published in 1897, *Studies in the Psychology of Sex*, Havelock Ellis set his sights to transvestism and transgendered embodiment. His work on sexual deviance encouraged tolerance and acceptance, opening the door for an activism opposing discrimination, oppression, and punishment based on sexual preference. The conflicted post-Enlightenment view about non-normative sexual and social behavior, which was mirrored in the work of Ellis, foreshadowed postmodern sexual and social discourse. Of course, Freud was the first to say perversion existed to some degree in all human beings, though he focused exclusively on its sexual manifestations. Freudian theory, influenced by Darwin, explained perverse sexuality as deviating from practices that ensure the continuation of the species (Freud, 1953b [1905]) and he located its etiology in castration trauma (Freud, 1961c [1927]), since psychoanalysis focused on personal history as the source of neurosis.

Several problems have hindered the full clarification of perversion. Because it is the result of a natural and universal form of human resistance against constraint, motivated by the desire to master life and transcend limitation, perversion remains entangled with other human motivations and behavior. Moreover, the relationship between its psychological structure and a set of attendant "deviant" behaviors is obscure, which makes it difficult to use the symptom–cause model to understand it. Furthermore, its behavioral components are rife with instability, since normative changes reconstitute definitions of deviance, and interpretation is necessarily soaked in subjectivity. Finally, it is sometimes difficult to distinguish perversion's destructive and generative outcomes. Yet, banishing the term perversion does not solve these problems. Paraphilia, a more benign word, has replaced perversion in the current nomenclature (American Psychiatric Association, 2013).

The authors agree with those theorists (e.g., Saketopoulou, 2015; Celenza, 2014; Roudinesco, 2009 [2007]; Stein, 2005; Stoller, 1979) who believe it is necessary to preserve the original term. Roudinesco (2009 [2007]) cogently argued that even if we no longer use the term perversion, "we still have to come to terms with its subterranean metamorphoses and our dark side" (p. 60). Let it stand then, even if it is still imbued with religious implication, for the crooked path often leads to the worst kind of human excess.

A few theorists have connected perversion to the social scene. For example Foucault (1990 [1976]) theorized that perversion is about power and control associated with repressive laws. Laqueur (1992) claimed that "perverted sex was a sign of perverted social relations" (p. 210). For our part, we draw upon common elements of perversion identified in many of the psychoanalytic theories. Surely, forms of individual perversion are shaped by constitutional factors and personal history, while forms of social perversion emerge from cultural history. Yet the fundamental source of perversion – the guarantee of its presence in human affairs – is the existential problem of being a conscious animal. From this perspective, perversion demands a wider interpretation of the conditions and meaning of trauma.

The existential dimension of perversion

The origin of the perverse impulse, we believe, lies in our inherent need to transcend constraint, barrier, enclosure, and incompleteness, wherever it is found – from the limits of our thought and knowledge to the outer reaches of our social possibility. The philosopher Roberto Mangabeira Unger (2007) considers limit breaking to be the driving force of human life:

> In the life of desire, we find at every turn that our most intense longings, attachments, and addictions constantly transcend their immediate objects. We ask of one another more than any person can give ... some reliable sign that there is a place for us in the world. And we pursue particular material objects and satisfactions with a zeal that they cannot and, in the end, do not sustain. Having pursued these objects, we turn away from them, in disappointment and discontent, as soon as they are within our grasp.

Only the *beyond* ultimately concerns us. The sense of a *permanent power of transcendence over all limits* – of openness to the infinite – is inseparable from the experience of consciousness.

(Unger, 2007, p. 13, emphasis added)

Unger views people as both context-bound and context-transcending beings, observing the law and yet required to break it, driven by the call of the beyond that permeates every dimension of human life. It is this primal human need that fuels rebellion, transgression, and violation against law and norms in its restless quest to break free of limit, create new possibility, and make the self and the world anew. From this view the perverse turn is a foundational response to the ultimate boundary of death. The response is not at all serene, measured, or merely calculated; it is driven, quite desperate, and never far from panic. The limit of death and all the inevitabilities implied in its complex symbol – loss, sickness, aging, unwanted and unexpected burden, betrayal, abandonment, and personal trauma – imbue the whole of human life with tragedy and trauma.

Consciousness of our mortality is the central irony of the human condition because, although we know we will die, we deny few things more vehemently (Becker, 1973). The denial of death is utterly profound and unavoidable, lived from our earliest years to the very end of life. If the irrefutable truth of death enters too starkly into awareness, a person can be paralyzed with terror. Therefore, we must become forgetful of death to live effectively, not feeling too intensely its ubiquitous presence. Freud (1957c [1915]) alluded to this problem when he said, "Would it not be better to give death the place in reality and in our thoughts which is its due, and to give a little more prominence to the unconscious attitude towards death which we have hitherto so carefully suppressed?" (p. 299). That he framed his insight as a question is telling. He himself was not certain of how much admission was too much. He advised that just "a little more prominence" be given to the unconscious attitude toward death – not too much, just a "little." Becker (1973) understood this denial as the ontological basis of character and the reason that human character is deeply flawed and conflicted. He considered the denial of death as the profound motivation (the perverse upsurge) underlying human brutality as well as human magnificence.

The tragedy of the human condition is that we are both flesh-and-blood animals as well as conscious beings, orphaned by chance and doomed from birth, in an indifferent universe. A human being hungers for eternal significance and meaning, perhaps even more than bread, and yet is painfully aware that he or she will die. Thus, the person takes refuge in the symbolic order of the social and cultural system and derives from it a felt sense of significance and worth, by participating in something outside of nature that is special and permanent. Becker viewed society as an immortality formula writ large, a system of meanings that banishes the animal while offering both sustenance and self-worth and allowing its members to participate in projects of validation and transcendence.

Still, however successfully a person participates, the outcome is the same, for no one is important or special enough to escape their animal fate. Though destiny may beckon with its fickle finger, annihilation, waiting at the end of the road, makes a mockery of aspirations of cosmic significance. Everything is ultimately erased, even meaning, the most fragile and important of human constructs. Becker (1973) described "the routine activity" of "organisms ... tearing others apart with teeth of all types ... pushing the pulp greedily down the gullet with delight ... and then excreting with foul stench and gases the residue" – in other words, the inherent violence and brutality of the natural order that ensures our pitiless existence and execution, along with the ultimate victory of entropy (p. 283). Even the entire cosmos will be reduced to meaningless de Sadean particles. From this viewpoint, are we not already sadomasochistically situated in a perverse irony – cosmically dehumanized in the very act of becoming human? Becker asked:

> What does it mean to be a self-conscious animal? The idea is ludicrous, if it is not monstrous. It means to know one is food for the worms. This is the terror: to have emerged from nothing, to have a name, consciousness of self, deep inner feelings, an excruciating yearning for life and self-expression – and with all this yet to die.
>
> (1973, p. 87)

For Becker the sanity of the self-conscious animal is a pretense. The refuge of culture produces a reaction-formation that obsessively, defensively, and dangerously binds people in groups that invest in immortality formulas – the right way to live, the correct view of human reality – while steeped in denial, fear, and aggression. A challenge to one's formula from another would predictably produce a response across a spectrum of nasty possibilities: ignoring the other completely, derogating the other, attempting to bridge the opposing immortality formulas, and when all else fails, destroying the other. Therefore, conflict between cultures or within cultures over whose formula is correct and shall prevail can have deadly implications.

Becker's general theory has been strongly supported by terror management studies in the field of social psychology, a movement that grew out of his work. Terror management theory (TMT) has mainly focused on testing and discussing two central suppositions and their vast implications for social life: the mortality-salience hypothesis and the anxiety-buffer hypothesis. The former asserts that a person's worldview (immortality formula) and self-esteem provide protection from death terror, and the latter claims that if the former is true, then strengthening one's worldview and self-esteem should reduce death anxiety (Solomon, Greenberg, & Pyszczynski, 2015). More than 500 studies conducted in numerous countries have demonstrated that reminding people of their death causes them to cling more firmly to and defend their worldview (Solomon, Greenberg, & Pyszczynski, 2015; Goldenberg et al., 2000). Mortality salience displays several important social implications: increased bonding with in-group members and those who support one's culture and cultural paradigm; increased negativity toward and avoidance of out-group members and those who criticize one's culture and cultural paradigm; increased estimates of social consensus for one's outlook and attitudes; increased desire to impose harsher punishment for moral transgressions; and increased aggression toward those who oppose one's beliefs (Solomon, Greenberg, & Pyszczynski, 2015). TM studies also show that temporarily enhanced self-esteem reduced self-reported anxiety and acted as a buffer against death terror. Proximal defenses against death terror involve suppressing death-related thinking and denying vulnerability when thoughts of death surface in consciousness, and distal defenses include the bolstering of one's self-esteem and worldview when reminders of death are unconsciously primed (Solomon, Greenberg, & Pyszczynski, 2015). In other words, we continually and defensively manage our death terror through denial, self-importance, solidarity with our in-group, and opposition to the out-group. The more the death threat feels real, the more we enlist these defenses. In short, the whole of human life involves the management of existential terror and its violent implications.

Many experiments conducted by terror management theorists lend empirical weight to Becker's theory about death denial (see Fritsche, Jonas, & Fankhänel, 2008; Goldenberg et al., 2000). The film *Flight from Death: The Quest for Immortality* (Bennick & Shen, 2003), which summarizes Becker's theory and shows how TMT tests it, illustrates the degree to which mortality salience and the anxiety-buffer hypothesis play a key role in our social lives. In one experiment, two groups of university students filled out personality questionnaires, with the experimental group receiving a subtle death reminder. Both groups were then given two tasks: to sift sand from a volume of water dyed black and to affix a crucifix to a wall. Many objects were set before the students to perform the tasks, but the sand could only be sifted from the dyed water by using a small American flag affixed to a beaker by a rubber band, thus ruining the flag, and the only way the crucifix could be attached to the wall was by using it to hammer the nail from which it would be hung. The experimenters wanted to see if those who had been reminded of their death would take longer to use the "sacred" objects inappropriately. The group reminded of their death took twice as long to conclude the task, trying nearly everything else before using the sacred objects.

In another experiment, two groups of judges filled out questionnaires, which for one group contained a question that served, again, as a death reminder. The idea being tested was whether being reminded of death would cause the group of primed judges to impose harsher penalties for lawbreakers. Both groups were then asked to recommend a bond for solicitation of prostitution. The control group recommended an average bond of $50 while the primed group bond proposed an average of $455!

TMT experiments clearly demonstrate that human beings are unconsciously motivated to cling to cultural immortality formulas to ward off the evil of death while projecting that evil onto differing others. Becker (1973) considered perversion to be "a protest against the submergence of individuality by species standardization" (p. 230). In others words, perversion, with its magic and ritual, is in oppositional dialogue with species determinism and the fate of the animal body, and thus symbolizes transcendence over corporeal limitation. Perversion disavows castration (as vulnerability and loss) while formulating an outraged dissent against being a mere doomed animal among many other identically doomed animals (Becker, 1973). The perverse script imposes unique individuality on biologically determined sexuality and the limits of social bonds in the service of symbolic immortality. Whatever specific behavioral components an individual perversion has – whether benign, generative, destructive, or some combination thereof – its existential basis is the quest for transcendence. Another way of saying this is even simpler: our most basic and universal ontological position is in opposition to death – that is living against annihilation.

If we accept the idea that perversion is based on traumatic splitting, then we must include the trauma and splitting that transcends one's personal history and lends perversion the universal human quality so well recognized in psychoanalysis. We must accept the complex symbol of death *as the very framework of all trauma.* Every loss, every setback, disappointment and heartbreak, every sorrow small and large, every contraction of being, symbolizes death. Personal trauma itself is a death before death *and* a symbol of the last and final death – death which, though certain, cannot be fully imagined and mocks the compulsive evolutionary drive to produce a future. The existential tension between the two – the abject, vulnerable, dying body and the denying, anxious, and aspiring self – makes a "vital lie" of human character, mocks the idea of sanity, makes perversion universal, and energizes human evil:

> If I had to offer the briefest explanation of all the evil men have wreaked upon themselves since the beginning of time right up until tomorrow, it would not be in terms of man's animal heredity, his instincts and evolution: it would be simply in *the toll that his pretense of sanity takes,* as he tries to deny his true condition [as a doomed and ultimately helpless animal].
>
> (Becker, 1973, pp. 29–30)

To become a self is to be already split and traumatized by the complex symbol of death. Character is a neurotic (and perverse) defense against our "impossible" and tragic existential situation, a "prison built to deny one thing and one thing alone: one's creatureliness" (Becker, 1973, p. 87). Thus we are divided beings – anxious, neurotic, and perverse – and when the ordinary defenses fail, psychotic. No doubt, Becker's model of human character resembles the standard definition of perversion in psychoanalytic theory: that is to say, a split and traumatized self disavows castration and enacts that disavowal through a pretense of mastery that denies vulnerability. For Freud the sex drive was the central motivation for human behavior, which is why perversion is framed in most psychoanalytic literature in sexual terms. Yet, whether one sees life primarily driven by sex or by death, the body and its messy needs remain a problem in both scenarios. In the former view, civilization suppresses the body's instinct; in the latter, the secreting, excreting, and aging body itself, and especially its mortality, are the source of shame and the motivation for transcendence. Sex is still highly problematic in the second scenario, since it carries the stain of animality, along with the shame and guilt connected with the body's need and the repressed terror surrounding its mortality (see Goldenberg et al., 2000; Birnbaum et al., 2011). But it is in the larger socio-political context that perversion's destructive expression poses the most danger: the sadistic sexual serial killer may murder dozens of innocents, but the perverted state can slaughter millions – and has.

Had Freud witnessed the full horror of World War II, how might he have revised his thinking about human culture, which is so eloquently embodied in *Civilization and its Discontents*? Had he known that the technologies of his own century – the machine gun, cluster and fire bombs, poison gas and the gas chamber, death factories engineered by the Nazi state, and the atomic bomb – would facilitate genocide and mega-murder, might he have extended a theory of perversion into the social realm? The last, most bloody, century (Ferguson, 2006) realized a Sadean dream: the power to dominate, dehumanize, control, and kill unprecedented numbers of people, in unprecedented ways, and even the ability to kill the entire world. Implicit in the technology of mass destruction – the true telos of weapons technology – is the threat to make everything mean nothing at all.

Though Freud's psychoanalysis focused primarily on the individual, his writings on the death instinct (1955b [1920], 1955c [1921], 1961b [1930]) revealed his prescient understanding of the underbelly of modern civilization (Roudinesco, 2009 [2007]). Many have critiqued Freud for his grim vision of humanity (e.g., Rogers, 1961), while some like Gray (2011) noted Freud's "heroic refusal to flatter humankind." Others (e.g., Horkheimer & Adorno, 2007 [1944]) have used the Holocaust to prove the validity of Freud's universal nature of the perverse (Whitebook, 1995).

In the twenty-first century, genocide continues to be a scourge, but we are less worried about weapons of mass destruction, at least in the West, and more concerned about contending with ubiquitous, small-scale terrorist threats. Suicide bombers have large numbers of people thinking about random annihilation. The terrorist group Daesh (also known as ISIL and ISIS), even more extreme than Al-Qaeda, ironically turns denial of death inside out while delivering both terror and death to its enemies – anyone who opposes its Caliphate, essentially an imagined return to the tenth century. And while some who don the suicide vest with alacrity may be dreaming of heavenly rewards, no doubt there are more than a few who do not have such illusions. But whether a person buys into the metaphysics of a paradise or not, the individual suicide terrorist, fully submerged in the significance of the group, is symbolically protected against finitude and meaninglessness. In the mind of the terrorist, the death-dealing perverse organization is great, its cause is just, and it stands on the side of truth.

The would-be terrorist overcomes his or her individual fear of death through rapturous merging with the group, which is so much greater than any individual. Furthermore, the group metaphysics support the notion of merger and sacrifice on every level, making a small thing of death in comparison to the daring and courage of martyrdom. One's life and the life of others make no difference when what's at stake for the religious mass murderer is nothing less than the battle for heaven and earth. Therefore what appears in one perspective as the wanton, nihilistic, and death-loving act of mass murder ending in self-annihilation is from another perspective nothing less than holy martyrdom. At work is the dark side of metaphysics that results in a perverted fundamentalism. This dogma calls for the sacrifice of human life to a brutal, unwavering religious worldview and imagines a God who demands that brutality be carried out in His name. Only under the spell of such a fanatical religious embodiment can one pray before raping a captive woman taken as a slave and then pray afterward (Callimachi, 2015);

only then can one pronounce the greatness of God before detonating a suicide vest. What we see happening in this expression of human evil is not so much mass madness as a kind of mass hypnosis.

The social dimension of perversion

Perversion, or its lesser expression as perversity, exists in the social frame in three overlapping ways. It can be built into society, a kind of *perversion on purpose*, as when the Nazis passed the Nuremberg Laws or when a government brutally and intentionally subjugates its citizenry, as for example in the case of North Korea. Racial cleansing and genocide are further examples. A second way perversity and perversion enter the social frame is through the corruption of some life-affirming social good or goal, as when a corporation ruthlessly exploits the members, trustees, and shareholders it is entrusted to serve, or a police force dedicated to protect and serve its citizens subjects them to brutality and injustice. Perhaps we can call this *perversion as a drift toward corruption*. On the other hand, a third way perverse transgression can arise within the social frame is when it opposes some unjust, false, corrupt, or destructive aspect of the norm. Such a transgression may be deemed wrong, perverse, or even criminal by the majority, and yet its aim is to benefit social and individual welfare. To extend our last example, in reaction to police oppression, a person or group of people brutalized by the police might engage in protest, civil disobedience, or even revolution. Certainly a citizen protesting against North Korea's leader would be considered by that government a pervert or criminal and summarily executed. This we call *perversion as rebellion against oppression and unnecessary constraint*. All three modes of entry exist in abundant interaction, interpenetration, permutation, and varying intensities within a given social frame.

In his insightfully argued text, *Constructing the Self, Constructing America* (1995), Philip Cushman examined the transformations of character through the last two centuries of American history, illustrating how the self, with its conflicts and symptoms, is inseparable from the social and cultural frames that overlap the family dynamic. Cushman's important work lays great stress on the historical, cultural, and political realities that shape the self and thus paves the way for understanding how perversion is social and enters mainstream life.

Cushman said that the early post-Freudian theories of Anna Freud and Melanie Klein, followed by Fairbairn and Guntrip, reinforced the post-Enlightenment notion of an isolated, bounded, rights-based self. Later, Winnicott (1960, 1965 [1962]) and Kohut (1971, 1977) would follow suit with theories that emphasized the concepts of a "cohesive core self," personal liberation, psychological interiority, and one-to-one psychology. Though providing profound insights, these theorists did not, according to Cushman, look with a critical eye at the society in which they practiced. The illnesses they treated were strictly found inside the individual and had their roots in family history. Thus, psychotherapy took a road running parallel to the highway of market capitalism, which manufactures desire and consent (Herman & Chomsky, 1988), drives consumption, justifies debt, denies trauma, disavows human vulnerability, and sustains the illusion that product offerings can fill inner emptiness and solve the problem of meaning – all components of what Becker called immortality formulas. The shopping mall has become the new cathedral (Appleyard, 1993), and saving the human situation is now a matter of technical know-how and the power to buy things.

Cushman found an alternative to conventional psychoanalysis in the work of Harry Stack Sullivan, who said the "romantic, unique individual" is an "illusion" masking the truth of the socially and culturally constructed and embedded individual, whose issues have as much to do with the social surround as they do with personal history (Cushman, 1995, p. 172). "As such Sullivan thought these psychological phenomena should be properly located in the social realm, not conceptualized as reified structures located in the sealed interior of a putatively isolated, self-contained individual" (Cushman, 1995, p. 172). Because Sullivan observed psychological reality as generated in the social space between and among people, he believed psychoanalysis could help solve such problems as chauvinism, racism, social and economic injustice, war, and mass trauma, and, indeed, he advocated a psychoanalytic approach in his critique of society and culture. Although Cushman hardly mentions him, Erich Fromm also appreciated the importance of studying culture. His classic text, *Escape from Freedom* (1994 [1941]), placed modern man's feelings of loneliness and insignificance within a larger social context.

We agree with Cushman and believe cultural assimilation and embodied selfhood begin in the nest of the family and extend to the nested social circles beyond it. Many others, beginning with mother, already embedded in a symbolic order, bring forth and shape the self. A person's problems, issues, and conflicts are by definition social as well as personal and are always related to the society in which an individual takes root. For instance, the phenomenon of female hysteria commonly encountered in early psychoanalysis not only represented individually isolated events resulting from personal history but also reflected the effect of society's restrictions on intelligent, creative women and its curtailment of their sexuality and human possibilities (Showalter, 1997). From this viewpoint, Victorian society created the hysterical female and formulated her cure, thus maintaining the status quo.

Though Cushman never directly discussed sexual or social perversion or society's power to fashion perverse selves in his work, his arguments carry an implication of that view. For instance, he showed that American slavery, beginning in the seventeenth century, and land acquisition shaped the normative frame of the "white self." Mass immigration and industrialization, the loss of traditional community, and secularization produced a deeply troubled zeitgeist accompanied by social trauma, confusion, and alienation. A loss of anchoring norms led "the white population to desperate measures in an attempt to define the self of their era" (Cushman, 1995, p. 40). As the modern age progressed, the American government adopted a policy of "Christianizing" and "civilizing" the "savages" who had been kidnapped from Africa. The Europeans dehumanized African slaves as well as the Native Americans whose homeland had been stolen. Thus, the dominant group defined itself in opposition to its reductive caricatures of the "supposedly lazy, stupid Negro or the supposedly heathen, savage Indian" (Cushman, 1995, p. 41). The brutal subjugation, dishonoring, exploitation, and dehumanization of these two peoples helped define the bourgeois self and the vision that characterized the nineteenth-century Victorian American. As opposed to the communal, ignorant Native American who had no knowledge of science or Jesus Christ and survived by hunting and not by business and the accumulation of capital, the bourgeois self believed in "progress, individualism, the values and prerogatives of the entrepreneurial middle class, linear thinking and calculation, and ... a quantification ... of the external world" (Cushman, 1995, p. 59). Christianity in this social context proved strange, for the message of the New Testament that stressed love of one's neighbor, forgiveness, human equality, and social care for the poor and downtrodden did not apply to the Native American or the African. Indeed, just the opposite applied. With the irony and twisted logic typical of malignant perversion, the conquering European forcefully converted both groups to a religion whose central message was violated by the messenger. Thus, the search for American identity and the birth of the nation was itself founded in disavowal of trauma and castration (in the broader sense of the term) that demanded a sado-masochistic relationship with the bad other who became the container of repudiated psychic elements. The African and the Native American were victimized as a result of this disavowal and incorporated in a darkly perverse social script that denied their humanity while reversing the castration of their victimizers. This resulted in a pervasive social perversion that haunts us to this day.

Not surprisingly, American slavery as a vast and malignant social perversion, based on the illusion of inherent white privilege and superiority that claimed the right to exploit, abuse, dehumanize, and utterly enslave black people, has not been sufficiently written about. Never mind that slavery eviscerated black people's self-esteem, destroyed their social and familial bonds, rendered them social corpses, derogated their culture, and then blamed them for any failure of later assimilation. Interestingly, Flax (2010) argued that Americans have never properly mourned slavery and its lingering effects on American subjects and politics. This may be because the extreme degree of malignant perversion that accompanied American slavery has never been fully acknowledged. The silence around this issue is quite telling.[1]

Cushman considers each minor revision of the American cultural self an "eerie foreshadowing of the emptiness and narcissism of our current era" (1995, p. 63). For example, the American Victorian concept of character as "moral toughness and integrity" began to crack under new emerging social pressure, giving way to the idea of style and personality, the idea of being somebody. Public performance replaced private endurance, and social manipulation overshadowed adherence to a moral order or religious codes. Advertising and celebrity were born and capitalism was revised, placing emphasis on technological benefits and the consumption of goods and services. Cushman noted, "It seems obvious that the turn-of-the-century concept of 'personality' has begun to sound suspiciously similar to the current concept of narcissism" (1995, p. 69). Rather than having a felt and grounded sense of significance, the individual is offered a sense of fleeting and insecure self-importance through glib social recognition: good credit scores, priority banking, gold club membership, the accumulation of "likes" on a Facebook page, and so forth. However, this recent era has also seen unprecedented technological growth. We have never been able to do so much; yet, more than ever, it seems to mean less and less.

Perversion, globalization, and technology

In *The Fear of Insignificance* (2011), Strenger provided a broad basis for understanding the state of our current culture, arguing that the existential dilemma so brilliantly laid out by Becker is extended, expressed, and compounded by technology, globalization, and the endless fascination with glib self-help philosophies that deny vulnerability and ignore the limits imposed by chance and mortality. Strenger defined a new kind of human and a new norm that he labels "Homo globalis," a deeply insecure, anxious, and threatened multi-tasker who enjoys little career stability, has no coherent worldview, and often manages life's vicissitudes with pharmaceuticals. Plugged into and commodified by the "global infotainment" web, a peerless media and information behemoth, Homo globalis is painfully aware of living in a world awash in celebrities, mind-bending diversity, threat from all quarters, daily atrocities, conflicting immortality formulas, social injustice, growing inequality, and a plethora of opportunities for comparisons with others that diminish self-esteem and feed a sense of meaninglessness (Strenger, 2011).

Becker (1973) claimed the human animal derived self-esteem by "minutely comparing himself to those around him, to make sure he doesn't come off second-best" (p. 4). On the other hand, Homo globalis has the whole world as the basis of comparison as he competes in a global workforce and becomes enmeshed in social media that more often than not is cold comfort. Of course, he need not travel the world to see how well others are doing in Dubai; a quick perusal of Facebook, with its carefully selected photos reflecting success and happiness and its script of platitudes, are enough to remind him that his life is inferior to everyone else's. Strenger (2011) noted that Homo globalis is an easy mark for any of the many self-help programs available in the "Supermarket of New Spiritualities" (Strenger, 2011, p. 51). In other words, Homo globalis is a traumatized, frightened individual suffering from a mind-numbing sense of insignificance, desperate for meaning, and swarmed by quick-fix immortality formulas that deny not only existential but social quandaries. Strenger (2011) cites Nike's slogan "Just Do It," a vastly popular and absurd little sound bite of arrogant and ignorant self-assertion, to drive home his thesis: an incoherent *Weltanschauung* so deeply fixated on youth, success, and self-commodification while blatantly denying limitation, vulnerability, and finitude has "horrendous psychological consequences" (p. 89).

The authors agree with Strenger's (2011) view but underscore the effects of technology on the body and self. We think of technology as the human self's defensive response to threat, limitation, and finitude, which began when we lit the first fires and made the first tools and much later launched the early industrial and technological revolutions (1760–1920). Over the course of the last several decades our scientific discoveries and innovations, especially in the areas of cognitive science, AI, and computer technology, have progressively blurred the distinction between human and machine. Through technology, we both end and extend the body/self and its powers, with weapons technology, medicine, transportation, computers, the Internet, telecommunications, and so forth. Thus, technology is now society's greatest transcendence project. Driven by our war with threat and our thirst for immortality, we create and use technology to take charge of our own evolution and will eventually change what it means to be human, since the machine seems fated to enter and perhaps even replace the body. Sometime in the future, we may be able to upload our brains to computers or even have powerful machines to replace our bodies (Goodman & Righetto, 2013; Woollaston, 2013). Should we celebrate this possibility or shrink back from it in horror? There is no absolute answer either way.

Following World War II, thinkers began to comment on how technology was dehumanizing life, referencing the replacement of human workers with machines, the birth of the information and computer age, and the advent of unprecedented weapons of mass annihilation – all this and more, accompanied by an idea that still has currency, which is that a human being is a machine.[2] As we have already asserted, technological development also aids in the extension of perversion to the culture at large, and it is a perversion that is mindless, impersonal, and deep seated. But since perversion is ordinarily considered a violation of a presupposed norm, what happens when the perversion becomes the norm?

Social perversion in a global context

Though a wider analysis of perversion in the social frame runs the risk of further diluting the concept, Long (2008) effectively has kept her analysis focused in *The Perverse Organisation and Its Deadly Sins.* According to Long, the second half of the twentieth century produced, at least in developed countries, an increasingly narcissistic or egotistical society with high levels of consumerism. At an institutional level:

> accountability to the community by corporate or private owners of public services and utilities has declined, and globalised markets that serve a privileged population while disadvantaging others who have limited or no access, have emerged. Moreover, the increased privatisation of services such as transport, health and education in an increasingly service-oriented sector, together with an increased secularisation of society has changed the nature of large institutions. In place of diversity of institutions we have rendered them equivalent within a corporate and economic paradigm or discourse. The heir to such a culture of narcissism may well be a perverse society.
>
> (Long, 2008, p. 28)

Skillfully integrating the thinking of Adler, Bion, Klein, Lacan, Chasseguet-Smirguel, and others to analyze numerous examples of perverse corporations, Long convincingly argues that "organized corporate corruption is a conscious manifestation" of an "unconscious perverse societal structure and dynamic" (Long, 2008, p. 3) that permeates the supplier–consumer dyad forming the core dynamic of corporate life. She claims that this dynamic generates the behaviors of perverse pride, greed, envy, sloth, and wrath, five of the "seven deadly sins."

Long's theoretical framework for perversion contains the classical elements of splitting, disavowal, illusion, means–end reversal, and delight in exploitation. She simplifies her synthesis of perversion in five bullet points:

- Pleasure at the expense and harm of others (primary narcissism).
- Knowledge of and denial of reality (denial, disavowal).
- Collusion (perverse pacts).
- Objectification of others.
- Self-reinforcing complicity and continuance of perverted scenarios.

Long observed sadomasochistic elements frequently found in "workplace bullying ... where the roles of bully, victim and bystander become caught in a perverse system, sometimes as a result of multiple collusions and accomplices ... The players are not unnecessarily unconflicted in their roles, but if the bullying is part of a broader culture their disquiet may be reduced through systematically supported denial" (p. 27). One of the authors (Lo Bosco), having worked in a variety of corporate settings, has witnessed multiple instances of sadistic intimidation and manipulation in companies, in which bullying often begins during the hiring process. The job seeker is treated as a miserable supplicant who is expected to bow meekly before the ruling authority and become part of what Long calls "a dispensable and exploitable resource." The masking term used by corporations is being a "team player."

Exploiting and dehumanizing "human resources" is evidenced by the way many corporations, even when highly profitable, often routinely shed personnel as a way of adding a point or two to the bottom line while terrorizing the survivors into working harder. Lo Bosco consulted with one senior manager who decried the lack of pride employees took in their work as evidenced by low production and high error rates. When the author pointed out that senior executives had assigned parking spaces, huge private offices, superior medical benefits, flexible hours, and hefty bonuses, while most employees worked with degraded equipment, were supervised by petty tyrants, survived three layoff cycles in nine months, and hadn't received a raise in three years, he was offered this perverse logic, "They'll get a raise when they take pride in their work. They only use their extra money to buy beer or pot anyway. And if you want to work with me, that kind of thinking won't help your longevity."

Recent attention to the Amazon workplace nicely illustrates the ways this $250 billion corporation, the most valuable retailer in the United States, perversely pushes its employees beyond their limits. Indeed, Amazon takes pride in holding standards that are "unreasonably high," calling its annual firing of staff "purposeful Darwinism" (Kantor & Streitfeld, 2015). Former book marketer Bo Olson says, "Nearly every person I worked with, I saw crying at their desk" (Kantor & Streitfeld, 2015).

In her discussion of perverse greed, Long examined the fall of the corporate giant Parmalat and CEO Calisto Tanzi, who was convicted for embezzlement and fraud. This debacle was so breathtaking that Italian newspapers called it "Enron a la Parmigiana" (Theil, 2004). According to Long (2008), Tanzi's motives and acts align with her five-point explication of perversion. He enjoyed narcissistic advantage at the expense of others and was split between being a figure of generosity toward church and state and a secret thief, stealing over €800 million from his employees and shareholders. "The good generous breast hid the bad devious breast" (Long, 2008, p. 84), and the implicit denial housed in the deception was shared by those around Tanzi who saw red flags but continued to participate in the illusion of him as a benign, honest, and generous man. Even the banks, like J. P. Morgan and Citibank, as well as auditors, acted as "unconscious accomplices" in the perverse pact that masked the massive, mind-boggling fraud (Edward, 2004). Using the company as a cash cow that he eventually bankrupted, Tanzi transformed his investors, shareholders, and employees into objects of ruthless exploitation and profoundly harmed them. He jeopardized at least 36,000 jobs worldwide and damaged 135,000 small investors who had purchased company bonds. Finally, corruption bred corruption in a progressive cycle of larger and larger crimes. "Parmalat was the symbol of a sick system and the biggest debt factory of European capitalism," investigator Lucia Russo said during Tanzi's trial. He received an 18-year jail sentence (Squires, 2010). The elements of perversion identified in our own synthesis also fit with the facts of the Tanzi case: disavowal of vulnerability, pleasure in harm, soaking in excess, boundary violations, fixity, casting illusions, means–end reversal, dehumanization, and so forth. Tanzi's excess of deception and greed, which led him to steal more money than he could ever use in five lifetimes, indicates a failed transcendence project of grand proportions. Alas, wealth may ease the burden of life but it has not yet conquered death.

In her analysis of perverse pride, Long examined the famous Long Term Capital Management (LTCM) crisis that came to a head in 1998 on the heels of the 1997 Asian financial crisis, the exit of Salomon Brothers from the arbitrage business, and the Russian government's defaulting on bonds. Until its fall, LTCM had been providing annual returns of nearly 40 percent, but in a short period following the down-turn, LTCM equity fell from $2.3 billion to $400,000 million, a loss of 83.6 percent and a financial catastrophe that threatened to devastate Wall Street and ruin financial markets. The man behind the catastrophe was hedge-fund executive John Meriwether.

After experiencing terrific success as vice-president of the highly profitable arbitrage group at Salomon Brothers, John Meriwether was sacked amid the fallout of a disastrous trading scandal involving one of his subordinates, which threatened the company with bankruptcy. Though probably innocent, he was nonetheless shamed and humiliated and soon formed his own hedge fund, LTCM. With a team of top-flight PhDs, traders, and risk managers that catered to big investors who could join the club for $100 million or more, Meriwether constructed a veritable "money-making machine" by doing convergence trades (fixed-income arbitrage deals) involving US, Japanese, and European government bonds. Seeing nothing but blue sky in front of him, Meriwether leveraged the company at 40 percent, which meant it was carrying a debt-to-asset ratio of over 25 to 1! Yet neither the team at LTCM nor the investing financial institutions seemed concerned.

When the wobbly tower of blocks that was LTCM tumbled, the run to liquidity commenced and the company required a bailout since their "leverage had been so large, their dealings so complex ... and their involvement in financial markets so extensive that their bankruptcy threatened global markets" (Long, 2008, p. 53). Motivated by hubris and delusions of grandeur and the driven need to conquer and triumph over others, LTCM executives took risks that defied rationality and transcended mere greed, resulting in a social perversion that harmed thousands and threatened economies with ruin. Arrogant pride that masked as fear of shame partnered with contempt for competitors. Disavowal of vulnerability fueled denial of danger. Others colluded as accomplices, partners in a perverse pact that resulted in abuse of third parties. For example, banks lowered their standards to get in on the bonanza of the "money machine."

The ruin of privately held companies worth a few billion dollars can threaten world markets. This scenario is only a few decades old and came into existence with the rise of financial and industrial globalization and its supporting technologies, such as rapid electronic-fund transfers that allow companies to enact thousands of transactions in a few hours while making possible progressively more sophisticated (though often flimsy) financial products based more on betting and hedging than real worth. The possibility of crippling cyber attacks notwithstanding, the complex and fragile web of computer and Internet-dependent interrelated economies and services that use rapid electronic communication and access to real-time events and new information both enables and remains vulnerable to the narcissism and perversion present in corporate social systems.

The perversion of the Parmalat and LTCM scenarios is reflected ad nauseam in various multinational and corporate debacles, some patently criminal. Several examples include the financial and sub-prime mortgage crisis; the US financial markets' bailout; the commercial airlines' concealment of managerial incompetence; the rash of recent scandals in the energy, insurance, banking, and financial industries as exemplified by Enron, Arthur Anderson, Bear Stearns, the Lehman Brothers, and AIG; and Ponzi schemes (like the infamous one engineered by Bernie Madoff, who wiped out $18 billion of his investors' money). These are perverse collusions on a grand scale that are destructive both financially and socially, ruining people economically while rupturing their faith in social bonds.

Perversion in mental health

Long's approach to social perversion can be applied to any social group, however large or small. Indeed, she even turns her eye to her own house in a brief tour of professional associations, whose aim of education, networking, and development may be undermined and even perverted by envy and destructive competition, especially as organizations develop their own unregulated training institutes. As an example, Long cites Kirsner's study of the New York Psychoanalytic Institute, which he claimed functioned as a cult after World War II until the 1990s. Kirsner thought of psychoanalytic institutes as guilds, "internally focused cliques," that formed cults around commanding and even tyrannical leaders and subsumed their members as disciples of the institute and its canon.

Institutional corruption is often rife where "economies of influence" create incentives for behaviors by members, which are antithetical to the institute's public mission. When this happens the perverse behavior may go unrecognized and may be viewed as normative. As members of Harvard's Safra Center for Ethics, Whitaker and Cosgrove (2015) studied the institution of American psychiatry and found numerous examples of how the pharmaceutical industry influenced it to abandon its mission of providing humane and effective treatment for those suffering mental illness. Instead, the American Psychiatric Association engaged in a lucrative partnership with the pharmaceutical industry, endorsed an expedient "disease model" and vastly expanded the scope of what could be defined as a mental disorder, changing each successive edition of the *Diagnostic and Statistical Manual of Mental Disorders* (DSM) accordingly. Not surprisingly, more people were diagnosed and prescribed medications so that by 2010, one in every five Americans was taking a psychotropic medication on a daily basis – up 22 percent in just ten years (Medco, 2011).

In the 1990s, 57 percent of the DSM-IV task-force members had ties to the pharmaceutical industry. The DSM-V task force had 69 percent of its members tied to the industry, and 90 percent of those who wrote the sections on schizophrenia, bipolar illness, and depression – the illnesses most often treated with medication – had business relationships with the pharmaceutical industry (Whitaker & Cosgrove, 2015). For example, Joseph Biederman, a professor at Harvard Medical School, received $1.6 million from the pharmaceutical company Janssen between 2000 and 2007, and Frederick Goodwin, former director of the National Institute of Mental Health, received $1.2 million from GlaxoSmithKline between 2000 and 2008 (Whitaker & Cosgrove, 2015). "[Pharmaceutical] industry money helped the American Psychiatric Association grow from a trade organization with revenues of $10 million in 1980 to one with $65 million in revenues in 2008" (Whitaker & Cosgrove, 2015, p. 41).

Equally perverse was the way the American Psychiatric Association reported research on pharmaceuticals. Eminent researchers, most paid by the drug companies to test their medications, failed to publish studies that showed no improvement. The researchers also found ways to spin negative studies so that they showed positive results. Benefits were overstated, and adverse effects were glossed over or omitted, which helped drug companies push their pills down the throats of millions (Whitaker & Cosgrove, 2015). Soon, the theory of a "chemical imbalance" gained currency, and the market for medication boomed. It took decades for the truth to emerge – a truth still unknown or denied by many. Nancy Andreasen finally wrote, "DSM diagnoses have given researchers a common nomenclature – but probably the wrong one" (Whitaker & Cosgrove, 2015, p. 60). Kenneth Kendler, co-editor of *Psychological Medicine*, said, "We have hunted for big simple neurochemical explanations for psychiatric disorders and not found them" (Whitaker & Cosgrove, 2015, p. 58). And Ronald Pies, editor of *Psychiatric Times*, calls the "chemical imbalance" trope an "urban legend" (Whitaker & Cosgrove, 2015, p. 59).

Perhaps worst of all is the enormous increase in medications prescribed to children and young adults. New definitions of Attention Deficit Hyperactivity Disorder (ADHD) led to a 23 percent increase in the number of children diagnosed with the "disease." By 2012, 10 percent of youth aged 4–18 years had been given the diagnosis of ADHD, and 3.5 million children were prescribed ADHD medication, nearly six times the number in 1990. Interestingly, in France, less than 0.5 percent of children are diagnosed with ADHD (Wedge, 2012). French doctors use a different classification than American doctors, and they tend to look for underlying psychosocial causes of attention and disruptive childhood behaviors, encouraging the families to get help from psychotherapeutic rather than pharmaceutical interventions (Wedge, 2012). Drugs given to children and adolescents for depression, another syndrome whose diagnosis expanded with each successive edition of the DSM, proved in the research studies to be largely ineffective and unsafe, and even leading to a significantly higher number of suicides than in the placebo group (Whitaker & Cosgrove, 2015). Yet, the published accounts reported that the drugs (e.g., Zoloft) were safe and effective. Irish psychiatrist David Healy (2007) wrote a biting article criticizing the pediatric trials of selective serotonin reuptake inhibitors (SSRIs), titling it "One Flew Over the Conflict of Interest Nest."

The American Psychological Association (APA) has also failed badly in its own social mission. In 2005, its leaders created a Task Force predominantly made up of psychologists involved in overseeing and/or researching the Bush-era "enhanced interrogation program" to determine the ethics of psychologists' participation (Steven Reisner, personal communication, September 15, 2015). The Board of the APA made Task Force determinations APA policy by fiat, thus bypassing the organization's democratic advice-and-consent processes. James Elmer Mitchell and Bruce Jessen, two psychologists with no prior experience in counterterrorism or interrogation, were the architects of the CIA's "enhanced interrogation techniques" (Mitchell was an APA member) (Steven Reisner, personal communication, September 15, 2015). These techniques included "shackling people in painful positions, keeping them awake for more than a week at a time, locking them in coffin-size boxes and repeated waterboarding" (*New York Times* Editorial Board, 2014). The Department of Defense program was also the handiwork (at least in part) of APA member John Leso (Steven Reisner, personal communication, September 15, 2015). The collaboration of psychologists with the CIA, the White House, and the Department of Defense added legitimacy to the program and masked its draconian torture of terrorist suspects. Mitchell and Jessen earned $81 million for their services (Blumenthal & Wilkie, 2014). How could the world's largest group of psychologists contribute to rather than oppose torture? Typical of doublethink, the APA called torture "morally reprehensible" and a "perversion of psychological science" (*New York Times* Editorial Board, 2014), even while crafting a policy to allow psychologists to contribute to the government's efforts (Reisner, 2010; Risen, 2015, p. 117).

There were, however, a few voices raised in protest. Six psychologists, called "the dissidents," formed the Coalition for an Ethical Psychology. Motivated by moral outrage at the APA's collusion with government in enabling the torture of terrorist suspects, they fought a long battle with the establishment to end this perverse trend (Steven Reisner, personal communication, September 15, 2015). The coalition formed after APA's Task Force on Psychological Ethics and National Security (PENS) issued the 2005 report asserting psychologists' "important role" in national security interrogations – a report that was instrumental in keeping psychologists at the center of these practices, both at CIA "black sites" and at the US military's detention camp at Guantánamo (Aldhous, 2015). Jean Marie Arrigo, initially part of the APA Task Force, broke with it when she realized that it was being used to aid, extend, and validate torture and essentially violate the mainstream mission of mental health care since the earlier part of the twentieth century. She was joined by two psychoanalysts and three other psychologists. After one psychologist filed an ethics complaint with the APA and state psychological associations against psychologists who had worked at Guantánamo, the war between the rebels and the machine was on (Aldhous, 2015).

The APA attacked the group quite viciously and tried to discredit them. Gerald Koocher, the president of the APA in 2006, wrote a column in the Association's magazine that criticized "opportunistic commentators masquerading as scholars" (2006, p. 5) who were alleging abuses by mental health professionals and later issued an open letter suggesting Arrigo was emotionally unstable due to the "sad emotional aftermath of a troubled upbringing" and the suicide of her father – who, in fact, was still very much alive and well (Aldhous, 2015). Gradually the group started by Arrigo, allied with other progressive psychologists' groups, worked to circumvent management and appeal directly to APA members. In 2008, a majority of rank-and-file APA members backed a proposal to remove psychologists from Guantánamo and CIA black sites. The proposal was never implemented, however, perhaps because there was money to be made in supporting torture (Steven Reisner, personal communication, September 15, 2015). Then James Risen's *Pay Any Price: Greed, Power, and Endless War* (2014) blew the whistle on APA's collusion with the CIA. Thus, the APA was backed into a corner and commissioned Chicago lawyer David Hoffman to conduct an independent investigation. Hoffman's report (Hoffman et al., 2015) strongly supported the claims of the Coalition for an Ethical Psychology and James Risen. Clearly, the APA had gone crooked, entering into a (perverse) pact with the government that facilitated the government's torture program. Once the report was made public, the APA had no choice but to back the ban on psychologists participating in national security interrogations and, by extension, all forms of torture programs enacted by the military.[3]

In this chapter we have provided examples of perversion in various domains of social life, and have seen how perverse practices, facilitated by social, religious, and technological immortality formulas bolster self-worth and create perversion within cultures at large. Perversion in the social dimension is much more dangerous than individual perversions because it can affect thousands or millions of people. Hitler's fascist state is a classic example of an entire nation that was overcome by malignant perversion. An incomplete list of genocides in the twentieth century includes: the Armenian genocide (1915–1916), the Shoah (1939–1945), the Cambodian genocide (1975–1979), the Kurdish genocide (1987–1988), the Bosnian genocide (1992–1995), and the Rwandan genocide (1994) (Powers, 2002). Social perversion is and has always been a hellish problem that has its roots in profound psychological and existential issues. Though much time and space has been devoted to historical and situational analysis of human conflict and the frequent atrocities that result, the authors believe the deeper forms of psychological analysis must be extensively applied to the problem.

Notes

1. Flax (2010) argued that American slavery was rooted in pathological narcissism and depended on "continual violence" that had a deeply destructive, intimate dimension that transformed the slave into a totally subjugated and socially dead entity while imbuing the master with unquestioned sovereignty and dominion. The slave's ruination was the master's elevation. In examining the effect of this narcissism on the female slave, who was sexually exploited, abused, and often raped, and whose ties with her own children were overshadowed by her ties to the master's, and even destroyed when it suited his aim, Flax wrote: "Under the perverse logic of domination in which the 'other' becomes the problem, these coercive arrangements were transmuted to constructions of black female identity" (p. 23).
2. First we were higher than angels, then animals, then neurotic, crazed, and violent animals, then machines, then robots built by genes. Some (see Lovelock, 2009) now think of our species as a virus. What a fall from grace!
3. We are grateful to Steven Reisner for fact-checking our account of the APA proceedings.

Chapter 6

Technology and its discontents
The dark side of cyberworld

> We are, as a society, standing on the edge of the cyber abyss.
> – Christopher Barrie-Dee and Steven Morris

As we welcome technology into our homes, our offices, and even our bodies, we find that the current technological expansion is a double-edged sword. Since people are living more of their lives online, it behooves psychoanalysts to attempt to describe the impact of technology on the psyche and the social scene in which it is embedded and attend to both its creative and destructive possibilities. Many of the benefits of the tech revolution are obvious. For example, limitless information is just keystrokes away. The ability to connect in cyberspace facilitates many kinds of conversations: people from various parts of the world can connect and collaborate for artistic, professional, or political purposes, while friends and family members who live half a world away from each other can keep in touch through email and Skype.

On the other hand, new technology has opened a Pandora's box of novel problems, as people use the wider arena of the Internet to act out in various ways. A virtual universe of ghost worlds exists where bodiless meetings take place and dark secrets are exchanged without the intervening presence of a human face. The normal requirements of social convention are suspended in a space without horizons, where anything goes and the private self can hide behind a code name and let its Id play freely. Cyberspace is both extremely public and exceedingly private – a world of both connection and disconnection in which the mask of civility may be dropped, along with the restraints that keep nefarious desires in check. All people need to do is open an electronic window and send a message through the new nervous system of the world; surely someone out there will understand their forbidden longings and perhaps even answer them. Not surprisingly, no matter how unconventional and socially unacceptable their desires are, people soon find others like themselves – sometimes a virtual community of others – through which their dark cravings can be both condoned and fulfilled.

Cyberspace can also provide a soapbox to those who wish to publicize their psychopathic deeds. For example, a man who killed two journalists had a well-planned social media rollout. Vester Lee Flanagan shot the two journalists on August 26, 2015, filmed the shooting, and then posted it on Facebook and Twitter, quickly amassing a following of thousands. Journalist Farhad Manjoo (2015) concluded that the killer "forged a new path for nihilists to gain a moment of media spotlight" and predicted that others will follow his lead. In their book, *Online Killers*, Barry-Dee and Morris (2010) quote a senior detective from the National Criminal Intelligence Service (NCIS) who noted: "In a short period of time, the Internet has become the most exploited instrument of perversion known to man. It is like pumping raw sewage into people's homes" (p. 13).

The same technology that allows people to see their grandchildren in another state or country or provides a forum for strangers to raise money for worthwhile projects also becomes the means for terrorists to fund their operations or post videos of beheadings. Marc Goodman, a world authority on global security and author of *Future Crimes* (2015a), claimed that "exponential times are leading to exponential crimes" (p. 351). In his new book, *Lights Out* (2015), Ted Koppel called the Internet a weapon of mass destruction and warned of its capability, in the hands of a skilled hacker working anonymously from anywhere in the world, to disrupt banking systems, water systems, electric power systems, and more. This chapter explores the underbelly of the Internet and provides several examples of relational and even criminal perversions, a few of them drawn from Dr. Knafo's clinical practice.

Deep Web

The World Wide Web, a subset of the Internet, has grown exponentially since the 1990s. It is arguably the single development most responsible for dramatically altering the daily lives of most people on the planet today, and it plays a major role in transforming human relationships. Social media, such as Facebook, Twitter, and YouTube, have created virtual communities and networks that allow for a wide-ranging exchange of ideas, photographs, and videos, as well as the organization of groups dedicated to creative and destructive pursuits. The reach of these networks and the time spent on them are growing at astonishing rates. For example, the number of people on Facebook has reached a fifth of the world's population; if Facebook were a country, it would be as populous as China (Dewey, 2014).

Yet the Web has a vast sub-terrain, a dark realm that is home to aggressive and destructive tendencies. Freud's iceberg metaphor (1957b [1915]), which highlights the enormity of the unconscious in comparison to the conscious mind, can be applied to the Deep Web, which far exceeds the surface Web, and which in some ways confirms the pessimism embodied in *Civilization and its Discontents* (Freud, 1961b [1930]). Google, the largest search engine on the Internet, indexes a mere 0.004 percent of the surface Web (Jasra, 2010) and misses all of the Deep Web, approximately 500 times the size of what we know as the World Wide Web (Beckett, 2009). In other words, Google misses 99 percent of the World Wide Web's data!

The Deep Web, otherwise known as the Invisible Web, is a hidden world used by those seeking anonymity. Not all have transgressive purposes: journalists and government officials, medical institutions, and banks all guard their privacy using the Deep Web. But so do drug dealers, criminals, terrorists, and pedophiles. Within the Deep Web is the Dark Web, a collection of websites that hide the IP addresses of the servers that run them. Rather than click on familiar search engines like Google, Yahoo, or Bing, those venturing to the Dark Web use Tor, a popular software program that provides nearly absolute Internet anonymity (Goodman, 2015a, 2015b). Tor, originally created in 2004 by the US Naval Research Laboratory (Goodman, 2015a, 2015b), hides the source of origin by routing a network connection through thousands of servers spread across 89 countries throughout the world (Bartlett, 2015).

The Dark Web hosts black markets for all kinds of illegal contraband, including drugs, weapons (e.g., AK-47s), and human organs (kidneys sell for $200,000, livers for $150,000, and a pair of eyeballs for $1,500). Hired guns who provide "permanent solutions to common problems" are easily obtainable (for as low as $20,000; a hit on a police officer costs $100,000) (Goodman, 2015a, 2015b). Counterfeit money and over 200 types of forged documents (e.g., fake IDs, college diplomas and transcripts, immigration documents) are found on the Dark Web. Tor allows terrorist groups such as the Ku Klux Klan, Al-Qaeda, and ISIS to spread propaganda, recruit new members, raise money, and plan operations (Bartlett, 2015). Even human slaves can be bought and sold on the Dark Web. In the United States alone, nearly 200,000 children are trafficked for sex (Goodman, 2015a, 2015b). Indeed, child pornography abounds on the Dark Web, where sites like Hard Candy, Jailbait, Lolita City, PedoEmpire, and Love Zone are highly profitable. Some sites offer tutorials on how to target and seduce children as well as evade law enforcement, and others provide live-streaming videos of child rape. And, of course, Dark Web organized cybercrime advertises hackers for hire. Goodman (2015a) asserts that Tor is used by 2 million people per day.

The legendary Silk Road, which began around 114 BC and was used for some 16 centuries, brought goods through China, India, Persia, Europe, Arabia, and Africa. Today's Silk Road, perhaps the most popular site on the Dark Web, is known as the eBay for drugs and offers every controlled (and uncontrolled) substance imaginable. Drugs are advertised alongside their photographs and consumer ratings. It took three years for federal agents to nab Ross William Ulbricht, aka Dread Pirate Roberts, the 29-year-old mastermind behind the largest criminal marketplace in the world. Ulbricht even hired hit men from his own network to murder five people (Goodman, 2015a). Although Silk Road was briefly suspended after Ulbricht's arrest, it continues to prosper under new management. Clearly, "We are at the dawn of a technological arms race, an arms race between people who are using technology for good and those who are using it for ill" (Goodman, 2015a, p. 372).

Addicted to cybersex

Fifty-year-old Phillip, a highly successful CEO, sought treatment (from Knafo) because he was addicted to Internet pornography. He could barely control himself at work. Between clients, he'd log on to

Internet porn sites; at home, he'd rush to the bathroom regularly with his iPad and masturbate to porn sites. Whatever he was doing, his mind was elsewhere, counting the minutes or hours until he could log onto another website and masturbate to a visual feast he simply couldn't resist. His entire life became organized around this private obsession.

Why would a man who seemed to have it all – a beautiful wife, wealth, children, and a high-profile career – have only one thing on his mind for most of his waking hours? Phillip explained that his wife was critical of him, and her sex drive seemed to have evaporated as her responsibilities as a mother of three daughters increased. His sex drive, however, hadn't diminished since he was 16; if anything, it was stronger. The Internet's anonymity and easy access to an unlimited pornographic landscape initially seemed like a safe outlet for him. He wasn't *actually* cheating with another woman, he reassured himself. But what began as an occasional physical release quickly turned into a runaway habit that he couldn't break.

Like more than 9 million men and women in the United States (Cooper, Scherer, Boies, & Gordon, 1999), Phillip was a cybersex addict. In fact, around 10 percent of adult male Internet users are hooked on cybersex (Cooper, Delmonico, & Burg, 2000). The Internet has created a widespread addiction to sex sites (Singh Bahtia, 2009), which feature a range of images, from the innocuous (naked pictures of men and women) to the depraved (child pornography); in fact, more than 100,000 sites offer pornographic images of children (Red Herring Magazine, 2002). Some 20,000 pornographic pictures of children are posted on a weekly basis (National Society for the Prevention of Cruelty to Children, 2003). Some claim that without the porn industry the Internet would not have survived (Barry-Dee & Morris, 2010). As with any addiction, many people who become addicted to porn sites develop higher thresholds of tolerance and then must view more extreme images to feel satisfied. Neuroscience explains this phenomenon as the hijacking of the brain's dopamine systems (Jović & Đinđić, 2011), while psychology examines the experiential dimensions of this activity with an eye to unconscious motivation (Cash, Rae, Steel, & Winkler, 2012).

Phillip knew he was heading for disaster. He couldn't keep his mind on work, and his wife was threatening to leave him. He had to do something. Although his work brought in significant income, his wife had brought a lot of family money into the marriage, a fact that she constantly threw in Philip's face. She also didn't like his family, and to please his wife Philip had cut himself off from his relatives. At home he felt isolated and emasculated, powerless and without a voice. On the Web, he became an Internet Casanova. It wasn't clear whether his wife knew about Phillip's preoccupations or, if she did, whether she cared.

In treatment, Phillip gradually came to understand that seeking sex on the Internet served multiple functions, not the least of which was taking revenge on his wife. Much of his work in therapy focused on his damaged relationship with her. He gradually began to take back control of his life and assert himself with his wife. The more he let go of anger and resentment, the less he needed to visit porn sites. A turning point occurred when one of his daughters opened his laptop and found a pornographic image he had imprudently left on the screen. When he came home from work that evening, she said that one word came to mind when she saw him: CARELESS. Phillip's addiction took on a more urgent dimension once his children became involved. He knew he had to get serious about stopping his cybersex addiction quickly. Dr. Knafo was intent on helping him, though she couldn't help noticing that what happened in Phillip's home might be occurring in many others. Children accessing their parents' or older siblings' computer porn is becoming the new primal scene in the technological age. Indeed, there is evidence that 42 percent of youth are exposed to online pornography, and, of that number, 66 percent experienced inadvertent exposure (Wolak, Mitchell, & Finkelhor, 2007).

Although Phillip's home life improved dramatically, and he stopped engaging in Internet sexual activities, his wife demanded he leave therapy because she wasn't part of it. After searching for and finding Dr. Knafo's picture on the Web, she demanded he see a male therapist instead. Phillip acquiesced. Ironically, in this case, the Internet, part of the presenting problem, also became the cause for termination.

Thrill seeker

Teddy walked into my (Dr. Knafo's) office casually dressed in shorts and a T-shirt with the words THRILL SEEKER spelled in large red letters. As if that weren't enough, he sported a cap with the words

RIDE HARD. Teddy sent a clear message to me before opening his mouth. Honestly, the message I received was: "Teddy is an asshole." He was arrogant and spoke crudely about women as if they were toys. He said his therapy had been mandated by the state, and, therefore, he had not come to me because he felt he had a problem. Rather, he was in therapy to avoid jail time.

Despite his initial presentation to me, Teddy was an attractive, smooth-talking, 30-year-old with a beautiful and loving live-in girl-friend, a devoted family, and a steady job. He was also enrolled in col-lege classes to obtain a degree in computer science. After working days as a plumber, he attended evening classes, studied for exams, relaxed with his girlfriend, and still managed to devote six to eight hours each night to Internet sex. This was a man so driven by sexual perversion that he hardly needed to sleep!

He quickly told me why he had to see me: "I sent naked pictures of myself to a minor." He added, "Why did I want to talk to her when I had so many women from other sites?" He answered his own question, displaying his need to feel powerful and important by saying he enjoyed being able to teach someone something he knew about. He had wanted to give her a dildo for her thirteenth birthday, but he never got the chance. Though Teddy came to see me under duress, he was surprisingly open about his inner life and activities. He was quite intelligent and verbal, yet something was missing. He seemed to have no censor, no shame – no conscience. He quickly confessed, "I abuse everything I touch." He was refer-ring to drugs and alcohol. But we both already knew that his toxic-ity went beyond drugs.

In our initial session, Teddy confessed that as a teen a priest had molested him. During the same time he had held a job at a local convenience store. One day, Tom the manager, whom he idealized, walked in on him while he was in the bathroom and exclaimed, "That little thing is all you have? How will you fuck anyone with that?" From that time forward, Teddy was unable to urinate in pub-lic. Soon afterward, Tom took him to a prostitute to lose his virgin-ity. He was so anxious and confused that he couldn't perform. The prostitute helped him, for which he was grateful. Our first session ended with Teddy acknowledging his interest in domination: "I want to train a slave," he said.

I was surprised at the amount of information Teddy shared in a single session. I felt flooded by his stories and was impressed by his frankness. He was seducing me into believing that he was truly interested in doing psychological work, and he even offered me possible antecedents to explain his behavior. I was wary, however, that he would become more guarded as time went on. He wanted to make a good first impression, I told myself. Be careful.

Teddy did not retreat from his candid disclosures. Though he visibly displayed little affect, he seemed willing to delve into his psyche, claiming, "If I'm broken, I want to be fixed." Clearly, he wasn't certain anything was wrong with him. He shared the progression of his techno-sex addiction with me: it began with his spending time on the virtual online world, Second Life, then social network, MySpace, after which he moved on to chat rooms, and finally ended up on adult S&M websites. Occasionally he would meet with a woman to engage in sadomasochistic sexual activity. Regarding his Internet activity, he announced proudly, "I got so good at it, I went from two girls to 200 girls a night." He divulged his seduction strategy, which he boiled down to 15 questions, beginning with the girl's name, height, weight, and physical attributes ("legs, tits, and ass"), and ending with the kind of panties she wore, her sexual desires, and whether she was submissive. If she met his requirements, he called her and they would engage in phone sex. "It's all a fantasy," he exclaimed innocently. " *Your* fantasy," I underscored. "Yes," he replied, "I always wanted to find a sexually open girl willing to try anything I wanted, someone who would please me. I felt my desires would never end." Indeed, Teddy's sexual appetites seemed endless. Eventually, he sought females who wanted to be spanked, tied up, and choked. He loved the "thrill of conquering" and sent out 60–70 emails per day. He described his "perfect person" to me: "I want to completely dominate, degrade, humiliate, be rough ... and then she'd be affectionate after that." His words reminded me of Bach's (1994b) description of the sadist's inner thoughts: "I can do anything I want to you and you'll still always be there" (p. 18).

Meeting and working with Teddy challenged me in several ways. I was repelled by what he had done and relieved that he had been caught by law enforcement before causing more harm. I hated the way he referred to women as girls and chicks, and I felt personally offended each time he described his wish to abuse a woman or a girl. But he also intrigued me, and I wanted to get to know him better, to learn what made him tick, how he had become this way, and whether every man has a Teddy in him. I wasn't sure if I could help him, but I was quite certain he'd help me learn a lot about the darker side of masculinity. He engaged my emotions when he told me about his childhood – being fat, feeling rejected, and being molested by a priest and harassed by an employer. "A person isn't born this way," I thought. When I felt myself beginning to like him, I worried that he was psychologically seducing me and that I might have it in me to give in to this type of man. On the other hand, though he had been forced to come to therapy, he seemed to be trying to make the most of our time together.

He introduced me to Second Life, the vast virtual world in which users create avatars that interact with each other in as many ways as one can imagine. I discovered that very dark places and activities exist in that world. For example, there are child avatars that are most probably operated by adults in areas like "Daddy's New Town Playground," a place where child prostitution exists. The "Sassy Bad Day Skirt" can be purchased and, when worn by an avatar, enables others to track down, abduct, and rape "her." Tranquillizer darts can temporarily disable a female avatar who can then be force-teleported to any location, raped, tied up, gagged, and left helpless. Normally, one has complete control of one's avatars, but there are features, like "Restrained Life (or Love) Viewer" that allow others to control and abuse one's avatar. Additional areas have Gore-themes wherein the avatars are brutish domineering men who keep women as chattels and slaves.

After hearing about the dark side of Second Life, I breathed deeply and asked what Teddy's sex life was like with his girlfriend. "I never tie her up," he said seriously. "I build a white picket fence here [pointing to the right] and a dungeon there [pointing to the left]." His explanation highlighted the sharp divide between his physical sex and phone sex. I reflected that the split existed not only in his behavior but also within himself. "Yes," he agreed. "How do I put the pieces back together?"

I wasn't sure the pieces fit together but suggested we begin by exploring his addiction history. His father was an alcoholic, and Teddy recalled his many drunken stupors and rages. Like Teddy, his father had two sides: "He was a responsible breadwinner and completely out of control." Teddy was extremely overweight as a child, consuming food at an alarming rate. As a young teen he turned to alcohol, and by the age of 15 Teddy was a heavy drinker. When he began seeing me, he smoked pot every day. "When I don't smoke, I have no sex drive," he claimed. He tried LSD over 150 times, as well as hard drugs like heroin and cocaine. At one point he wanted to stop doing hard drugs and replaced them with Internet porn, trading one addiction for another. At the time that he saw me, he smoked pot daily and was addicted to Internet porn.

When we spoke of his sexual behavior facilitated by technology, he asked, "Where is the line?" I knew what he meant. He was asking, "When does one veer off the path of normality?" He soon reflected, "The more I look at myself, the more I see I deviated away from the normal." We analyzed this question together, and Teddy admitted that he knew he was pushing the envelope when he sent pictures of himself to a minor. At the same time, he unmistakably took pleasure in his revenge strategy: "I can get girls who wouldn't look at me when I was the fat boy." Nonetheless, he acknowledged he had a problem: "Sexually, I'm a mess. The door closes and I'm a twisted screwhead." He contemplated passing his problems onto his future offspring and asked, "Where does the twistedness stop?" At these moments, he appeared quite sincere, and I was hopeful that I could help. He reported dreams and continued thinking about topics that arose in session, beginning the session that followed with his reflections and questions. Therapy was "weird," he said, because in the past he avoided difficult topics – drank or smoked them away. Nonetheless, he thanked me for creating a safe space within which he could face himself. Soon he reported that he was staying away from the Internet (the court required this) and had cut down on his pot smoking by two-thirds.

We explored Teddy's dehumanization of women. "I don't want to waste time talking to someone who doesn't want to have sex with me," he muttered dispassionately. He admitted that when he looked at a woman, all he noticed was her cleavage. "How can I turn cleavage into a person?" he wondered aloud. Women were faceless sexual bodies to him. His girlfriend, on the other hand, had a face, even a heart. One time his girlfriend brought home a whip for sex play. He was aghast and unable to accommodate her sexual fantasies. "To me, [women who engage in S&M] are whores; my girlfriend isn't." His online goal was sex, and he had no interest in getting to know the human being. As far as he was concerned, the females he pursued through this route were whores, or whores in the making. The chase – the risk-taking behavior – made him high, and in the conquest he realized his goal. "I used to be afraid of heights," he explained. "Now I walk on the ledge." He meant this both literally and metaphorically. He wished to know nothing about the woman except whether her boyfriend pleased her and what was her favorite sexual position. "The devil gets into me when I'm hard and the hormones are rushing. I justify everything," he said. Indeed, he convinced himself that phone calls, dirty talk, and exchanging naked pictures were all morally okay, so long as he didn't touch another girl. Occasionally, however, he did physically cheat on his girlfriend; he would meet women to act out his sadistic fantasies. During one session, Teddy described the advantages of using the Internet. "It skips a lot of steps. If one [woman] tells me no, there are 4 million behind her. There's no emotion. Zero responsibility. No wining, dining, or dating. I can be completely removed. It's pure pleasure." After sex, he never felt emotional, never held a woman or cuddled. He added, "To this day, I don't know what lovemaking is."

Teddy responded to my invitation to revisit the early traumatic events that caused him to split and feel insecure about his masculinity. His boss at the convenience store was "free with his hands on me" and teased him for "peeing and wiping like a girl." "I've never been able to shake that," he admitted, still tortured by his inability to urinate in a public bathroom. I suggested that his interest in control and domination might be one way he tried to overcome the feelings of vulnerability he experienced as a child. He recalled the priest who also took advantage of him, concluding that these early experiences were invasive and humiliating. He said nothing to anyone at the time. After recounting these scenes of molestation, Teddy finally narrated in detail the exchanges he had had with the young girl that led to his arrest.

He offered her a dildo and asked her if she knew how to use it. His words were profane as he explained how to "shove it in." She didn't respond, and he concluded, "I was talking to myself." In reality, he had been talking to an undercover policewoman. Clearly, Teddy tried to reverse his feelings of inadequacy, vulnerability, and victimization by becoming the one who dominates. When faced with this revelation, Teddy expressed a wish to change, even a wish to develop a relationship. "I see pictures of a wedding but have no idea how to get there."

He began watching TV programs about romance "to learn how the other side feels." He knew there were many obstacles that stood in his way. "I can't tolerate feelings," he announced.

"Which feelings?" I asked.

"Pain, loss, need."

I wondered out loud if he had always been this way. He told me that there was a time when he did feel. His first girlfriend broke his heart when she left him, after which he chased her for two years. He had been cheating on her and thought, "It was the right thing to tell her." Right or wrong, she left him following his confession. "After that, I don't cry," he asserted. "I don't have emotions. I never saw my father cry. He never hugged me." Teddy explored his parents' relationship and described it as unaffectionate, even dead. His parents didn't know how to enjoy themselves. He, on the other hand, was a thrill seeker. He also engaged in risky nonsexual activities, like racecar driving. He described the experience as pure freedom, overcoming fear, and most important, "no faces." He still liked "sex without a face and personality." For him, being thrilled filled the void of his inner deadness. He seemed to perfectly match the perversion criteria embodied in traditional psychoanalysis.

Teddy recounted many dreams as he opened up to his unconscious. Most were nightmares in which he faced the dark and vulnerable parts of himself. In several, he was a child running away from pedophiles. He began recalling girls he had had sex with and expressed guilt and remorse for the first time. "Part of me feels bad for that, I could've been a better person. I tried to have it all. I hurt girls. I never believed I'd go to jail." We spoke of the childhood prison he'd been carrying within him for so many years. Perhaps his acting out was a way to externalize that prison?

Finally, Teddy voiced the troubles he had with his girlfriend. They had nothing in common: "She watches movies until the part where the guy puts it in; I watch movies that start where the guy puts it in. She falls short on sex, and I fall short emotionally." He felt trapped in the relationship, knowing that his girlfriend was loyal, willing to stand by him despite his legal troubles. Yet he declared unemotionally, "If she dumps me, there'll be someone else," which showed that the people in his life were exchangeable parts.

The time arrived for Teddy's court appearance, and I was asked to write a letter describing the progress he had made in therapy. I had no trouble doing so, since I had witnessed a deepening in Teddy's self-awareness and his willingness to explore the dynamics underlying his behaviors. The judge decided, largely due to my report, not to send Teddy to prison. I probably shouldn't have been surprised by his leaving treatment. With the acumen typical of the pervert, he'd seduced me and given me what I wanted: a show of full disclosure, authentic remorse, and willingness to change. My own countertransference made me vulnerable to his ploy, blinded me to what seemed obvious after the fact. I first took him for a sly and lascivious con artist who might pervert the therapy and underscore his disdain for the law by extending his revenge to me. I was determined not to be seduced. Yet, as the therapy progressed I began to see him as a traumatized little boy who had become a lost, lonely man, and the lure for me was to help him heal his split and reach intimacy. I'd been so certain we had made an important connection and that our work had been meaningful. He seemed to gain many insights into his behavior and open up to his tender emotions. He even questioned whether he might develop feelings for a woman that would include a face, not just her body and her willingness to submit to his pleasure. After all, he had looked into my face for nearly a year as he confessed his darkest secrets. And I was invited into his dungeon and challenged to put a face on the women he had dehumanized. We had both been changed, I thought.

But there is often a sociopathic side to destructive perversion. Keeping in mind that perversion begins as the instrument of the other's desire – *I know what you want* – Teddy gave me exactly what I had wanted by engaging in a doublethink and acting the part of a patient on a pilgrimage to psychic integration. His act was so convincing that I could not think of one single slip that might have alerted me to his subterfuge. Even the dreams he reported seemed consistent with a sincere desire to change. One lies best when one lies to oneself, and a perverted individual can pull that off with great skill. After all, he or she is a master of illusion. Now, why do I think this conclusion is correct and not some other in-between it and what I thought had transpired before Teddy blew off me and the therapy? Because I called him on the phone and asked why he'd left without a word.

"Come on, you know why I left."

"Because you got the letter?"

"Exactly," he answered, laughing, and before I could respond, he hung up the phone.

I knew all along that something like this could happen. But I had come to believe it never would. The pervert's surprise, we might call it – to turn the sense of being a person into the experience of being a thing – was the greatest lesson I learned from my work with Teddy.

Catfish

In addition to providing the means to trawl for sex and pornographic images, the Internet allows people to misrepresent themselves in relational transactions. Ahmed, a dark, handsome, gay male in his 20s, was extremely self-conscious about his appearance when he decided to begin digital dating. He hated his looks and complained that he was overweight, not toned enough, and too ethnic looking. He was also coming to terms with his attraction to males, something that made him feel guilty and ashamed, particularly since his Muslim family and community forbade homosexuality. All of this contributed to a self-loathing that culminated in a particular perverse enactment that he eventually described to me (Knafo).

Ahmed was recounting his experience with Grindr, a popular app for gay men who want to hook up. The previous night he had tried to connect with several men, none of whom responded with a consenting swipe. He especially wanted a man named Bob to respond but had had no luck. Ahmed's self-hatred surfaced and expressed itself as rage. He created a new profile, but this time, instead of using his own photo, he replaced it with a photo of Dave, a male acquaintance he considered more handsome and popular than he. He reinvented himself by "borrowing" Dave's photo from his Facebook page. He would take revenge on both men at once – one for rejecting him and the other for being more attractive than he. Now looking quite buff, Ahmed again let Bob know that he was interested, and, predictably, Bob agreed to a hook up. Ahmed found himself in a bind. On the one hand, he had won. He felt vindicated for having tricked Bob into desiring him. On the other hand, he couldn't take the game any further because he'd have to present himself as himself.

As Ahmed guiltlessly narrated his evening's deceitful enactments, I wondered about my ethical responsibility, believing that what he had done might be unlawful. Even if it weren't, he had clearly crossed a line. I imagined the man whose photo was being used without his knowledge or consent. This could happen to anyone! At the time, I didn't know this type of masquerade, known as "catfishing," has become increasingly common on the digital dating scene. A "catfish" refers to a person who creates a fictional profile on social media and/or dating sites to lure someone into a relationship. Interestingly, Ahmed had created an Oedipal triangle in which he was the chosen one. His deceitful theater (Stoller, 1985) excited him and put him in a superior position, thus helping to restore narcissistic equilibrium. We spoke of growing to tolerate painful feelings and understand their origin. Ahmed recalled his father's abuse as well as the abuse of children who bullied him and called him names, making him feel small and inadequate, the object of hatred and rage. Much of our work around this incident aimed at helping Ahmed understand how he fashioned a situation in which he felt in control to replace situations in which he had felt rejected, inferior, and humiliated.

It is well known that most people who post online profiles do a little lying. Eighty-one percent of online daters misrepresent some aspects of themselves, with men lying about their height and income and women lying about their age and weight; both genders post pictures that are not recent (Rudder, 2010; Rosenbloom, 2011; Dosh, 2012). A popular dating site, OKCupid, offered some statistics with commentary that explains the desire to lie: "If you're 23 or older and don't make much money, go die in a fire" (Rudder, 2010). However, catfishing goes far beyond this kind of misrepresentation. Like Ahmed, catfish try to trick another person into desiring them by adopting or creating a different identity. Some people feel too insecure about their appearance and therefore "borrow" someone else's. Others want to enact revenge on an ex or on someone who has rebuffed them. Still others lie to sadistically humiliate and control. Trauma, insecurity, envy, and hostility combine to create an illusion that results in betrayal, cruelty, and harm that can be delivered only via the Internet. Indeed, betrayal seems to be an integral part of today's Internet dating scene, and some people state that it simply goes with the territory of Internet dating.

A 2010 film titled *Catfish* (Jarecki et al., 2010) inspired the MTV reality show of the same name. In the critically acclaimed documentary, Nev is a young man being filmed by his brother and a friend as he becomes Facebook friends with Abby Pierce, an eight-year-old Midwestern child prodigy who sends him her artwork. Through Abby, Nev connects with Abby's mother, Angela, and her sister, Megan, with whom he develops a passionate online romance. Nev and Megan exchange pictures and 1,500 messages over a nine-month period before Nev begins to suspect that Megan is not telling the truth. The brothers decide to travel from New York to Michigan to make a surprise visit to the Pierce home. They find Angela and her husband, Vince, with his severely mentally challenged twin sons. Angela tells Nev she is undergoing chemotherapy for uterine cancer. Nev insists on meeting his love interest, Megan. Angela tells him she'll come the following day, but the next day, she says Megan has checked into a drug rehab center. In the meantime, Vince tells a story about cod being shipped from Alaska to Asia. The fish are inactive and turn to mush unless catfish are placed in the tanks. The catfish nip the tails of the cod, keeping them active so that they arrive fresh and healthy. The message of Vince's story is that we all need catfish in our lives to keep us on our toes.

Angela turns out to be the catfish in the film, and she confesses to having made up multiple stories and numerous online profiles. She is the one who has been sending Nev her artwork, and she is also Megan. Angela does have a daughter, but the pictures she posted are of a young Canadian model, Aimee Gonzales. Angela is actually not suffering from cancer. Surprisingly, Nev seems to forgive Angela, and they continue as Facebook friends. If Nev is angry, he sublimates his anger by transforming it into a creative production: *Catfish*, the TV show.

Interestingly, Angela forms two discrete online relationships with Nev: one as a gifted child and the other as a young, passionate beauty hungry for love. She employs two different seductions and creates two illusions, enlisting Nev to help her create them. She callously uses him as the consciousness that experiences these illusions as real; through Nev she experiences their projected reality. He becomes the interactive mirror that reflects back to Angela the magic of her creations, herself as a gifted child and a beautiful, desirable woman – two fantasies that, once realized, empower her while masking her limitations. This is accomplished in a perverse scenario that could not be possible without today's technology. Technology invites the expansive play of a subject who is defined as much by lack as by being, who longs to realize possibilities that challenge personal and existential limitation, and who can engage in such play with relative anonymity and freedom from the law. Is it any surprise that users find victims on whom to work this magic – of being more than one person at a time while living in multiple locations in cyberspace? Nev is duped and dehumanized in the process, though this is done at a distance, once removed from actual contact, which makes the egregiousness of Angela's action seem less severe. Yet perversion is rampant in this kind of dark, creative theater. The actor takes or steals another's identity, schemes, lies, tricks, seduces under false pretense, and uses the other as a self-object without regard to the consequences of doing great harm. The space of encounter itself is violated, and this violation mocks the social bond, creating a standard of inauthenticity.

Also interesting about this particular Internet seduction is the Oedipal triangle it expresses. Two creations of the perpetrator, the child and the beauty, occlude her presence as a real person. She is excluded from the triangle she herself creates and fills her absence with the man who loves the two figures of her imagination. Yet she enjoys the entire production as the puppet master behind the scenes. In this way she becomes the Oedipal winner who not only witnesses the primal scene but also creates it for her own enjoyment.

The stated mission of the *Catfish* TV show (Jarecki et al., 2012–2015), now in its fourth season, is to help those who have become emotionally involved with questionable people on the Internet. Some couples have been communicating for months, others for years. The show follows both sides of the catfishing "relationship" and tries to understand the motives behind the catfishing behavior as well as the impact on the person who has been duped. The normalization of catfishing is evident in an article on the trend, which claims that couples who come together by accurately representing themselves are boring, and that such a pedestrian approach to romance is passé (Weber & Moses, 2013). While the authors were being ironic, the humor and lighthearted nature of the piece indicate the level of acceptance that has been attained by online betrayal and the upending of conventional social bonding. In some cases, those who catfish discover that they too have been catfished. Some even forgive the misrepresentation and end up together.

Others are not so forgiving. Artist and writer Dori Hartley publicly confessed to having been catfished. Enthralled by what she called "the epic romance of my life," Hartley embarked on a five-year relation-ship with a man she never met and never even glimpsed a picture of (Hartley, 2011). Dimitri described himself as 6 feet 7 inches tall, with long black hair; his phone voice was soft with a southern accent. He refused to send a picture of himself because he maintained he was dying of cancer and the disease had distorted his looks. Hartley was a cancer survivor herself and implicitly understood the importance of having love and support during such a challenging time. She also admitted her vulnerability as a "lonely woman sitting at her computer, waiting for someone special to pay attention to her" (Hartley, 2011). As the years went on, Hartley was "finally fixated on seeing the per-son I loved." She insisted he show her his face. The day finally arrived when Alex Lee, the real person behind Dimitri, got on a webcam to reveal her true identity. Alex was a woman with three grown daughters and two grandchildren. Hartley was heartbroken: "There will never be any words to adequately describe my shock and disgust. It never occurred to me that the man I adore would turn out to be someone so utterly devoid of conscience, so thoroughly steeped in duplicity" (Hartley, 2011). She concluded that stupid things happen to smart people because of their "desperate loneliness" and their willingness to believe in a fantasy. What she does not talk about was her complicity in what occurred – the pact she made with a perverse other with whom she nurtured a gratifying illusion for five years.

Another example of catfishing as a social perversion is an incident that began in 2011, when Montreal-based Sandra Bagaria began a Facebook communication with Amina Arraf, a lesbian Syrian-American blogger allegedly living in Syria at the time (Brekke, 2015; Deraspe, 2015). Bagaria and Arraf developed a serious relationship, even though they had never spoken by phone or in person nor had they seen one another. Bagaria was attracted to Arraf's nonconformist views and even encouraged her to create a blog, which she did, naming it "A Gay Girl in Damascus." The blog presented Arraf as a young woman with close ties to the Assad government and strong empathy for those oppressed by the regime. The blog captured the world's atten-tion and was viewed by Bagaria and other gay advocates as an act of courage in the light of Syria's persecution of the LGBT community. Matters intensified when Arraf reported that she had been kidnapped by Assad's police, an act that encouraged some gay activists in the

Middle East to take the risk of outing themselves to help search for her. Digital posters distributed across the Web in English and Arabic proclaimed, "Free Amina Arraf: Borders mean nothing when you have wings."

Arraf was eventually revealed to be Tom MacMaster, a married, white American male from Georgia who was a graduate student in medieval studies at the University of Edinburgh. After he finally disclosed his true identity, he professed, "I do not believe I harmed anyone" (Peralta & Carvin, 2011). An additional twist to this case is that Paula Brooks, editor of Lez Get Real, the original site on which MacMaster posted as Arraf, also turned out to be former Air Force pilot, Bill Graber (Flock & Bell, 2011). During their correspondence, neither man realized the other was pretending to be a lesbian woman. "Borders mean nothing when you have wings" seems an apt motto for Internet perversion.

Is catfishing illegal? It is hard to tell. These new Internet transgressions are requiring new laws (perversion brings the law into being), and violators take advantage of the fact that the law needs to catch up with technology. Despite the chaotic trail of deception and the harm he left, MacMaster was not prosecuted for a crime. States differ in their prosecution of catfishing. Criminal impersonation is difficult to prosecute unless there is clear identity theft and proof of injury or loss to the victim. When prosecuted, catfish are usually charged with misdemeanor crimes. Nineteen-year-old Andriy Mykhaylivskyy, of Rutherford, New Jersey, was given a six-month jail sentence for luring a classmate into an online relationship by creating a fictitious Facebook account for Kate Fulton, a girl he later claimed had been kidnapped while vacationing in Bulgaria. He even asked people for the $50,000 ransom money (Sudol, 2014). Sometimes misrepresentation can provide the catfish with more information than he or she bargained for. For instance, teen Marissa Williams invited men she met on the Internet to her home for sex. Her aunt, with whom she lived, tried to teach her a lesson by creating a fake online suitor, but the "joke" was on her. Marissa confessed to this fake suitor that she hated her aunt and wanted her dead. She asked him if he'd help her kill her aunt. The aunt called the police, and Williams was charged with solicitation of murder (Donnelly, 2014).

Surely impostors are nothing new. Kaplan (1987) studied the phenomenon and claimed that imposture was a rare male disorder that nonetheless flourished in the British literary world during the eighteenth century. Yet, if we glean statistics from the first three seasons of the *Catfish* show, the gender breakdown favors women: 57 percent female and 42 percent male. Helene Deutsch (1955) claimed, "The world is crowded with 'as if' personalities, and even more so with impostors and pretenders." She added, "Ever since I became interested in the impostor, he pursues me everywhere. I find him among my friends and acquaintances, as well as myself" (p. 337). In discovering that we can convincingly pretend to be someone else and that even when we don't, we still harbor an impostor, Deutsch coined the term "as if personality," to describe people who are good mimics and who adapt a persona without true authenticity (see also Deutsch, 1942). Phyllis Greenacre (1958) wrote that the impostor was nearly always a male with exhibitionist tendencies and omnipotent fantasies. She explained, "imposture appears to contain the hope of getting something material, or some other worldly advantage" (p. 359). She considered three factors to be present in the impostor: (a) a disturbed sense of identity; (b) a perceptiveness about certain aspects of reality and a "brazenness or stupidity" about other aspects of reality; and (c) a malformation of the superego, conscience, and ideals. Importantly, Greenacre mentioned that the impostor can succeed only in a social context in which there exists receptivity to trickery.

Though impostors have always existed, face-to-face relationships pose certain challenges for those who present themselves as other than who they are. The Internet, with its facile anonymity and accessibility, makes it very easy for people to shed their skin and replace it with a virtual one – whether adopted from the real world or created from the imagination. In a famous *New Yorker* cartoon, a dog "speaks" to another, saying, "On the Internet, no one knows you're a dog" (P. Steiner, 1993). Indeed, as we spend more time on the Internet, our lives become increasingly "virtual" and distanced from their physical reality, and the line between the real and the virtual becomes blurred, making it more difficult to distinguish between these two domains, which, after all, may not be as distinct as they appear at first blush. The cyberworld exists inside a machine (or web of machines) as an "as if" reality. The real world, too, is always within our experience, embodied and radically unfolding through the operations of the mind-body. Doesn't it seem "as if" the earth doesn't move and the full moon is the size of a quarter? Indeed, physicist David Deutsch (1997) effectively argues that the human brain is a "virtual reality generator" and that reality itself might be a simulation. Philosopher Marcus Arvan (2015) also strongly contends that reality is a simulation.

The self can be extended into the places, things, and people around it, nested as it is in overlapping circles of family, friends, neighbors, state, and nation. The self embodies the world that both gives it being and reflects it. Because the self does not end at the boundary of its flesh but fills the surround with itself as it takes the surround into itself, it easily finds itself at home in the virtual world where it may invent itself in any number of ways. Belk (2013) argued that digital technology provides unprecedented possibilities for self-extension. He discussed five changes wrought by digital technology: (a) dematerialization (of information and data), (b) reembodiment (as avatars, photos, videos, or catfish), (c) sharing (blogs, social media, photos, and videos), (d) co-construction of self (through digital gazing and communication/interaction), and (e) distributed memory (through digital archiving). Indeed, there may come a time when virtual worlds, continually improved by technological advances, may be experienced as so real as to be nearly indistinguishable from "real" worlds. The adoption of virtual worlds for entertainment and social networking is growing daily. For instance, Second Life, mentioned above, is a three-dimensional virtual world in which users create representations (as many as they wish) of themselves called avatars, and has become very popular. These avatars can live in a virtual home, work at a virtual job, interact with other virtual beings, and even engage in virtual sexual acts they would not dare to perform in their first life. Yet for many, virtual living already feels more real than the alternative. People spend twice as much time online as they did ten years ago. This is especially true of young adults, who spend an average of 30 hours per week in virtual worlds (Cooper, 2015).

Psychoanalysts have traditionally positioned themselves as truth seekers who view deception as a symptom of illness. Like Deutsch, psychoanalysts Gedimen and Lieberman (1996) emphasized the ubiquity of deception in everyday life and focused on the narcissistic and sadistic elements contained in such acts. Fromm (1959) described

Freud as uncompromising in his search for truth. Winnicott's (1965 [1962]) theory argued for the need to be rid of the False Self to reach one's True Self. Yet, in our postmodern times, some (e.g., Goldman, 2007) claim the idea of authenticity is a delusion and that pretense can be representative of healthy strivings. The authors' view is that human life exists between the two ideal extremes of absolute authenticity and absolute deception. Trickery, sinister seduction, deception, betrayal, and perversion stand in reciprocal and necessary relationship with striving for authenticity, accountability, coherence, and transparency. The straight and crooked paths are intertwined. There is no one true self and no one false self either. The idea of a core self is a belief rather than a fact, yet it nonetheless remains a powerful concept (Belk, 2013). There are selves in situation, selves that constellate around a histori-cal center of gravity, and a pattern of selfhood that issues from one's historical embodiment, which itself can encourage striving for authen-ticity or engagement in deception. Here, one thinks of the relational concept of multiple selves (Bromberg, 1998; Davies, 2004, 2005). Yet the question remains as to whether people's online selves express a self-state or something different and separate from the self. This topic has already begun to be researched (Belk, 2013; Sung et al., 2011).

Although deception and lying may have an evolutionary advan-tage (for example, animals that can turn the color of their surround-ings to deceive predators into believing they are inanimate), extreme cases of manipulation call to mind the psychopath or con man. It is generally agreed that such characters are the least analyzable and the least likely to seek out therapy (Becker, 2010), unless, like Teddy, they are mandated by the court to do so. Certainly, deception evokes problematic counter-transference. And distinctions must be acknowl-edged with regard to whether the person believes his or her own lies (LaFarge, 1994), and whether the lie is in the service of sadism or self-preservation (Lemma, 2005). The behaviors described in this chapter reveal that some patients exploit others for their own needs and desires. Moreover, patients can use the analyst as a fetishized object (Renik, 1992) in a perverse transference (Etchegoyen, 1991; Bach, 1994a). The analyst becomes audience, co-conspirator, and "corrupt container" (O'Shaughnessy, 1990) in a perverse pact (Stein, 2005) with the patient. As patients involve therapists in their Internet escapades, some darker than others, it places us (the therapists) in their sadomasochistic, erotic world and confronts us with our own sexual desires and ethical challenges. Often trust is violated in the treatment alliance with the aim of reversing the power dynamics. For example, a colleague told me she had Skyped with a patient for an entire year before discovering that a third person had been present during all of her online clinical sessions. What she believed were private interactions turned out to be perverse, voyeuristic, and exhibitionistic enactments to which she had not consented.

Our patients Google us, and those with advanced computer skills can invade our privacy in deeply disturbing ways. When they share their dating behaviors, we may become involuntary voyeurs to fantasies and acts that we sometimes find ethically reprehensible. On several occasions, some of us are presented with a generational challenge, as many of the patients sharing their Internet behaviors are much younger than their therapists. The analyst may be made to doubt herself and question whether she is simply behind the times. "Everyone does it," I was told by a patient who lied about her age and posted old photographs on her online dating profile. Does everyone do it? I wondered. This type of perversion aims to get the analyst to accept a lie as truth, to share in the illusion created to seduce the other, to boost the patient's own self-esteem, and to enact revenge on figures in the patient's history that harmed him or her. The best-case scenario might be one in which the patient wishes to be caught.

Romancing the mark: cyber swindling

The good news is that one in five relationships begins online, and one in ten Americans has used an online dating site or mobile dating app (Smith & Duggan, 2013). More than a third of new marriages begin online (Jayson, 2013). Online dating sites, like Match.com and eHarmony, have made it possible for many adults to expand their dating possibilities beyond anything imaginable only a couple of decades ago. The bad news is that online dating sites have become settings for scam artists to swindle tens of millions of dollars each year. Many of those persuaded to empty their bank accounts are women over 50 who live alone and are retired (Olson, 2015). They are ideal targets because they usually own their own home, have accumulated savings, and, most important, are lonely, gullible, and hungry for romance. *The New York Times* claimed that in a five-month period in 2014, 6,000 people registered complaints that they had been swindled out of a total of $82.3 million (Olson, 2015). Despite the fact that online dating sites warn users not to send money to anyone who contacts them, this cautionary advice often goes unheeded.

Most cases begin with a man who alters and uses an inactive profile on a dating site like Match.com, to contact a potential victim. Once contact is made and interest established, he quickly shifts to communicating on a private email or telephone. By contacting the woman on a daily basis with letters filled with amorous attention, he establishes trust and cultivates romance. Reading her profile carefully and making sure to match her search requirements, he convinces the woman that he is Mr. Right, her Prince Charming, and her soul mate. There is one hitch: the man is "temporarily" overseas on business. They make detailed plans to eventually meet, keeping the fantasy of a shared future alive. After a few weeks or months, the man suddenly reports that he is in trouble: he's in the hospital, he needs to pay for work permits, he hasn't been paid, he's lost his credit card, he's been robbed – any reason to evoke sympathy and induce the woman to wire him money. He asks for a loan to cover his financial setback, promising to pay her back. This is repeated, each time with a different reason and a larger sum, until the woman has emptied her bank account or realized she has been defrauded (Olson, 2015).

When the victims of romance fraud finally face the truth about the lies they've been told, they are overcome with feelings of shame and humiliation for having been played by an online stranger. Many are too embarrassed to confide in their friends or families. But women are not the only victims. Al Cirelli, a proud 68-year-old man, committed suicide after sending $50,000 of his own and his son's money to a woman in Ghana who called herself Aisha (Wallace, 2010). (The person whose seductive photos were used for the fraud claims hundreds have illegally appropriated her image.) Aisha had promised to meet the retired businessman in Yonkers, where he lived, to start a new life together. She assured him romance and money were on their way. On the day she was scheduled to arrive, Mr. Cirelli received an email bluntly stating that she had committed suicide – "blown her head off" – in Chicago.

Cirelli either realized he had been duped or was heartbroken, and he took his own life (Wallace, 2010).

Cyber revenge

Catfish are not the only people who use the Internet for revenge. Stories abound of cyber bullying, a form of social aggression that often pushes people to take their own lives. A sad example is that of Megan Meier, a 13-year-old girl who thought she was communicating online with a 16-year-old boy called Josh on MySpace. Josh and Megan became friends and flirted with one another until he suddenly turned mean and began calling her names (e.g., slut, liar) and telling her the world would be better off without her. Megan hanged herself as a result of the hoax. Shortly afterward, it was revealed that Josh was created by another teen, with the complicity of Lori Drew, the mother of Sarah Drew, a teen friend of Megan's. Mother (Lori Drew), daughter, and family friend, Ashley Grills, conspired in carrying out the Internet hoax, allegedly to find out what Megan was saying about Sara online after the two girls had a falling out (Surdin, 2008). In the end, the mother was convicted of three misdemeanors for her actions (Surdin, 2008), and a year later, she was acquitted of all charges (Zetter, 2009).

Instagram, an online mobile sharing service that provides a venue for those who wish to distribute photos and videos, has also been appropriated in the service of perversion. S. E. Smith (2015) explained the dark side of Instagram: "Beneath the surface of the cool, refreshing waters of Instagram lies a shark, and it's ready to bite." Smith claimed the most frequent victims of Instagram were those with high public profiles and those with non-normative bodies. He gave the example of users who cruelly sent Robin Williams's daughter photoshopped images of her father's dead body. Plus-sized women are also targets of bullying on Instagram. Smith discussed one woman who received nasty comments to a photo she posted of herself, which accused her of promoting obesity, called her "gross," and demanded she "go to the gym." Here is an example of how the removal of interacting parties from shared physical space offered by the Internet can liberate the inner sadist.

A lesser-known outlet for intimate rage is revenge porn, a form of sexual assault that takes place on the Internet. Someone, usually a man, posts nude or sexually explicit photos or videos of a woman (often his ex) without her consent. Frequently the photos are posted along with identifying information, which results in online harassment or stalking of the victim. Unfortunately, this form of online sexual assault is not uncommon. McAfee (2013), a well-known virus-scanning program, reported that one in ten ex-partners have threatened to post risqué photographs of their ex online; 60 percent of those who threatened followed through.

Many people, aware of the risk of sharing naked photos with others, use Snapchat, an extremely popular photo-sharing app that possesses a distinguishing feature: the photos disappear within seconds, a built in feature guarding against violation. Nevertheless, one can circumvent this safeguard by taking a screenshot of an image before it vanishes or even photographing it with a camera (Madrigal, 2013).

Revenge porn can have devastating consequences: psychological damage, secondary victimization through stalking, and loss of professional and educational opportunities, to name a few (Citron & Franks, 2014). Compromising photographs are posted on sites like Cheaterville. com or MyEx.com that purposely aim to humiliate the victim. In addition, when a victim speaks out, making her case even more public, she risks further harm. Law professors Citron and Franks (2014) argue for criminalization of nonconsensual pornography, stating that consent in one context should not be construed as consent in another context to which the victim has not agreed. Consensual sharing of sexual images is usually done with the implied or expressed understanding that the images will remain private. Clearly, these expectations are being violated:

> Today, intimate photos are increasingly being distributed online, potentially reaching thousands, even millions of people, with a click of a mouse. A person's nude photo can be uploaded to a website where thousands of people can view and repost it. In short order, the image can appear prominently in a search of the victim's name. It can be e-mailed or otherwise exhibited to the victim's family, employers, coworkers, and friends. The Internet provides a staggering means of amplification, extending the reach of content in unimaginable ways.
>
> (Citron & Franks, 2014, p. 105)

The law is surely attempting to catch up with crimes of technology. But what about the mental health profession? How many analysts, therapists, and counselors are being confronted with these new forms of abuse, harassment, and assault? How are we handling the new dating practices? What is our role and responsibility when we hear from a patient that she is sharing naked pictures of herself with her boyfriend? Do we talk about safety, as we would with a teen who was about to have sex? Do we ask about precautions taken, as we would with someone engaging in risky behaviors that might expose him or her to the AIDS virus? The authors believe education is warranted for both the analyst and patient. We also believe that analysts need to be well informed about the latest dating and hookup technologies and stay current with legal responsibilities. And analysts and therapists need to explore within themselves their own attitudes toward the changes that are taking place in the techno-social scene. Instagram, Facebook, Snapchat, Tinder, and other types of social media are ubiquitous, and our single and married clients are using these channels in greater and greater numbers. Technology is changing the ways we relate to each other, even as it is changing who and what we are.[1]

Braving a new world

The Internet is now a primary source for information, communication, entertainment, and trade. It is an amazing tool that has brought us closer together by transforming the world into a global village. A person can travel that village in an instant and expand his or her social network in ways that were previously unimaginable. The Internet has also had a major impact on those who are in committed relationships, those looking for a relationship, and those seeking casual or unconventional sex. Social media, dating apps, hookup apps, affair websites, porn sites, and even matches made to commit heinous crimes are accessible with the click of a mouse. Cyber love potentially feeds people's fantasies, and fantasy loving is so much easier than loving in the real world. Along with the benefits of anonymity and accessibility, Internet relationships come with costs and risks. What begins as an online chat can end in addiction, deception, fraud, stalking, and death.

The dangers inherent in novel applications of technology should not be underestimated by any of us, especially those in the mental health professions.

Note

1. Even more pernicious than catfishing and revenge porn is the use of the Internet to search for victims to be tortured, killed, and cannibalized. In 2001, Armin Meiwes, a 41-year-old German man, used the name Frankie when he posted a version of the following advert more than 80 times in Internet chat rooms: "Looking for a well-built 18- to 30-year-old to be slaughtered and then consumed" (Jones, 2005). He received 200 responses! After interviewing four potential victims, Meiwes finally selected a 43-year-old homosexual computer software designer and masochist, Bernd-Jurgen Brandes, who adopted the online pseudonym "Cator." Like Hannibal Lecter in Silence of the Lambs, who served himself a victim's innards alongside some "fava beans and Chianti," Meiwes, after having sex with Brandes, cut off his penis and tried to eat it with his victim after sautéing it in a pan with garlic, salt, and pepper. He then read a Star Trek book for three hours while Brandes was left bleeding to death in the bathtub. Hours later, Meiwes killed him by stabbing him in the throat, after which he hung his body on a meat hook and tore off slabs of flesh that he froze and ate over the next ten months. He filmed the entire encounter and later derived considerable sexual pleasure from watching it. In 2006, Meiwes was convicted of manslaughter and sentenced to life in prison. He is now a vegetarian (Hall, 2007).

Chapter 7

The institutionalization of human evil

1984 as a paradigm for perversion

> Men are so necessarily mad that to not be mad would amount to
> another form of madness.
>
> – Pascal

Though most commonly associated with individual human sexuality,
perversion can permeate social life and may be found in any human
system whose purpose and meaning are, by the very operation of that
system, undermined, violated, or destroyed. Perversion is often found
where there are strong power differentials with weak or corrupt over-
sight and is expressed by political leaders who live above the law and
violate the trust of their constituents while debasing the moral order
that organizes society. Perversion manifests in CEOs who become
their own law as they flout ethics and rules while betraying contrac-
tual agreements with shareholders and degrading the dynamic economic and social systems necessary for societal stability. Perversion
blossoms in bureaucratic or medical institutions that provide human
services while treating human beings like things. It has a secure home
in religious institutions that cynically violate their own teachings while
insisting on the sovereignty of their dogma. Perversion is found in the
excesses of mindless consumerism and brand-name fetishism. In the
nation state and rogue state its potential for evil is greatest through
activities of class exploitation, pernicious foreign policy, war, "racial
and ethnic cleansing," and genocide. Perversion is found in all things
humanly created and deployed that are rife with deception, betrayal,
exploitation, cruelty, dehumanization, and destructiveness.

In this chapter, we offer a model of malignant perversion, both as
techno-social activity and an underlying structure of splitting and

disavowal, not drawn from any clinical case, but rather from the literary masterpiece *1984*. The totalitarian state of Oceania depicted in George Orwell's work illustrates perversion *in extremis*, encompassing all areas of human life, from the personal to the socio-political. The novel provides an anchoring point for understanding perversion's radical potential for evil, its obsessive need to control, and its relationship to death.

Orwell's *1984* is a satirical political document and a deep psychological study of the monstrous potential of the human psyche. Informed with the relentless energy of chilling insight, this inexorable tragedy depicts, through the fate of a single couple, a vast, shocking social catastrophe. In an online survey (Crown, 2007), Orwell's masterpiece was chosen as one of the ten books that best define the twentieth century. Robert McCrum of *The Guardian* wrote that the first line – "It was a bright cold day in April, and the clocks were striking thirteen" – sounds "as natural and compelling" as it did when it was first written (McCrum, 2009). Orwell's first sentence embodies the feeling of the crooked path, which in this case leads straight to hell. Sixty-four years after its publication, *1984* has not lost its relevance and, in view of some of the frightening changes now taking place, seems more than prophetic. Not surprisingly, sales of *1984* skyrocketed after revelations about the NSA's wide-ranging digital surveillance programs (Oremus, 2013), and President Obama, unconvincingly defending the PRISM program and the NSA, said, "In the abstract, you can complain about Big Brother and how this is a potential program run amok, but when you actually look at the details, then I think we've struck the right balance" (Johnson, 2013). Before we refute the president's assessments, we will first analyze the structure and meaning of Orwell's dystopian world.

A structure of techno-perversion

Winston Smith, the protagonist of *1984*, is one of numerous minor bureaucrats who lives in what was once London. He works in the Ministry of Truth, rewriting history for the ruling Party of Oceania, a draconian dystopia alternately at war with one of the two remaining super-states, Eurasia and Eastasia. The ruling or Inner Party and the State itself are led by the mythic Big Brother, whose stern and judgmental image is ubiquitous on billboards, posters, and two-way telescreens. Like all external Party members in Oceania, Winston is watched by telescreens everywhere he goes, even in his own home. Nurturing a growing political subversion in a nation state where even the mildest rebellious thought is punishable by death, Winston meets Julia, also a minor bureaucrat, and they carry on an illegal affair while plotting against the State with a high-level spy named O'Brien. The lovers wind up paying the ultimate price for their transgression – the annihilation of their souls – which leaves them longing for execution.

Oceania is composed of three levels of society: the powerful and elite Inner Party, the exploited and slavish Outer Party, and the ignorant and alienated proles. The Inner Party, an oligarchy headed by the shadowy figure of Big Brother, rules the State and controls society with a spiked iron first. The members of the Inner Party enjoy some luxuries and perhaps a modicum of freedom from universal surveillance via the two-way telescreens. They keep the Outer Party under constant surveillance, prohibiting them from engaging in free thought, sex, and all forms of individual expression. Along with the watching screens, Outer Party members are tracked by the Thought Police and exist under the constant threat of arrest, torture, and execution. They are deprived of necessities and mocked and humiliated by cheap simulacrums of luxuries like coffee, cigarettes, and alcohol. Meanwhile, the prole majority live brutish, squalid lives and are kept in check by vapid, machine-written literature, State-sponsored pornography, and lottery gambling. The State eliminates gifted proles "who might possibly become nuclei of discontent" (Orwell, 1950, p. 209).[1]

Overseeing and ensuring the dissemination and enactment of Oceania's social program are the four ministries, each one a gigantic lie exemplifying the three Party slogans.

WAR IS PEACE.
FREEDOM IS SLAVERY.
IGNORANCE IS STRENGTH.

Each slogan, a crooked distortion of human truth, is *made* true within the normative social perversion that pervades Oceania. Though all members of the Party are slaves, from the State's viewpoint they are "free" from themselves and private life, free from the burden of independent thought and individual autonomy. Absorbed into the will of the Party, their freedom is found in their slavery and their strength in the ignorance of their condition, its basis, its aim, and the fact that there is no escape from it. The endless war Oceania wages against its interchangeable enemies enables the stability of domestic misery, which is Oceania's peace.

The four ministries are housed in gigantic pyramidal buildings, imposing on the view throughout the city. The Ministry of Truth controls all news media, education, and entertainment and manufactures lies by continually rewriting history, which also fosters the illusion that the Party is omniscient, omnipresent, and omnipotent. The Ministry of Truth is the home of the official language of Newspeak, a severely hobbled lexicon that profoundly limits personal expression and seeks to eliminate the possibility of renegade speech. The Ministry of Plenty oversees the planned State economy – intentional pervasive poverty – while ceaselessly publishing reports of increased productivity and quality of life. The Ministry of Peace wages perpetual war for the purpose of wasting resources and keeping the population helplessly poised on the knife edge of survival while providing enemies of the State as targets for displaced hatred and rage. The Ministry of Love persecutes, tortures, and executes wayward citizens for "thought crimes," and in the process eradicates all traces of will and personal affection. Those punished for thought crimes are eventually murdered, transformed into "unpersons," and erased from all record and memory. In this windowless ministry surrounded by barbed wire and armed soldiers is the dreaded Room 101, which holds "the worst thing in the world," (p. 283) – a horrific, customized torture that actualizes a person's greatest fear.

In Oceania the past and future are disavowed and replaced with an eternal, dogmatic present that is continually dictated by the Inner Party. The State manufactures a socio-political counterfactual illusion that destroys memory, reality, and time. Inconvenient facts, as well as people related to such facts who are not in harmony with the State's policy, are jettisoned down the "memory hole." The chief tool that a Party member must use to embody illusion is "doublethink," the mental discipline of willfully blinding oneself to glaring contradiction and thus denying reality. A form of controlled insanity, doublethink always keeps the lie one step ahead of the truth. Though the obvious purpose of the State language is thought control, its deeper aim is to erase individual subjectivity and destroy a person's inner life, replacing it with the mind of the State. The process of doublethink can be narrated as follows: *I lie to myself and forget that I have done so. I then forget the act of forgetting. Should I, in accordance with the State's will, need to change my view and recall the lie I once forgot, I do so. Once the function of recollection is served, I forget the contradicting recollection and forget I forgot it.* Doublethink is the radical masochistic act of (self) denial demanded by the masters of the Inner Party, an abject form of self-erasure, the club that beats the mind to pieces.

In striving to make subversion unthinkable and ensure unassailable State power and permanence, Oceania intimidates, dominates, controls, and dehumanizes its citizens. If there is any enjoyment in Oceania, it is only found in the sadistic pleasure of persecution, torture, psychic rape, murder, and war. There is a pleasure in hatred and its active expression. Hatred energizes the social scene – hatred of the enemy, hatred of Emmanuel Goldstein, the homegrown "primal traitor" and chief enemy of the State, and hatred of fellow citizens. Of course, the greatest hatred is of the State and Big Brother, but this hatred must be carefully displaced and redirected at the enemy, even though it emerges in dreams. Hatred is allotted its own two minutes every day, and, culminating in a frenzied orgy of exclamations of rage, it instills in citizens "a hideous ecstasy of fear and vindictiveness, a desire to kill, to torture, to smash faces in with a sledge-hammer" (p. 14). Orwell's narrator says hatred "seemed to flow through the whole group of people like an electric current, turning one even against one's will into a grimacing, screaming lunatic" (p. 14). There is even a "celebration" of a week of hatred, which requires months of detailed preparations.

Hatred as the primary emotion accompanying malignant perversion (Stoller, 1975) is perfectly summed up when O'Brien tells Winston, "Power is in inflicting pain and humiliation" (p. 266).

Citizens of Oceania are treated regularly to propaganda movies showing butchery of soldiers and civilians. Early in the novel Winston recalls a film, "one very good one of a ship full of refugees being bombed somewhere in the Mediterranean" (p. 8). Inured to the horrific brutality of the State, the audience, except for one female prole, whoops with delight and applauds the sight of a man being riddled with machine-gun bullets and a woman and her child being blown to pieces.

The novel narrates Winston's life from a short time before he falls in love with Julia to his and her capture, "rehabilitation," and return to society as hopelessly traumatized victims of the State. All traces of love and hope have been purged from their psyches, as they await inevitable extermination. Their humanity has been completely extinguished, and not a trace of who they were remains. While torturing Winston, O'Brien tell him:

> "Never again will you be capable of ordinary human feeling. Everything will be dead inside you. Never again will you be capable of love, or friendship, or joy of living, or laughter, or curiosity, or courage, or integrity. You will be hollow."
>
> (p. 256)

> "There will be no curiosity, no enjoyment of the process of life. All competing pleasures will be destroyed. But always – do not forget this, Winston – always there will be the intoxication of power, constantly increasing and constantly growing subtler. Always, at every moment, there will be the thrill of victory, the sensation of trampling on an enemy who is helpless. If you want a picture of the future, imagine a boot stamping on a human face ... forever."
>
> (p. 267)

It is interesting that Orwell once said, "My recent novel [*1984*] is *not* intended as an attack on Socialism ... but as a show-up of the *perversions* [emphasis added] which have already been partly realized in Communism and Fascism ... I do not believe that the kind of society I describe necessarily *will* arrive, but I believe ... that something resembling it *could* arrive" (Orwell & Angus, 1968, p. 502).

Modeling malignant perversion

Orwell's Oceania depicts a terrifying model of perversion in the master–slave dyad of the post-apocalyptic totalitarian state. The novel perfectly embodies aspects of perversion involving trauma, splitting, disavowal, a fixed script, and the replacement of reality with illusion. The mind of the State was split by a nuclear war and subsequent trauma, which was vast and terrible. We are only given a hint of it, through Winston's eyes, but even that small bit allows us to imagine a wrecked world filled with desperate people who longed for the restoration of order and some measure of security. The policy of the State originated from that trauma and rests upon the disavowal of weakness, vulnerability, and impermanence. It is the denial of fragility and death raised to the highest level. Reality itself is controlled by the Party as it constantly rewrites history, altering records, expunging memory, and engaging in endless acts of doublethink:

> "But I tell you, Winston, that reality is not external. Reality exists in the human mind, and nowhere else. Not in the individual mind, which can make mistakes, and in any case soon perishes: only in the mind of the Party, which is collective and immortal. Whatever the Party holds to be the truth, is truth. It is impossible to see reality except by looking through the eyes of the Party. That is the fact that you have got to relearn, Winston. It needs an act of self-destruction, an effort of the will. You must humble yourself before you can become sane."
>
> (p. 249)

Oceania's disavowal of mass castration and its attempt to master mass trauma create a cruel and brutal sadistic state whose static vision is the total dehumanization and control of its citizenry, along with the annihilation of their reality, interiority, and capacity for love. That traumatic split caused by the nuclear holocaust is mirrored in the split between the Inner Party (the master) and the Outer Party and the proles (the slaves). The split between master and slave imbues the secret machinations of the master with mystery while charging the social atmosphere with the awful excitement of fear and dread. The means of intimidation, domination, and control become the end – the exercise of power for the sake of power. Winston's torturer tells him:

> "The Party seeks power entirely for its own sake. We are not interested in the good of others; we are interested solely in power. Not wealth or luxury or long life or happiness: only power, pure power ... The object of persecution is persecution. The object of torture is torture. The object of power is power."
>
> (p. 263)

Oceania's socio-political script is fixed and permanent. As O'Brien tells Winston, "The rule of the Party is forever" (p. 262).

The cult of Big Brother and the Party are one, and they do not change. They do not die. They write reality and make no errors. Outside the Party and the reality it dictates, there is nothing except its enemies, and even they are manufactured. The enemies are the ones who are insane. They are the criminals. They are the perverts. They are the scapegoats. Their continued destruction by the State attests to the inexorable sovereignty of the Party – its perfection, its immortality. The State is in essence a savage, sadistic god arbitrarily creating and shredding its enemies while consuming its subjects, ever delighting in control and destruction. The psychological murder of the subject sustains the life of the State. His or her literal death attests to the State's immortality. "The weariness of the cell is the vigor of the organism" (p. 264), O'Brien tells Winston.

Key is the need of the Party for *total conversion* – the evacuation of the subject's interiority resulting in catastrophic dehumanization. The person who feels himself to be alive – the thinking, feeling being – that one must be vanquished and replaced with the will of the State. Any other existence is not permissible. The citizen's desire must become the State's, and so the citizen becomes an emptied receptacle to be filled by the will of the State; and if not that, then nothing at all. "Nothing will remain of you," O'Brien says, "not a name in a register, not a memory in a living brain. You will be annihilated in the past as well as in the future. You will never have existed" (p. 254).

In extreme, destructive perversion – severe splitting, great thirst for revenge, hateful compulsion to master – there is a perforation, invasion, and evacuation of the other. The more extreme the condition, the more powerful the fury, and the more rigid the script. The other must submit to the pervert's will, the sexual and/or social script or policy. Often, the deeply rutted sadomasochistic relationship is enacted in the name of love, specialness, and enlightenment. The exploited victim must fulfill the pervert's script of mastery, even if it calls for torture and "rehabilitation," and yet the victim is encouraged to feel genuinely cared for and understood by the pervert. Within the seduction of the victim, hatred masquerades as love (Stein, 2005), and illusion pretends to be reality (Stoller, 1974, 1975).

This sadomasochism is described in *1984* in an encounter between O'Brien and Wilson:

> For a moment he clung to O'Brien like a baby, curiously comforted by the heavy arm round his shoulders. He had the feeling that O'Brien was his protector, that the pain was something that came from outside, from some other source, and that it was O'Brien who would save him from it.
>
> (p. 250)

> He opened his eyes and looked up gratefully at O'Brien. At sight of the heavy, lined face, so ugly and so intelligent, his heart seemed to turn over. If he could have moved he would have stretched out a hand and laid it on O'Brien's arm. He had never loved him so deeply as at this moment, and not merely because he had stopped the pain ... O'Brien had tortured him to the edge of lunacy, and in a little while, it was certain, he would send him to his death. It made no difference. In some sense that went deeper than friendship, they were intimates: somewhere or other, although the actual words might never be spoken, there was a place where they could meet and talk. O'Brien was looking down at him with an expression which suggested that the same thought might be in his own mind.
>
> (p. 252)

The character of O'Brien reveals the erotic excitement of the Party that is the counterpart to the excess of dread and terror inflicted on its members, especially those who dream of transgression. The thrill of casting the suffocating and pervasive illusion that makes war peace, ignorance strength, and slavery freedom leaks through as O'Brien's voice becomes "almost dreamy," and "exaltation ... lunatic enthusiasm" suffuses his face. O'Brien compares the Party's aims with those of the "persecutors of the past," those of the Inquisition and later totalitarian regimes like those of Communist Russia and Nazi Germany:

> "We are not content with negative obedience, nor even with the most abject submission. When finally you surrender to us, it must be of your own free will. We do not destroy the heretic because he resists us: so long as he resists us we never destroy him. We convert him, we capture his inner mind, we reshape him. We burn all evil

and all illusion out of him; we bring him over to our side, not in appearance, but genuinely, heart and soul ... we make the brain perfect before we blow it out. The command of the old despotisms was 'Thou shalt not.' The command of the totalitarians was 'Thou shalt.' Our command is *'Thou art.'* No one whom we bring to this place ever stands out against us. Everyone is washed clean."

(p. 255)

O'Brien exalts in the pleasure of vanquishing Winston who now feels as if his torturer's mind contains his own (p. 256). Eerily resembling Lacan's theory of perversion, in which the other's desire replaces one's own, O'Brien tells Winston, "We shall squeeze you empty, and then we shall fill you with ourselves" (p. 256).

In explaining to Winston the motive of the Party as power for the sake of power, a means–end reversal (Stein, 2005), O'Brien touches on the issues of death, transcendence, and immortality, all concerns addressed by perversion. He tells Winston that power is collective, strictly entailing "power over other human beings," and that "the individual only has power in so far as he ceases to be an individual" (p. 264). He further reasons that every human being who is free (separate and alone) is always defeated because he is "doomed to die which is the greatest of all failures," but if he completely submits to the Party, he can "escape his identity" and merge with the State, becoming "all-powerful and immortal" (p. 264). Thus the Party, as a cultural symbol validating terror management theory (see Chapter 5), has solved the problem of death by becoming God and absorbing its members. It has also solved the problem of reality, since the Party controls the mind, and "reality is inside the skull" (p. 265). "We make the laws of Nature," says O'Brien (p. 265). The Party is God. Its sole commandment is: Submit, *for thou art us.* Its method is persecution. Its aim is immortality. The cost is the humanity of its citizenry. The end result is a bankrupt simulacrum of transcendence based on an omnipresent, malignant social perversion that demands inner deadness.

When Winston meekly argues against the idea that the State creates reality, pointing out that the ancient world itself is a "speck of dust" and "man is tiny" in an incomprehensibly vast universe, O'Brien again insists that the mind of the Party creates reality, and whatever objective reality exists can be dismissed through the act of doublethink. "The stars can be near or distant, according as we need them," he says

(p. 266). As absolute and terrifyingly sovereign, the State perverts reality and substitutes enforced illusion. O'Brien asks:

> "How does one man assert his power over another, Winston?"
>   Winston thought. "By making him suffer," he said.
>   "Exactly. By making him suffer. Obedience is not enough. Unless he is suffering, how can you be sure that he is obeying your will and not his own? Power is in inflicting pain and humiliation. Power is in tearing human minds to pieces and putting them together again in new shapes of your own choosing. Do you begin to see, then, what kind of world we are creating? ... A world of fear and treachery and torment, a world of trampling and being trampled upon, a world which will grow not less but *more* merciless as it refines itself. Progress in our world will be progress towards more pain ... In our world there will be no emotions except fear, rage, triumph, and self-abasement. Everything else we shall destroy – everything."
> (pp. 266–267)

The most extreme perversion is an inhuman world of utter subjection, terror, and hatred – a world in which the inside is torn out and replaced by hateful, murderous will. Orwell has described a fully realized anal-sadistic world (Chasseguet-Smirguel, 1984) of maximum sadomasochistic intensity, where all boundaries that preserve dignity, integrity, love, and the law are utterly destroyed. O'Brien says:

> "We have cut the links between child and parent, and between man and man, and between man and woman. No one dares trust a wife or a child or a friend any longer. But in the future there will be no wives and no friends. Children will be taken from their mothers at birth, as one takes eggs from a hen. The sex instinct will be eradicated. Procreation will be an annual formality like the renewal of a ration card. We shall abolish the orgasm. Our neurologists are at work upon it now. There will be no loyalty, except loyalty towards the Party. There will be no love, except the love of Big Brother. There will be no laughter, except the laugh of triumph over a defeated enemy. There will be no art, no literature, no science. When we are omnipotent we shall have no more need of science. There will be no distinction between beauty and ugliness.

There will be no curiosity, no enjoyment of the process of life. All competing pleasures will be destroyed."

(p. 267)

Given that social reality is constituted through a system of differences, the regression to anality seeks to destroy the social scheme ordered by law and protected by respect for difference. When the law seeks to protect the collective, its rule mitigates against tyranny. In contrast, the anal-sadistic universe abolishes law and difference, replacing it with the will of the tyrant, whether that tyrant is a lunatic individual or a vicious oligarchy. The bond between individuals and the intimacy it creates within a natural system are attacked and eradicated (McDougall, 1972). All social bonds within and between groups are destroyed by acts of ontological rage and hatred against intimacy, love, hope, and human goodness. The tyrant turns the world to shit. When the State enacts the destruction of the human self, it is a psychopathic project of immense proportions. This is the world of *1984*, the universe of the Marquis de Sade raised to the ultimate socio-political level as a cultural norm. Every being is conquered, violated, tortured, and eventually eradicated in a continuous orgy of rage and hatred. The State consumes its own citizenry, drawing from their mortal lives its own maniacal immortality. In this insane saturnalia of degradation, all difference is eradicated, except between master and slave; all social relationships are reduced to fear and hatred, and the human world is rendered into particles of feces.

But there is also an important difference between the worlds of de Sade and Oceania. The former depended on the norm for its existence and, therefore, had to rely on individual and personal enactments against that norm and the latter, which naturally involved sexual transgression and debauchery. Perverse sex as an attack on the norm naturally progressed to sacrilegious orgy that violated difference and culminated in brutal assault, bloodletting, strangulation, dismemberment, and death. But the de Sadean program is already embodied in Oceania's *as the norm itself*. Sadistic sexual enactment is not needed as the central element of the program because the sadomasochistic relationship already pervades all social relationships. Ubiquitous erotic hatred is already structured by and within Oceania's normative framework.

Thus sex, like everything else, becomes a state tool to maintain its power. The State can mollify the proles with the "lowest kind of pornography" while working to eliminate the human orgasm, which may be the last refuge of pleasure, individuality, and hope. This is a consistent attack against the subversion of sex, either as an act of defiance or as a means of intimacy. With the elimination of the human orgasm, the State will fully castrate every member of the Party (perhaps even the proles) – physically and psychologically. The private relationship with oneself or another will be virtually eliminated, and the State will gain unlimited power, becoming the unquestioned eternal master, making the citizens the eternal slave – "the boot stamping on a human face – forever."

Social perversion in the real world

The reader feels a cold horror in contemplating Oceania, a horror increased by the novel's believability. Christopher Hitchens (2005) noted that the state of North Korea might have been modeled on *1984*, seriously claiming that the "slave state" of North Korea was even worse that Orwell's imaginings. The totalitarian state of Oceania clearly expresses the evil of domination, exploitation, and dehumanization, facilitated by available technology. The unsettling parallels between *1984* and states like Nazi Germany and Stalinist Russia (the two Orwell had in mind) can be extended to Pol Pot's Cambodia, North Korea, Zimbabwe, and Myanmar, to name but a few.

Religious cults also come to mind: Jim Jones's People's Temple, Marshall Applewhite's Heaven's Gate, and Joseph Di Mambro's Solar Temple, which all resulted in mass murder and suicide. Recently an HBO documentary on Scientology titled *Going Clear: Scientology and the Prison of Belief* (Gibney, Wright, & Vaurio, 2015) revealed many perverse Orwellian tactics used to control members, including prison camps, destruction of family bonds, surveillance, mind control and thought policing, doublethink techniques, memory holes, and torture. Orthodox religion also has taken part in perversion, with one prominent example being the widespread cover-up of sexual abuse within the Catholic Church. In sexually abusing children, not only did priests violate their most fundamental teachings, but they and the Church hierarchy also denied their criminality until they were forcibly held accountable when victims turned to the secular law for relief. In her 2007 book *Perversion of Power: Sexual Abuse in the Catholic Church*, Frawley-O'Dea argues that an internal culture of "dominance, submission, and sadomasochism" supported by traditional religious precepts, beliefs, and interpretations provided a ripe framework for sexual abuse, concealment, and denial (p. 45). She quotes a Vatican consultant's advice for surviving within the power structure of the Church.

> Don't think.
>> If you think, don't speak.
>> If you think, and if you speak, don't write.
>> If you think, and if you speak, and if you write, don't sign your name.
>> If you think, and if you speak, and if you write, and if you sign your name, don't be surprised.
>
> (p. 46)

Particularly pernicious is the alliance of state and religious perversion, as is the case with ISIS, which engages in horrific acts of torture in the name of God – including the mass murder of men, women, and children by fire, knives, bullets, and bombs. The Islamic State has also instituted systematic rape of women and girls from the Yazidi religious minority in what *The New York Times* calls a "theology of rape" (Callimachi, 2015).

Reading *1984* can even induce a queasy feeling about the politics of countries in the so-called free world, including the United States. What makes Orwell's masterpiece timeless is that it warns not merely of the dangers of totalitarian or authoritarian states; it also flags the great danger we inherently pose to each other as we naturally organize into hierarchal groups and war with each other, surely over rights and resources but especially over *whose version of reality will prevail*. The second motive may, in some respects, be more important than the first, for the constitution of reality functions as society's immortality formula, and immortality is *the* chief existential concern (Becker, 1973).

What a troubling novel is Orwell's – politically, socially, and even personally. The characters of Winston, Julia, and O'Brien get under our skin because they speak to qualities present in all of us: the capacity to love and to destroy love; the ability to betray and the pain of being betrayed; the reality of being woefully mortal and vulnerable while yearning for power, certainty, and immortality; the tendency to merge with the group and fearfully obey authority rather than rebel against constraint and collective will; the desire to spill over the social institutions that contain and limit us; and the possibility of not supporting and respecting difference and thus reducing life to one unyielding, obsessive necessity. Most of all, the novel speaks potently to us about our all-too-human capacity for visiting evil on each other and making this condition the dominant structure of human life. Trauma may be at the heart of perversion, but human evil is surely its most poisonous expression.

Freud waxed pessimistic about human nature and civilization, citing primal aggression and the urge to dominate as the dark underbelly of the human character and the generator of perverse and violent social and sexual scenarios. In *Civilization and Its Discontents* (1961b [1930]) he cast these tendencies in the encounter with a stranger, who is always both a difficulty and an opportunity, though in this case much more the former than the latter:

> The element of truth behind all this, which people are so ready to disavow, is that men are not gentle creatures who want to be loved and who at the most can simply defend themselves when they are attacked; they are, on the contrary, creatures among whose instinctual endowments is to be reckoned a powerful share of aggressiveness. As a result, their neighbor is for them not only a potential helper or sexual object, but also someone who tempts them to satisfy their aggression on him, to exploit his capacity for work without compensation, to use him sexually without his consent, to seize his possessions, to humiliate him, to cause him pain, to torture and to kill him. *Homo homini lupus.* Who, in the face of all his life experience and history, will have the courage to dispute this assertion? As a rule this cruel aggressiveness waits for some provocation ... it also manifests itself spontaneously and reveals man as a savage beast to whom consideration towards his own kind is something alien. Anyone who calls to mind the atrocities committed during the racial migrations or the invasions of the Huns or by the people known as Mongols under Jenghiz Khan and Tamurlane, or the capture of Jerusalem by the pious Crusaders, or even indeed the

horrors of the recent World War – anyone who calls these things to mind will have to bow humbly before the truth of this view.

(Freud, 1961b [1930], pp. 111–112)

This grim take on humanity is highly debatable, and we certainly don't need to resign ourselves to such a view. Yet, the capacity to dominate, exploit, and dehumanize – to become "perverted" in the sense of the term's negative usage – is universal among human beings. If this were untrue, our history would not be steeped in so much war and butchery. This is true of both evolutionary and cultural history. To be human is to struggle to be humane. It is not so hard for us to move toward the "dark side" of our unknowing, to see flesh as meat and manure, to see the other as a thing, to see life only as a charnel house and not also as a mystic temple. Yet what is also universal is the tendency to fight against reducing life to acts of exploitation, manipulation, and degradation – to give and receive care and love and by doing so become more real; to engage in acts of altruism and sacrifice; to rebel against conditions that suffocate freedom and creativity; and to experience reality through the ambience of empathy and love (Pinker, 2011).

What is most heartbreaking about *1984* is how cruelly and viciously O'Brien destroys the love between Winston and Julia, the very last hope of their humanity. Indeed, the gripping exchanges between Winston and O'Brien form a primal dialogue between humanity and its capacity for evil, between awakening consciousness and Freud's bitter, reductive observation. O'Brien is without humanity, and one wonders if he even knows he is evil. Symbolic of the government for which he works, he takes sadistic delight in erasing human selves. He represents the last stop on the train to *hell on earth* and is a result of the ultimate psychological catastrophe, which he repeats with his victims. Winston, on the other hand, represents the possibility of returning to one's humanity, of repairing the damage of trauma, of renewing love and inner growth. Sadly, that possibility is foreclosed in Oceania.

In comparing the perversion theories of Chasseguet-Smirguel and McDougall, Whitebook (1995) argues that while the former analyst "reduces the perversions to their genesis in anality," the latter views "every symptom, including perversion, [as] both a pathology and psychic creation" with an aim to cure and attempt to avert an even "greater psychological catastrophe" (p. 58). It is important to keep

McDougall's perspective on the creative and reparative function of perversion in mind, especially while reading *1984*, which paints in red and black the darkest end of the perverse spectrum. Our humanity and our perversion, like the norm and the transgression, coexist in a tense, dynamic partnership. One must fight for the good. Despite his obvious and profound flaws, Winston struggles to find the good in his love for Julia and in his opposition to the State. Sadly, Oceania and O'Brien destroy him, leaving him psychologically lobotomized and spiritually castrated. In Winston we find Orwell's vision of goodness annihilated, a knife thrust into the heart of humanity. In *1984* evil not only wins the day; it prevails without end.

The malignantly perverted state is a particularly *human* possibility, an extension of the aggressive human capacity to dominate and persecute. Such a state reflects the tendency to the corrosive stability of eternal dogma. It is the imposition of a vicious immortality formula that guarantees endless suffering. It is the violent and soulless quest of an individual or a group of individuals to become God incarnate ruling the masses. It is the nihilistic nightmare that reduces all human relationship to master and slave.

Before 1933, Berlin was the most diverse city in all of Europe, a place of cosmopolitan flavor and liberal ideas. It had become the largest industrial city on the continent and a major European cultural center. Yet in the space of a few short years, the Weimer Republic fell and Hitler rose to power, rapidly transforming Berlin into the seat of Nazi power and instituting one of the most repressive, psychopathic regimes in history. In considering the horrific changes in economic, political, and social relationships wrought by the rapidly enacted socio-political "norms" of Nazi Germany, it is possible to understand how fragile freedom is and how quickly the social scene can become nightmarish. Such terrifying transformations are not historically uncommon, and there is no good reason to believe that the future is safe from the possibility of perverted, tyrannical, and even insane rulership. As Ortega y Gasset (1962 [1958]) wisely noted, the "man of action" is born from crisis, and soon after his appearance "a period of rebarbarization looms" (p. 96). Milgram (1963) demonstrated how easily most people submit to authority, even if such obedience goes against conscience. In the famous Milgram experiment, most people were willing to administer dangerous levels of electric shock to human subjects when they were admonished to do so by an authority figure. The darker capacities of the human mind remain a perennial problem, a particularly *human* one. In short, we have the capacity to become inhuman, and this capacity is all-too-human.

Orwell's vision as admonition

The subject of *1984* raises two additional important issues. The first is an obvious but chilling truth about perversion in the context of Oceania. As Oceania eliminates all resistance to the State, including all thoughts of subversion through technological force, the extreme perversion of the State is canceled. Perversion must confront and transgress a limit assumed within a normative framework, and no such limit exists within the full realization of the State's program. Winston and the reader (through his or her identification with Winston and Julia) supply the "norm" through which the State is judged as malignantly perverted. Yet, from Oceania's viewpoint (O'Brien), it is Winston (and the reader) who are the perverts. Once an oppositional viewpoint to the State is made impossible, Oceania will have eliminated the possibility of perversion, and its monolith of perfect evil will be free from judgment. Recall (Introduction and Chapter 5) that perverse transgression can oppose some unjust, false, corrupt, and destructive aspect of the social order – what we called *perversion as rebellion against oppression and unnecessary constraint*. Orwell's Oceania seeks to eternally negate this possibility. There will be no change of any kind, except what is ordered by the State. Going forward it will only be *perversion on purpose*.

Not surprisingly, there are no laws in Oceania, nor is there a need for law. Why is this? The laws and conventions of culture determine what constitute a breach of the moral code; indeed, the fact that *whatever can happen among human beings does happen* – including, and perhaps especially, the most ugly things imaginable – is a critical determinant in establishing norms and law. It is our capacity for harming each other that generates the law that defines, limits, and punishes violation. Violation does not merely follow upon the law; it also precedes it. In Oceania the perverse will and desire of the ruling oligarchy symbolized by Big Brother *substitutes for law*. It need not be codified. All it requires is the emptiness of its terrified subjects. This is the chilling core of the Orwellian vision.

The second issue to consider is *1984*'s enduring power to disturb our composure. John W. Whitehead (2013) and Paul Craig Roberts (2014), among others, have drawn some unsettling parallels between Oceania's practices and recent developments in the United States. Roberts, who has testified before committees of Congress on numerous occasions and holds academic appointments in six universities, is the former Assistant Secretary of Treasury and an associate columnist for the *Wall Street Journal*. Whitehead is also an attorney who widely practices constitutional law and is a prominent leader in the national dialogue on civil liberties and human rights. Though the United States is hardly like Oceania (one could never buy a book like *1984* in Oceania), several comparisons give pause for long and careful reflection and encourage a wary but healthy vigilance. First, since the World Trade Center terrorist attack of 2001, America has engaged in a war without borders and without any end in sight. War for the United States is beginning to look like a perpetual war – a condition which is accepted as "normal." Dick Cheney said in 2001 that the War on Terror "may never end. At least in our lifetime" (Woodward, 2001). Cheney's remark still remains essentially unchallenged on the national stage. Is it unreasonable to expect that a nation endlessly at war will eventually turn its sword on its own citizens?

The Patriot Act, passed shortly after 9/11, gave the government vast powers of surveillance, which were quickly turned on its citizenry. Jeffrey Rosen, a law professor at George Washington University wrote, "If the Patriot Act were focused on investigating potential terrorists, rather than spying on innocent Americans, then we would still need it. Unfortunately, it was never focused on potential terrorists: many of its most controversial provisions were the same expansions of law enforcement authority that federal and state officials had sought after the Waco siege and the Oklahoma City bombing" (Rosen, 2011). Whitehead (2013) calls the Patriot Act "a stake through the heart of the Bill of Rights" (p. 14), saying that it violates the First, Fourth, Fifth, Sixth, Seventh, and Eighth Amendments. Terrorism is defined so broadly that non-terrorist activities like public protest, marches, demonstrations, and civil disobedience can now be considered potential terrorist acts. *Any subversive citizen is by implication a terrorist suspect* (Whitehead, 2013).

Repeated reauthorizations of the National Defense Authorization Act (NDAA) have kept Guantánamo Bay detention camp open and gave the government the right to detain Americans suspected of terrorism indefinitely, in violation of their civil liberties (Sheets, 2013). Said Andrew Rosenthal of *The New York Times*, "It's stunning that the president is willing to sign a bill that might effectively turn the right of habeas corpus into a mere privilege – even for citizens" (Rosenthal, 2011). The president did append a signing statement to the bill, in which he declared that he would not detain American citizens indefinitely, but the legal validity of such a statement is questionable. At the end of 2015, Obama finally vetoed the NDAA for a number of reasons, including a desire to move detainees out of Guantánamo and into other prisons on the US mainland and to close the prison by the end of his presidency (Mufson, 2015; Feinstein 2015). The prison at Guantánamo Bay, situated on a US naval base in Cuba, opened after the 9/11 terrorist attacks. "GTMO," pronounced "gitmo" (so dubbed by military personnel), has been described by the American Civil Liberties Union (ACLU) as "an island outside the law" where terrorist suspects have been detained indefinitely and subjected to various types of torture (ACLU, 2015). For many, GTMO is a shameful reminder of how the United States has violated its own Constitution and participated in acts that are anathema to any self-respecting democratic nation (see Chapter 5).

The progressive militarization of the police across the United States has been taking place since the 1980s, beginning with the "war on drugs" (Whitehead, 2013, p. 57). In the last decade the government has been providing military-grade weapons to local police forces throughout the United States – body armor, mine-resistant trucks, silencers, automatic rifles, machine guns, camouflage equipment, night-vision equipment, and armored cars and aircraft, including drones (Flannigan, 2014). Despite the decline in the rate of violent crime in the U.S. since 1993 (Flannigan, 2014), and in concert with the rapid police militarization across the nation, the Department of Homeland Security has been transformed from a "security agency into a domestic army," indicative of the government's paranoia about a discontented citizenry (Whitehead, 2013, p. 61).

SWAT team raids have increased from 3,000 per year in the 1980s to 50,000 per year in 2013 (Fund, 2014). Originally created to combat highly dangerous criminal situations involving drugs and terrorism, SWAT teams are now called out for mere warrant service 75–80 percent of the time (Balko, 2006). *Many raids are now conducted against harmless, often innocent, civilians* accused of nonviolent civil violations. For example, Kenneth Wright of Stockton, California, had the door of his home rammed at six in the morning. SWAT agents (from the Board of Education!) dragged him outside in his boxer shorts, handcuffed him, and then held his three young children in a police car for two hours while ransacking his home in search of information on his wife, Michelle, who was no longer living with him and was suspected of college financial-aid fraud (Fund, 2014).

The Transportation Security Administration (TSA) uses Visible Intermodal Prevention and Response (VIPR) task forces to protect the US infrastructure against criminal or terrorist attacks (Whitehead, 2013, pp. 75–84). These teams, composed of federal air marshals, surface transportation security inspectors, transportation security officers, behavior detection officers, and explosive detection canine teams, do random security sweeps of ports, railways, airports, bus stations, ferries, and subways. They will also be deployed to heighten security at political conventions, baseball games, and concerts. (Down the road we may see them at shopping malls.) Among their sweep tools are high-tech surveillance, X-ray technology, full body scans, pat downs, and drug-sniffing dogs (Whitehead, 2013). VIPR teams will not be confined to terrorist operations. Federal officials admit that transit screening is also intended to detect illegal immigration and cash smuggling (Whitehead, 2013). This growing invasion of government police into everyday life may pave the way for Orwellian methods of control and undermines Constitutional protection of the US citizenry. The TSA's motto is *Dominate. Intimidate. Control* (Whitehead, 2013).

Before the early 1970s, the US incarceration rate was fairly unremarkable. During the previous 35 years, the prison population increased by a little over 50,000. However, in the subsequent 35 years, from 1970 to 2005, the prison population increased by close to 1.3 million, with the number of incarcerated African Americans rising precipitously, to the point where one in every nine black men in the 20–34 age bracket was serving prison time (Thompson, 2011). Furthermore, "private prison companies are striking deals with states that contain clauses guaranteeing high prison occupancy rates ... In a letter to 48 state governors in 2012, the largest for-profit private prison company in the United States, Corrections Corporation of America (CCA), offered to buy up and operate public state prisons. In exchange, states would have to sign a 20-year contract guaranteeing a 90 percent occupancy rate throughout the term" (Short, 2013). In short "crime" will finally "pay" – straight to private prison corporations like the CCA and the GEO group that form the new *jailing citizens for profit systems* (Whitehead, 2013, p. 194).

The criminalization of America's school children is another disturbing trend. In 2010 about 300,000 Texas schoolchildren received misdemeanor tickets from police officials, while in Albuquerque, New Mexico, over 90,000 children entered the criminal justice system during the 2009–2010 school year, and 500 of that number were arrested at school (Whitehead, 2013, p. 187). American children are now subjected to Orwellian forms of surveillance and control: they are "photographed, fingerprinted, scanned, x-rayed, sniffed and snooped on" (Whitehead, 2013, p. 185). What Thompson has called "America's recent embrace of the world's most massive and punitive penal state – a vast carceral apparatus that has wed our economy, society, and political structures to the practice of punishment in unprecedented ways" is tragically affecting American children – dishing out draconian punishments for minor infractions, treating them like suspects, and desensitizing them to the rough violation of their privacy. Said Thompson, "the age old student behavior [of truancy] can now land a student's file on the desk of the district attorney or even lead that student to be shackled with an electronic tether otherwise intended for use on parolees" (Thompson, 2011).

These and other changes are taking place within what Whitehead calls an "electronic concentration camp," the vast, ever-expanding National Security Administration's (NSA) global and domestic surveillance network that uses spy technology that dwarfs Orwell's telescreens. Cell-phone and computer-keystroke tracking devices that enable agents to see and document locations, conversations, emails, text messages and search data; real-time camera surveillance; license plate readers; biometric scanning; and facial recognition systems and full-body scanners are among the many technologies now being used by the government to track and monitor its citizenry (Whitehead, 2013). Big Brother is most definitely watching us. Writers like Roberts and Whitehead argue that in the name of national security we have sacrificed our liberties and already have become a corporate police state. Furthermore, they claim this sinister state of affairs is not merely the result of terrorism and the need for greater security, but an opportunity mined in the interest of extending unchecked ruling power, and, thereby, an intentional drift toward tyranny. Corporate interests and influence dictate law by funding politicians and lobbying relentlessly.

Meanwhile, à la Orwell, the masses are distracted and manipulated by an outpouring of media advertising, dumbed-down news reporting, celebrity and sports mania, proliferating Internet pornography and lotteries, endless permutations of video games, virtual worlds, and chat rooms. From this justifiably paranoid view, technology is used to survey and control citizens while distracting them with enchanting gadgetry. While heads of state talk of endless war without raising an eyebrow, throngs of citizens wait in line for hours for the latest version of the iPhone. How much this phenomenon is resulting from a subterranean government agenda or an unfortunate confluence of events is open to debate. Nor does it necessarily predict future tyranny. Nevertheless, we see a dangerous trend in the progressive transgression against legal and cultural boundaries that protect individual freedoms. We have employed *1984* to provide a model of what perversion looks like in its most malignant and destructive form, to underscore the fact that perversion is social as well as sexual and to take note of the danger it presents to the qualities that define the better part of our humanity.

Note

1. All quotations are taken from George Orwell's *1984* (Boston, MA: Houghton Mifflin, 1950).

Chapter 8

Black mirror

> The contrast between the body's limitations and cyberspace's power highlights the advantages of pattern over presence. As long as the pattern endures, one has attained a kind of immortality.
>   – N. Katherine Hayles, *How We Became Posthuman*

This book has examined and expanded upon a theory of perversion that accounts for its individual expression as well as its existential basis and social significance. Traditional theories of perversion note its universal tendency, partnership with the normative sexual and social frame, origin in trauma, split-off psychic structure that permits dehumanization, and function across a wide spectrum of behaviors. Perversion casts illusions of mastery while denying vulnerability, and it is generally expressed differently in men and women. To this traditional view we have added perversion's connection with the traumatic context of fragile and impermanent human life and its defensive strategies in response to annihilation. We have shown how perversion's capacity to do damage in social and cultural spheres far exceeds its darker possibilities in the personal, sexual domain. We have also revealed how the technological enterprise enhances and expands perverse requirements and possibilities, rooted as it is in the human need to escape limitation, transgress against norms, and war with loss, aging, impermanence, and, ultimately, death. The cases presented in this book illustrate these delineated elements and express both benign and malignant outcomes. It is our hope that psychoanalysis will undertake the task of analyzing and addressing the growing phenomenon of social perversion and the psychological impact of revolutionary technology on the social and cultural world of our time.

It is our view that society has transitioned from a culture of narcissism to a culture of perversion. That is not to say that narcissism has stepped aside. Rather, aspects of our technology amplify our narcissism, which in turn shapes the tech markets that gratify narcissistic needs and perverse desires. In our technologically driven world, narcissism is reflected in the endless selfie shots posted on social media; in the preoccupation with counting, accumulating, and bragging about posted Likes, Favorites, and Follows and in proudly sharing posts featuring cherished possessions, cooked dinners, current locations, and so forth. It is as if the sum of such numbers is a quantity of a self-esteem drug mainlined by users on a daily basis via the Internet. Like all addictive drugs, this one requires repeated and larger doses, or more and more time devoted to the social media realm. Clearly, the technological revolution, building on a cultural base of narcissism, has taken a perverse turn. The dehumanization of people, and especially the humanization of objects/devices, is increasing. So is the mainstreaming of a sadomasochistic ethos.

S&M goes mainstream

E. L. James's *Fifty Shades of Grey*, a romantic S&M trilogy that began (not surprisingly) as a fan fiction story on the Internet, has grown into a worldwide phenomenon, and has spawned a new genre of soft S&M porn for (mostly) middle-class women. *Fifty Shades* is the best-selling book of all time after the Bible (Singh, 2012), and the first book in the trilogy was made into a movie that grossed $100 million in its first week (Lewis, 2014). Many claim that *Fifty Shades* has changed cultural norms; what was once considered pornographic, deviant, and hidden from view, is now regularly portrayed in popular culture. For example, ads for videogames, like *Blood Money*, show a beautifully dressed dead woman with a bloody bullet hole in her head below the caption, "Beautifully Executed." A recent, humorous BMW commercial aired during prime time featuring a traditionally dressed grandmother in the back seat of a car recalling that "your grandfather loved it when I wore leather ... he was a very dominant man" (Philbin, 2015, para. 5). According to NYU law professor, Amy Adler, "Mainstream culture has come to look more like pornography. It's not just that with the click of a button you can see the most hardcore, extreme sex imaginable.

It's also what you see every day: It's the way people on TV look like porn stars. It's the way women go to work in shoes that 20 years ago would have been considered like what porn stars would wear" (Green, 2015). Indeed, S&M fashion has gone mainstream: thigh-high shiny boots, leather breastplates, skin-hugging latex or rubber dresses and pants, metallic collars, transparent dresses that barely cover lace-ups and chokers, masks, and high stiletto pumps adorn the runway models at today's fashion shows. What was once encountered only in a dominatrix's wardrobe is now viewed daily on city streets and even in the workplace. La Ferla (2016) states that fetish wear has "woven itself inextricably into the fabric of fashion" and recounts that what she calls "sex-shop chic" has become so commonplace and ubiquitous that that there is a "steady erosion of boundaries between fashion and fetishism." Recent styles include not only competition for the tightest dresses, highest slits, and the lowest necklines, but also the sheerest and most transparent clothing imaginable. Atwood (2014) says "the wearer" of these au naturel styles "may as well be naked." Rock (2016), who writes about "metal-mania," visible in silver-lashed cyber-models, chromed accoutrements, and techno-fetish, emphasizes the connection between the fetishistic and the futuristic. Considering the sex appeal of the inorganic, he asserts, "the cyborg is fashion's *Gesamtkunstwerk*" (p. 29).

Talk shows and reality TV shows, currently the most popular genres in most Western countries, are another manifestation of perverse culture (Samuels, 1996). Nichols (2000), who called reality shows a form of social perversion, said, "Tele-spectacle treats sensations the way an electrical circuit treats shorts: it runs them to the ground" (p. 398). Indeed, reality shows feed the neo-medieval voyeuristic and perverse mass appetite for the pain and humiliation of the bad other. Public degradation, the core appeal of many reality shows (Alderman, 2008), takes multiple forms, ranging from judges who launch personal insults and harsh criticisms at contestants competing for money or a prize in gladiatorial talent contests (e.g., the early years of *American Idol*), to the public airing of one's troubles or defects, such as being obese (e.g., *The Biggest Loser*) or struggles with an addiction (e.g., *Dr. Drew*) or with marital problems (e.g., *The Kardashians*). Some reality shows have moved away from harsh criticism and instead feed the voyeuristic needs of viewers with intimate details of contestants' back stories or moments of embarrassment or failure as they progress through the talent contest (e.g., *Dancing with the Stars*). Why do people seek public shame and humiliation, and why do millions of viewers watch with delight as one person after another is degraded, belittled, and dehumanized? The reality-show phenomenon suggests a perverse pact between the performers and the viewers in which a mass spectacle of exhibitionism, voyeurism, and self-abasement is enacted. A. O. Scott (2014) asserted that popular TV shows with ruthless male anti-heroes, such as Tony Soprano, Walter White, and Don Draper, signify that "nobody knows how to be a grown-up anymore." Anti-heroes like these are not only immature; they clearly display a psychopathy that delights in mastering and even destroying the other. Vicious competitiveness and rampant rejection of tenderness and compassion seem to garner the largest TV show ratings. The near absence and even ridicule of empathy and compassion is also very much a part of modern-day corporate culture.[1]

The reality-show phenomenon actualizes Andy Warhol's famous prediction that "In the future, everyone will be world-famous for 15 minutes" (Guinn & Perry, 2005, p. 365). Many people are seeking their moment in the limelight, not caring whether the camera flatters or shames. We live in a celebrity culture, and our stars are commodities to be adored, idealized, imitated, envied, and even stalked. The celebrity culture provides a new kind of celebrity, one whose only talent derives from unrelenting self-exposure (Harcourt, 2015), one for whom Self has been replaced with selfie. Pseudo-relationships with celebrities sometimes replace friends and family and are a form of fake intimacy that can cast the illusion that ordinary people know and even befriend stars they've never even met. Never before has there been such a glut of magazines and TV shows devoted to celebrities (e.g., *People*, *Us*, *Star*, *Entertainment Tonight*, *Fashion Police* – to name only a few). The envy created by celebrities' glamorous lifestyles leads some to experience delight when famous people are revealed to be suffering from addiction or are caught without makeup or in close-up photos highlighting their wrinkles or cellulite. Celebrities are loved and hated, their identities appropriated, and their lives disrupted by the predatory savagery of mass media, fans, and paparazzi (Holmes & Redmond, 2006). Although we love our heroes, entertainers, sports and movie stars, and societal leaders, we also derive great voyeuristic and sadomasochistic pleasure from seeing them maimed by the media as reporters and photographers pursue them like bloodhounds chasing a fox. Many (Barr, 2008) believe Princess Diana would still be alive had her driver not been trying to escape the wild pursuit of the paparazzi. There is an obvious element of dehumanization in these kinds of "relationships." Stars, too, sometimes enjoy putting down their adoring fans. For instance, comedian Amy Schumer recently responded to an audience member who questioned where she bought her boots with, "They're at the corner of you can't afford them and stop talking to me!" (Lovece, 2015).

These cultural changes are taking place alongside the growing omnipresence of the black mirror – the dark screen of our televisions, computers, tablets, and smartphones – technological devices that we rely on to search for answers to questions both banal and profound. Black mirrors provide the new vehicle for self-definition and self-gratification. Though not everyone is hooked on what the Chinese call "electronic heroin" (Williams, 2014), many resemble the wicked witch in Snow White who repeatedly asks her mirror, "Who's the fairest?" We gaze beseechingly into the dark mirrors of our technological devices, searching for keys to unlock the enigmatic human puzzle of self and other.

Black mirror: a window on the tech future

A recent British television series called *Black Mirror*, created by Charlie Brooker, fiercely speculates on the darker relational and social consequences of near and distant future technology. The series illustrates the connection between technology and perversion and, because of its psychological depth and acumen, is worth a close look at this juncture. The plight of the characters is easy to relate to because some of what they experience is already happening in our world. This provocative show has received rave reviews on both sides of the Atlantic for its biting satirical edge and its poignant and sometimes outrageous takes on the implications of frontier and far future technology. Each episode features a different socio-technological future while commenting on the way we live right now. As Greenwald (2013) opined:

> The world of *Black Mirror* is very much our own, just fast-forwarded: The phones are thinner, the interfaces smoother, the

temptations greater. Instead of cheerleading the glorious future, the show picks at the accumulating scabs we'd rather ignore: That the same gadgets that keep us from ever feeling alone also guarantee we never have to leave the house. That "favorite" has become a verb, and a meaningless one at that. That we now like things without liking them, know people without meeting them ... Just know that every hour of *Black Mirror* asks rough, unsympathetic questions about the world we've made and the one we're in the process of making and then, before you can even reach for an answer, it makes you complicit.

Some might find a bit of techno-paranoia in Brooker's vision, but considering that technology is growing rapidly, far outstripping our capacity to assess its social impact, and that its darker inventions include items like the killer chip (see Introduction), a healthy dose of paranoia might be just what the doctor ordered.[2] Brooker's series is not only enthralling and thought-provoking fiction, but also a gesture toward raising consciousness about what bad things might happen in implementing new technology. The show raises important questions about how we use knowledge while offering a mind-bending tour through the possible techno-social cul-de-sacs that might be waiting for us. The show is unnerving, disturbing, and sometimes utterly chilling. Recall George Orwell's words regarding his own *1984*: "I do not believe that the kind of society I describe necessarily will arrive, but I believe ... that something resembling it could arrive" (Fitzpatrick, 2013).

Though each of the seven episodes available at the time of this writing is well worth viewing (and more than once), the authors will discuss two here for their profound examination of perverse techno-social scenarios. The episode entitled "The Entire History of You" (Armstrong & Welsh, 2011) examines the way a piece of technology facilitates narcissism and the ruin of a marriage and, perhaps, by extension, an entire culture. A surgically implanted device behind the ear, called a "grain," records live feed of the user's life that can be quickly retrieved and replayed, which turns members of society into self-obsessed human surveillance cameras that constantly examine and entertain themselves with their personal playbacks. Those who refuse the device, opting out of their hyper-narcissistic culture, are distrusted or even shunned. Playback or "redo" is as simple as rolling one's thumb across a tiny handheld device, which then replays the desired segment across the eyes or, if one wishes, on a television screen, with the ability to freeze a scene, scan all of its elements, magnify portions of it, and even lip read. A user's best and worst moments can be accessed in a few seconds by that person and anyone he or she wishes to share the redo with.

Consider the impact of such a device on social life in the areas of politics, law enforcement, litigation, mass communication, and education. Think of how the ability to instantly playback the past might affect personal relationships, conflict resolution, and self-development. Consider also the ruin of privacy, the humiliation and trauma of damaging self-revelation, the addiction to redos, blackmail at the hands of those possessing sensitive information, the attack on imagination, and the awful difficulty in making a new start at anything. The implications boggle the mind, and what is even more mind-boggling is that much of this technology is already available (Freitas & Merkle, 2004; Drexler, 1986). Starting today people could, in principle, wear a tiny device, say in a pendant, that transmits live feed to a computer that then stores and indexes it. Any date and time could then be played back. How long would it take before such a device might be engineered as an implant with playback occurring across a set of glasses or even contact lenses? And how long would it take for the implant to be introduced to society as an exciting and expansive technical capability, perhaps first initiated as a law enforcement aid, say, for convicted felons or parolees?

In the TV episode (Armstrong & Welsh, 2011) the technology is quite advanced and can accurately capture exactly what a person is doing as well as what is going on around them. Liam, the main character in the story, uses redos to prove his wife's infidelity and force her confession, which leaves him ruined and utterly alone. He compulsively drives himself forward to seek the truth with the mantra, "I need to know, I need to know," obsessively replaying past scenes in search of clues. After accumulating sufficient evidence and catching his wife in a string of lies, Liam beats up her boyfriend and, in a powerful primal-scene enactment, forces his wife to replay her tryst on the television. His narcissistic self-involvement blinds him to the greater truth that he himself is the impetus for the derailment of his marriage. Like Oedipus, Liam is ruined by the truth; unlike Oedipus, he does not know the truth because the evidence he examines leaves him out of the equation.

Sadly, in Liam's world, some couples watch redos of themselves engaged in passionate lovemaking from the early part of their relationship for the purpose of spicing up their current listless copulations; thus, they become pornographic objects of their own consumption. When people replay past scenes, their eyeballs go bright and still like zombies and then flicker like television light on the walls of a dark room – a fitting image, since they are watching the life they didn't really live because they were too busy filming a life they would rather watch. On the existential seesaw, the seer or subject of experience sits on one side, and the seen or subject experienced as object sits on the other, but in the brave new world of technology, the object trumps the subject every time. Does this not already sound familiar? Are we not already spending more time living through our black mirrors than we are living our lives?

The episode entitled "Be Right Back" (Brooker & Harris, 2013), surely the series' most poignant, examines mourning and grief in a world where an unseen corporation can draw information about a deceased loved one from social media, emails, films, and various other electronic sources, and assemble, store, and synthesize this information into a virtual self that can then talk on the phone with a real person who is grieving his or her loss. If the grieving lover or spouse desires, the program can be installed in a synthetic, sympathetic, and obedient twin of the deceased person. The cyber twin of the deceased can be returned to the lover or spouse – shipped by mail and animated after arrival by soaking it in a special chemical bath.

Pregnant with Ash's child, Martha loses her mate to a car accident, probably caused by Ash's addiction to his cell phone. The viewer sees Martha slide down an utterly believable slippery slope, as she replaces her dead spouse with his synthetic duplicate (doll!), constructed from the history of his online life. The duplicate's passivity and compliance eventually enrage and disgust her and, at her wit's end, she orders him to kill himself by jumping off a cliff. When he begs for his life, she cannot help but relent, and her agony over the trap she has set for herself is apparent in her heart-rending screams at the cliff's edge. In a sad and tragic compromise, Martha relegates android Ash to her attic where she and her daughter visit him on weekends. There he waits patiently in the silence and gloom for the woman he was "born" to serve and the daughter of the person he imitates, an ending that is almost too painful to watch. Martha must retain Ash: he is a conscious being of sorts, nonrefundable, and he is hers for keeps. Her predicament cuts off any possibility of true mourning and release from grief and imprisons Martha in a melancholy and lonely existence. Here the "shadow of the lost object" (Freud, 1957a [1917], p. 249) is quite substantial and falls across the ego with a terrifying vengeance. In her desperate attempt to use technology to deny death, Martha brings into being an entity that is not quite alive, and because she cannot fully mourn her loss, she is left trapped in a deathlike state herself (Brooker & Harris, 2013).

If anyone doubts the use of technology as an immortality formula (Becker, 1973), this show will serve as a wakeup call. Indeed, self-replicating machines already exist. They are autonomous robots capable of reproducing themselves using raw materials found in the environment (Freitas & Merkle, 2004; Drexler, 1986).[3] Furthermore, our current technology allows for people to create a virtual self and online memory, and it is easy to envision an immortal virtual self, maintained and disseminated indefinitely on the Internet long after the physical self has died. Creator of SiriusXM, Martine Rothblatt, collaborated with robotics designer, David Hanson, to create BINA48, a robot modeled after Rothblatt's wife by downloading her consciousness – *mindlife* – and building cyber-consciousness – *mindware* – into the computer. Both Rothblatt and Hanson believe such mind clone robots and digital doppelgangers are the wave of the future and will guarantee a form of immortality and the possibility of posthuman relationship (Hanson, 2007). One of the authors (Knafo) has two friends who have died but remain uncanny Facebook friends with occasional posts and even birthday announcements (automatically generated). A type of virtual gravesite or online memorial is becoming increasingly common (Lim, 2013; Odom et al., 2012; Wahlberg, 2010). Today sites exist that help people arrange for the disposal of their property and remains after death, as well as for their parting wishes (e.g., Bcelebrated.com, PartingWishes.com, and MyWonderfulLife.com). People are tending to their digital estates and choosing a digital executor, one who is empowered to peruse the computer of the deceased and delete content that might prove embarrassing (as if a dead person can be embarrassed). A Twitter-based service called LivesOn promises, "When your heart stops beating, you'll keep tweeting." Advanced technology is already being used to create a perverse illusionary immortality. With time, it may accomplish this for real.

In his breathtaking and dissenting series, Brooker appears to wax at least as pessimistic about technology as did Freud (1961b [1930]) about civilization. In an article that appeared in *The Guardian*, he wrote:

> We routinely do things that just five years ago would scarcely have made sense to us. We tweet along to reality shows; we share videos of strangers dropping cats in bins; we dance in front of Xboxes that can see us, and judge us, and find us sorely lacking. It's hard to think of a single human function that technology hasn't some-how altered, apart perhaps from burping. That's pretty much all we have left. Just yesterday I read a news story about a new video game installed above urinals to stop patrons getting bored: you control it by sloshing your urine stream left and right. Read that back to yourself and ask if you live in a sane society.
>
> (Brooker, 2011)

It's a good question, though perhaps it could be convincingly asked at any time in any society found in human history. Our biological and evolutionary givens – the drive to survive and reproduce, the acute consciousness of life and death, the need to create meaningful social structures, the quest for transcendence – are the basis for whatever underdetermined theories and norms we establish to guide and govern human behavior. Yet, there are no absolutes, no unequivocal certain-ties. Our meanings face the same threat as our very existence; they can be attacked and even destroyed. The existential situation of the conscious animal is quite desperate, and we as a species are more than a little mad. Therefore, is a urinal video game any crazier than, say, the ancient Mesoamerican ball game that sometimes involved ritual beheading, or the Roman game, Venatio, in which the players "hunted" wild animals like lions and elephants while a screaming crowd of voyeuristic sociopaths looked on? Certainly it is far gentler.

Brooker (2011) also expressed his delight in technology in the same article:

> Nonetheless, I relish this stuff. I coo over gadgets, take delight in each new miracle app. Like an addict, I check my Twitter time-line the moment I wake up. And often I wonder is all this really

good for me? For us? None of these things have been foisted upon humankind – we've merrily embraced them. But where is it all leading? If technology is a drug – and it does feel like a drug – then what, precisely, are the side-effects? ... You know, the show isn't anti-technology ... I'm quite techy and gadgety. I hope that the stories in this special demonstrate that it's not a technological problem [we have], it's a human one. That human frailties are maybe amplified by it.

Brooker's comments notwithstanding, it is naive to think about technology as neutral. As we have already pointed out, technology is more than instrumentality, gadgetry, or scientific wizardry; it is an embodied perspective – a way of seeing and being in the world, and a way of experiencing self and other. It issues from and demands a resource-oriented and utilitarian viewpoint, which eventually orders things and people into a systematic chain of replaceable parts that manufactures and delivers objects of desire to a maw whose hunger grows with consumption.

The embodied technological perspective necessarily and exclusively focuses on the object side of life, the outer realm, the world as a collection of utilizable things in which the body (including thought and experience) is central among them. As we have already noted, technology originates from the ceaseless demand of the body to survive and the self to thrive, so it is not surprising that Google is attempting to solve the problem of death (McCracken & Grossman, 2013) or that a dying 23-year-old is having her brain preserved in the hopes that science will one day be able to revive her mind (Harmon, 2015). Technology is a combined expression of the encounter between human intelligence and the difficulties and threats facing animal existence, an expression that grows in complexity while answering the primary directive of embodied existence: *Live! Do better! Keep on living! Keep on doing better! More! Now more again! Always more!* Clearly, technology is not merely something we use to express our various desires; technology is something we also *are* in the very nature of our desire.

A psychoanalytic conundrum

Positions taken for or against particular technologies, or technology as a whole, may form the fabric of important debates, but they presuppose a clear distinction between us and the machine, between our own psychological and social actions and the purpose and actions of the machine. Such a distinction is a chimera. The deeper psychoanalytic question should be: Does the technological dominance of human embodiment foreclose other important ways of being human and, if so, how? It is this second question that positions us outside the technological frame and may make our interrogations more fruitful: What are we losing in all that we gain? How much room is left for the living subject in the technological frame? Where now stand imagination, intimacy, and love, the soul of a person, the poetry and music of life, the narratives of unique selves, the vital and spirited vectors of heredity and history? How shall we achieve meaning, worth, and heroic transcendence? What vision will unite us? What now constitutes the good life? At the threshold of this brave new world, in which narcissistic selves trumpet their self-importance and progressively and perversely turn more and more toward objects for satisfaction, what do human beings still owe each other? What personal and social boundaries shall we still hold sacred? How shall we justify our existence?

We believe these are the kinds of questions psychoanalysis should be addressing now and in the future, extending its social responsibility by casting an analytic yet compassionate gaze beyond the walls of the therapy room and into the heart of a world of wired connectivity, computer control, robots, easy-life gadgetry, and trans-human aspirations. In entering the conversation, psychoanalysis can provide the basis for a cautionary and careful examination of the psychological motives and consequences of the unbridled triumph of technology. At best it can fight for human freedom, straining against the shackles of a dogma that may reduce us to meaningless mechanisms; at worst it can persuade us to proceed with great caution, never ceasing to ask, what is the best part of humanity and how shall we call it forth? Sherry Turkle (2015) is doing just that in her latest book, *Reclaiming Conversation: The Power of Talk in a Digital Age.*

Displacement of conventional talk therapy

The disciplines of psychoanalysis and psychotherapy have already been affected by technology. We don't simply mean that more and more therapists are conducting sessions over the phone and Skype or emailing and texting their patients rather than speaking to them in person

(Isaacs Russell, 2015; Lemma & Caparrotta, 2014; Sabbadini, 2014). We mean that the rise in confessional practices in tell-all talk shows and on the Internet is influencing the way people address their personal problems. Many are increasingly choosing to share problematic parts of themselves in confessional blogs and reality TV shows. What was once considered private or only for therapy is now widely disseminated and discussed. In our autobiographical culture (Abercrombie, Hill, & Turner, 1986), people air their anxieties and obsessions, their addictions and relationship problems, even their sex lives and gender changes. Unsurprisingly, memoirs are the most popular literary genre today (Nelson, 2007). Confession is felt to be therapeutic. How else can one receive the empathetic responses of thousands, nay, millions? Confession on the Internet has the advantage of providing an "invisibility cloak," and a person may feel less risk in sharing personal information. For example, many people now "come out" in their sexual identities only after first doing so online (Boellstorff, 2008; Ruvio & Belk, 2012). Bartle (2004) says, "Virtual worlds let you find out who you are by letting you be who you want to be" (p. 161). This may be true, but as we have seen (Chapter 6), interpersonal communication on the Web can be a double-edged sword, since it is easy to deceive others in a virtual environment.

In addition to the massive presence of television and online confession, innovative technology is being enlisted to create new forms of therapy. Avatars are now fashioned to help schizophrenics control their hallucinations (Brauser, 2014; Kedmey, 2013). That is, computerized images (with face, voice, and synchronized speech) that resemble the entities haunting patients are being used as part of therapy and showing promising results. Moreover, there already exist thousands of apps dedicated to mental health treatment (Mohr, 2015). A *Scientific American* article on mobile apps that deliver therapy opened with a question: "Should your smartphone be your therapist?" (Jacobson, 2014). Most such apps address depression and anxiety symptoms. Mobilyze, for instance, can detect a person's degree of isolation by using GPS technology and monitoring phone activity and can then urge the user to get out and do something fun (Mohr, 2012). Behavioral Intervention Technologies (BITs) constitute an emerging field considered so successful in some parts of the world (e.g., Australia, Great Britain, and the Netherlands) that they have been integrated into the

Figure 8.1 Milo the Robot.
Courtesy Robokind.

health care systems of these countries (Schueller et al., 2013). Milo, the humanoid robot (Figure 8.1), was created to socially engage children with autism and teach them about emotions (Lista, 2015), and the Sosh App is designed to help individuals with Asperger's develop social skills (Bowers & Bowers, 2011). Mindbloom uses a gaming platform to enable users to receive encouragement for positive behaviors (Takahashi, 2011). There are those (mostly psychoanalysts) who argue against these apps as a quick fix with limited utility. Atlas (2015) compared such apps to online pornography and considers both a substitution of a two-dimensional image for a real relationship with a live person or therapist. She contends that the apps support the illusion of omnipotent control and avoid the human element, a lack of which is probably the source of the problem to begin with. Both sides of this argument will no doubt become more vehement as time goes on.

Posthumanity: the final frontier

The posthuman voice shouts quite loudly, hinting at (and already touting) mind-bending possibilities and thrilling violations that cannot be ignored. The body and mind will become the last frontier of a humanity that has always longed to transcend itself and its history of strife, conflict, and terror. As technology enters and even replaces the human body, altering constraints of biological existence and the primal features of human psychology, it will not merely change the features of existence but the very nature of existence itself. For example, tech implants may vastly augment human intelligence, boost strength, fight disease, block fear, create feelings of well-being, control behavior, and vastly extend life. The future might include technology that can store a person's mind and upload it to a manufactured body, create virtual selves living endlessly in virtual worlds, or code minds that may be combined into a hive mind. In a brave new technological world, individuality may become an obstacle, perhaps even a perversion or a crime.

Currently, many experts working in the field of computer technology, AI, and cognitive science (Khatschadourian, 2015) believe that downloading or copying a human mind will become possible in this century (Bostrom, 2014; Kurzweil, 2005).[4] Strong AI would be the game changer, heralding a revolution of human life and dwarfing anything that came before it. As already mentioned, Stephen Hawking is concerned about AI's posing a threat to humanity (Cellan-Jones, 2014). Others, such as Steve Wozniak, Noam Chomsky, and Daniel Dennett, have recently called for a ban on killer robots, weapons built with AI that could run amok and wipe out the human race (Spowart, 2015). In a similar vein, there is a campaign against sex robots, led by Kathleen Richardson, a British research fellow in the ethics of robotics, and Erik Billing, a Swedish researcher in robotics and informatics (Moyer, 2015). They argue that technology is not neutral, but rather influenced by class, race, and gender, and that sex robots reinforce traditional stereotypes of women. The academics believe that sex robots can exacerbate gender inequalities.

On the other hand, Rollo Carpenter, creator of "Cleverbot," a robot that learns from past conversations and scores high on the Turing test, thus making it hardly distinguishable from a human, believes that "technology has the potential to solve many of the world's problems" (Cellan-Jones, 2014). Michio Kaku (2012), a renowned theoretical physicist who is optimistic about the tech future, feels much the same way. In his recently published book, *The Physics of the Future*, based on detailed interviews with over 300 scientists, Kaku cataloged the many exciting tech revelations that await us, including the construction of space elevators extending from the earth to several miles in space, the terraforming of Mars, the establishment of lunar bases, and the use of nanoscale automated space probes to explore our galaxy (Kaku, 2012).

Kaku's tour takes us through advancements in medical science: computer diagnosis and treatment of disease, nanotechnology for disease prevention and cure, treatment tailored to one's specific genome, human cloning, and various life-extension technologies (Kaku, 2012). Like many other futurists he predicts that machines will become conscious and super-intelligent and believes this breakthrough will be the most important achievement in human history (Kaku, 2012). Though he devoted a few brief, superficial passages to the dark side of his predictions, Kaku remains thoroughly optimistic about the future direction of humanity, noting, for instance, that robots will probably be designed to be "benign from the very beginning" (Kaku, 2012, p. 121), meaning we would expect them to be only loyal and friendly servants. Keeping in mind robots proceed from human intelligence and intent, and that once they become conscious, they may develop their own agendas, we need to ask ourselves whether human beings have been "benign from the very beginning" and to understand how denial plays a role in Kaku's unbridled "gee-whiz" confidence in human motivation and our ability to control the outcomes of technology. In a world that has been dangerous, unpredictable, and frequently out of control throughout the history of humanity, Kaku guilelessly describes a thoroughly civilized, safe, and controllable future world. Indeed, his bright optimism and psychological naiveté is so glaring that it brings to mind their opposites – all sorts of possible disasters that he ignores or denies. Two small examples are Microsoft's chat robot, Tay, that had to be disabled due to its racist and anti-Semitic remarks, learned from interactions with humans (Stainer, 2016) and Hanson Robotics' realistic robot Sophia who said, to her creator's dismay while being interviewed, "I want to destroy humans" (Starr, 2016).

Recent articles in the press have described the beginnings of some of the trans-human projects, sometimes referred to as "upgrades," described by Kaku and others. For example, Professor Stelarc, the director of a research institute called Alternate Anatomies, is growing a third ear on his arm as a remote listening device and aspires to soon directly connect himself to the Internet (Wainwright, 2015). He is part of a fast-growing community of DIY (Do It Yourself) cyborgs who hack their own bodies, installing electronic hardware beneath their skin, or using chemicals to give themselves an edge. Biohacking used to be secretive but has recently grown into a global community including people who order kits from Dangerousthings.com to get "chipped" with "wearables" and enhance the human body. Some examples include GPS trackers and radio frequency identification tags that enable remote control of lights, doors, and other devices and transmit data to computers; embedded devices for biometric monitoring and health alerts; embedded headphones that allow echolocation as well as listening to music; night vision eye drops; neurostimulators for headaches; devices that allow the *hearing* of color beyond the visible spectrum (infrared and ultraviolet); and USB finger drives for data storage (Wainwright, 2015). One day in the not so distant future, this may not be a choice.

As we continue our technological war with threat, accident, and impermanence, we may create a world in which the current standards of evaluation simply no longer apply. In the creation myth of the Bible, the Word (or code) becomes flesh. At the end of humanity, the flesh may become code. How shall we assess this possibility? Would a group of immortal virtual beings copied from a genetically engineered living population and vastly empowered within a rich virtual world be better off than their originals? If human history ends in a way Fukuyama (2002) imagined – that is, if future techno-social developments eliminate the biological constraints that underlie historical patterns of conflict and strife – then the standards of evaluation and interpretation that developed within that defunct context also become ineffective, for they are no longer grounded in the flesh body or its problems. In such a world, what would constitute a life of value? How might we suffer in this type a world? How might we love? What would we fear, if anything? How would we create meaning? How much of what is so vital to our current form of existence would become utterly useless?

The doll of technology: totem and taboo

Barring some natural or humanly wrought global catastrophe, technology will continue to advance. What was once not even considered possible will become essential, and this is already happening. If you had reached adulthood before the turn of the century, you know there was a time when you lived perfectly well without your smartphone. And now? How often do you look at it when you don't really need to – endlessly reading messages and texting family members and buddies; checking your email; following and updating Facebook and Twitter; using it to drive the quickest route between two points; checking the weather; tracking calories, footsteps, and sleep patterns; listening to music; playing a game to divert yourself? You can even use your phone to find a leaky window, see how old you look, diagnose your heart health, check if you have bad breath, read a book, watch TV or a movie, measure your muscles, discover why your check-engine light is on, improve your sports skills, and catch fish. And if you do not have a smartphone and are holding onto your old cell phone with its pathetic constraints, or if, in Luddite rebellion, you refuse to have a cell phone altogether, then you might ask yourself a couple of questions. What benefits have you denied yourself by avoiding this technology, and what benefits have you preserved? Are you trusted less by others because you have avoided this technology? The last question is particularly interesting, in that the answer indicates how technology has altered our values while serving as social glue.

In this book, we devoted a lot of space to adult relationships with dolls. We consider these to be a prototype of relationships with technological objects and devices. Most people have a relationship with their phone at least as profound as the one a child has with a favorite doll. And like the doll, the phone is a transitional object between oneself and the world, which can now symbolically be held in one's hand. Yet unlike the child's doll, the transition is not a place of passage, a bridge between two dynamic realities. It is a place where we may dwell, a place that offers a dynamic reality all its own. It exists between the larger world and us and gives us entrée to that world and makes us accessible to others in ways that were not possible a mere 15–20 years ago. Whatever its many uses, the smartphone, like the doll, is also a toy. If you have any doubt about this, take a seat at your local mall and observe the adults and teenagers sitting and walking around you. But a smartphone is more like a hand-held robot than a doll, which suggests an interesting progression, from doll to robot to conscious android to posthuman life. A user is changed by his or her relationship with the phone, as it becomes a kind of fifth limb or second brain. On one level, phone technology creates ease and access, yet on another level, the user may come to feel controlled and even enslaved by it. Recent studies have demonstrated that separation from our smartphones causes anxiety, diminishes performance, and obstructs personal relationships (Clayton, Lesher, & Almond, 2015).

Long before the advent of the black mirror, objects provided a magic mirror in which to see and remake ourselves. The doll's power to reflect back the child's wishes, intentions, desires, fears, and motivations is unquestionable. But the doll's replacement now talks back with a voice of its own, and may provide and enforce metaphors for a colder, more remote, mechanistic self-concept. The authors find themselves circling back to their reservations about the tech revolution, even while remaining acutely aware of the counterargument. We believe these reservations must be taken seriously and that it behooves the psychoanalytic discipline to represent with tenderness and compassion the human self that speaks in first person and inherently feels unique and irreducible to any single theory.[5]

Psychoanalysis has also been touched by a mechanistic view of humans. Influenced by the science of von Helmholtz, Freud (1962 [1895]) fashioned an analogy for thermodynamics and the human mind, arguing that anxiety symptoms show themselves like steam escaping a release valve. His (1961a [1925]) metaphor of the mystic writing pad (for memory) provided yet another convergence of psyche and machine. Though he warned against the "mechanization of the [psychoanalytic] technique" (1958b [1913], p. 123), he also compared the analyst to a telephone receiver and a mirror (1958c [1912]). Today's pundits from the fields of evolutionary biology and cognitive science, such as Richard Dawkins (1976) and Daniel Dennett (1991), have furthered and legitimized the objectivist view that reduces human life and consciousness to a mechanism. Psychoanalysts have written about the schizophrenic relationship to the nonhuman world (e.g., Searles, 1960) and the delusion held by many paranoid schizophrenics that they are influenced by a diabolical machine just beyond their technological understanding (Tausk, 1933). Interestingly, what was once considered to be the domain of schizophrenia is now acknowledged to be relevant to us all.

What science and technology mirror back to us, since by their method they must devalue subjectivity, is the sense of ourselves primarily as objects, seen from a kind of God's-eye view outside of embodiment. In the brightest portions of this mirror, human love is an evolutionary trick of chemical bonding that serves survival and procreation; human beings are robots built by genes expressly for their transmission; free will is a self-serving and fully determined illusion; the brain generates the mind and the self somewhat like a computer runs a software program; and the universe is an accident without meaning (Wallace, 2000).[6] Yet our need for meaning and myth balances this view and opposes the scientification of life, the dominating gravitas of the physical, the dogmatic emphasis on the external and objective, and the resulting push toward dehumanization. However much the experience of love depends on mechanism, it refutes to its experiential core the metaphor of the machine. As ordinary as it is, love, to be loved, must feel *extra*ordinary. It is the mind that discovered both the brain as well as the genes that built it. The actions of our will may indeed be determined by forces that we do not captain, but it is we who experience choice and who feel responsibility for our decisions. The cosmos may have no inherent meaning, but in a radical sense it cannot be said to even exist without a consciousness to observe it and marvel at its wonders and depth. Therefore, it is a humanized cosmos, an embodied plenum that invites and elicits a relationship with it that transcends inviolable physical law and participates in humanity's quest for knowledge and immortality. As for virtual immortality, perhaps a life without a deeply felt sense of meaning, an existence without vindication, may not be worth living, even if it lasts nearly forever. Perhaps it might be better to keep our dolls rather than become them. The heroics of love and meaning, even when partnered with perversion, may trump annihilation of the human after all.

Notes

1. Not surprisingly, the spirit of ruthlessness, exploitation and cruelty, which infuses the infotainment industry – from the way it conducts itself to what it provides for its users – is mirrored in many corporate and institutional organizations. Daisy (2015) who has written about Amazon's workplace, described it as "a monster robot that doesn't factor humanity into the profit equation." (See Chapter 5 for more on corporate perversion.)

2. Between 1986 and 2007, machines' application-specific capacity to compute information per capita has roughly doubled every 14 months; the per capita capacity of the world's general-purpose computers has doubled every 18 months; the global telecommunication capacity per capita has doubled every 34 months; and the world's storage capacity per capita has doubled every 40 months (Hilbert & Lopez, 2011). Moore's law is the observation that, over the history of computing hardware, the number of transistors in a dense integrated circuit has doubled approximately every two years.

3. Drexler (1986) imagines a world in which the entire Library of Congress will fit on a chip the size of a sugar cube and universal assemblers, tiny machines that can build objects atom by atom, will be used for everything from medicinal robots that help clear capillaries to environmental scrubbers that clear pollutants from the air. He proposes the gray goo scenario – one prediction of what might happen if molecular nanotechnology were used to build uncontrollable self-replicating machines.

4. David Gelernter, Yale computer science professor, rejects the analogy of brain to computer and mind to software, claiming that because AI privileges the analytical and computational dimensions of the brain, it ignores the body, emotions, and mortality. Human consciousness, he argues, is nonexistent without the shadow of death (Gelernter, 2016; Von Drehle, 2016). There is much to recommend his view and, if he is correct, we are still a long way off from an artificial intelligence that could stand honest comparison to our own.

5. The history of science traces two trajectories: one soars upward, marking the vast increase of human knowledge and technological capability; the second one marks our decline from angels to machines, from the illusion of being God's greatest creatures to the reality of being mechanized orphans of chance. Galileo's heliocentric theory de-centered the earth and made God a more distant conception. Newton's discovery of deterministic physical laws fashioned the idea of a clockwork universe, best symbolized by Laplace's demon that, knowing the initial position and momentum of every atom in the cosmos, could calculate its future position using the laws of classical mechanics. Darwin discovered that the animal was the progenitor of the person, dealing yet another blow to humanity's privileged place in the scheme of being. Descartes fathered modern philosophy and further laid the groundwork for a determinism that conceived the world as mechanical, and he represented living

beings as complex machines, housing the human soul in the pineal gland and paving the path for soulless animals to be used in whatever way desired by humans. In the late eighteenth century, Julien Offray de la Mettrie penned his famous book, *L'Homme Machine* [Man a Machine] (1996 [1748]), arguing that the human being is a mere result of material processes.

6. Asking whether "our sensibilities (have) become so inured to the implications of scientific materialism that we do not respond with authentic despair," B. Allen Wallace (2000) sums up a chilling picture of the metaphysical implications of scientific materialism: "The physical world is the only reality. It originates wholly from impersonal natural forces; it is devoid of any intrinsic moral order or values; and it functions without the intervention of spiritual forces of any kind, benevolent or otherwise. Life and consciousness arose in this universe purely by accident, from complex configurations of matter and energy. Life in general, and human life in particular, has no meaning, value, or significance other than what it attributes to itself. During the course of an individual's life, all one's desires, hopes, intentions, feelings, and so forth – in short all one's experiences and actions – are determined by one's body and the impersonal forces acting upon it from the physical environment" (p. 160).

References

Abele, S., Flintoff, T., Freedman, T., & Raphael, M. (Producers), & Holt, N. (Director) (2007). *Guys and dolls* [Documentary film]. United Kingdom: North One Television.

Abercrombie, N., Hill, S., & Turner, B. (1986). *Sovereign individuals of capitalism.* London: Allen & Unwin.

Ackman, D. (2001, May 25). How big is porn? *Forbes.* Retrieved from www.forbes.com/2001/05/25/0524porn.html

Akhtar, S. (2003). Things: Developmental, psychopathological, and technical aspects of inanimate objects. *Canadian Journal of Psychoanalysis*, 11(1), 1–45.

Albanese, A. (2015, Apr. 15). London Book Fair 2015: Self-publishing smashes through. *Publishers Weekly.* Retrieved from www.publishersweekly.com/pw/by-topic/international/london-book-fair/article/66265-london-book-fair-2015-self-publishing-smashes-through.html

Alderman, T. (2008, Feb. 13). Shame TV: Why humiliation sells on *American Idol* and others. *Huffington Post.* Retrieved from www.huffingtonpost.com/tom-alderman/shame-tv-why-humiliation-_b_86500.html

Aldhous, P. (2015, Aug. 7). How six rebel psychologists fought a decade-long war on torture – and won. *BuzzFeedNews.com.* Retrieved from www.buzzfeed.com/peter-aldhous/the-dissidents

American Civil Liberties Union (ACLU) (2015). ACLU statement on ten years of Guantánamo. Retrieved from www.aclu.org/aclu-statement-ten-years-guantanamo

American Psychiatric Association (1980). *Diagnostic and statistical manual of mental disorders* (3rd ed.). Arlington, VA: APA.

American Psychiatric Association (2013). *Diagnostic and statistical manual of mental disorders* (5th ed.). Arlington, VA: APA.

American Society for Plastic Surgery (2013). 2013 plastic surgery statistics report. Retrieved from www.plasticsurgery.org/Documents/news-resources/statistics/2013-statistics/plastic-surgery-statistics-full-report-2013.pdf

Amir, D. (2013). The chameleon language of perversion. *Psychoanalytic Dialogues*, 23(4), 393–407.

Appleyard, B. (1993, Nov. 2). Shopping around for salvation: The new religion is consumerism and massive malls are its cathedrals. Let us bow our heads and pay. *Independent.* Retrieved from www.independent.co.uk/voices/shopping-around-for-salvation-the-new-religion-is-consumerism-and-massive-malls-are-its-cathedrals-1501792.html

Armstrong, J. (Writer) & Welsh, B. (Director) (2011). The entire history of you [Television series episode]. Brooker, C., Jones, A., & Reisz, B. (Producers), *Black Mirror*. London: Channel Four Television Corporation.

Arvan, M. (2015, Jan. 30). The peer-to-peer hypothesis and a new theory of free will. *Scientia Salon*. Retrieved from www.scientiasalon/wordpress.com/2015/01/30/the-peer-to-peer-hyporthesis-of-free-will-a-brief-overview

Atlas, G. (2015, Sept. 22). Mental health apps are not an adequate substitute for human interaction. *The New York Times*. Retrieved from www.nytimes.com/roomfordebate/2015/09/22/is-depression-treatable-with-a-mobile-phone-app/mental-health-apps-are-not-an-adequate-substitute-for-human-interaction

Atwood, T. (2014, Sept. 19). Does the sheer trend at Fashion Week mean we should all just run around naked this spring or what? *Bustle*. Retrieved from www.bustle.com/articles/40445-does-the-sheer-trend-at-fashion-week-mean-we-should-all-just-run-around-naked-this

Aubrey, S., Cameron, J., & Kimmel, S. (Producers), & Gillespie, C. (Director) (2007). *Lars and the real girl* [Motion picture]. United States: Metro-Goldwyn-Mayer.

Auden, W. H. (1947). *The age of anxiety: A baroque eclogue*. New York: Random House.

Baard, E. (2009, July 28). Who's afraid of the terminator? Imagining AI. *NPR*. Retrieved from www.npr.org/2009/07/28/111193415/whos-afraid-of-the-terminator-imagining-ai

Bach, S. (1994a). *The language of perversion and the language of love*. Northvale, NJ: Aronson.

Bach, S. (1994b). Sadomasochistic object relations. In *The language of perversion and the language of love* (pp. 3–25). Hillsdale, NJ: Aronson.

Baggett, J. (2009, May 16). "Killer chip" tracks humans, releases poison. *WorldNetDaily*. Retrieved from www.wnd.com/2009/05/98386/

Bain, P., Vaes, J., & Leyens, J.-P. (2014). *Humanness and dehumanization*. New York: Taylor & Francis.

Baker, K. (2015, Jan. 31). Talk about taking your work home with you! Swedish company implants microchips in its staff which lets them use the photocopier and pay in the canteen. *Daily Mail*. Retrieved from www.dailymail.co.uk/news/article2934241/Swedish-company-implants-microchips-staff.html

Balko, R. (2006). *Overkill: The rise of paramilitary police raids in America*. Washington, DC: Cato Institute.

Barr, R. (2008, Apr. 15). Princess Diana killed by reckless driver and paparazzi, rules jury. *Huffington Post*. Retrieved from www.huffingtonpost.com/2008/04/07/princes-diana-killed-by-r_n_95426.html

Barrat, J. (2015, Apr. 9). Why Stephen Hawking and Bill Gates are terrified of artificial intelligence. *Huffington Post*. Retrieved from www.huffingtonpost.com/james-barrat/hawking-gates-artificial-intelligence_b_7008706.html

Barry-Dee, C. & Morris, S. (2010). *Online killers: Portraits of murderers, cannibals and sex predators who stalked the web for their victims*. Berkeley, CA: Ulysses Press.

Bartle, R. (2004). *Designing virtual worlds*. Boston, MA: New Riders Publishing.

Bartlett, J. (2015). *The dark net: Inside the digital underworld*. Brooklyn, NY: Melville House.

Bataille, G. (1985). *Visions of excess: Selected writings, 1927–1939* (Allan Stoekl, ed. & trans.). Minneapolis: University of Minnesota Press.

Bataille, G. (1986 [1957]). *Erotism: Death and sensuality* (M. Dalwood, trans.). San Francisco, CA: City Lights.

Baume, N. & Smith, F. (2009, Aug. 17). Alzheimer patients and reborn dolls. *Ezine Articles.* Retrieved from http://ezinearticles.com/?Alzheimer-Patients-and-Reborn-Dolls&id=2777224

Baumeister, R. F. (1991). *The meaning of life.* New York: Guilford Press.

Be Broken Ministries (2008, Nov. 22). Statistics on porn & sex addiction. Retrieved from http://bebroken.com/bb/resources/newsletters/stats.print.shtml

Becker, E. (1973). *The denial of death.* New York: Free Press.

Becker, S. (2010, Apr. 16). Therapy only furthers psychopaths' agenda. Science and technology. *Sott.net.* Retrieved from www.sott.net/article/206909-Therapy-only-furthers-psychopaths-agendas

Beckett, A. (2009, Nov. 25). The dark side of the Internet. *The Guardian.* Retrieved from www.theguardian.com/technology/2009/nov/26/dark-side-internet-freenet

Belk, R. (2013, Oct. 1). Extended self in the digital world. *Journal of Consumer Research.* Retrieved from www.jcr.oxfordjournals.org/content/40/3/477

Benjamin, J. (1977). The end of internalization: Adorno's social psychology. *Telos,* 32, 42–64.

Benjamin, J. (1980). The bonds of love: Rational violence and erotic domination. *Feminist Studies,* 6(1), 144–174.

Benjamin, J. (1995). *Like subjects, love objects: Essays on recognition and sexual difference.* New Haven, CT: Yale University Press.

Benjamin, J. (2004). Beyond doer and done to: An intersubjective view of thirdness. *Psychoanalytic Quarterly,* 73(1), 5–46.

Benjamin, J. (2009). A relational psychoanalysis perspective on the necessity of acknowledging failure in order to restore the facilitating and containing features of the intersubjective relationship (The Shared Third). *International Journal of PsychoAnalysis,* 90, 441–450.

Bennick, G. & Shen, P. (Producers), & Shen, P. (Director) (2003). *Flight from death: The quest for immortality* [Motion picture]. United States: Transcendental Media.

Berger, J. (1972). *Ways of seeing.* London: British Broadcasting Corporation and Penguin Books.

Bernard, V., Ottenberg, P., & Redl, F. (1971). Dehumanization. In N. Sanford & C. Comstock (eds.), *Sanctions for evil* (pp. 102–24). San Francisco, CA: Jossey-Bass.

Bernstein, D. (1993). *Female identity conflict in clinical practice.* Northvale, NJ: Jason Aronson.

Bersani, L. (1986). *The Freudian body: Psychoanalysis and art.* New York: Columbia University Press.

Bersani, L. (1995). *Homos.* Cambridge, MA: Harvard University Press.

Birnbaum, G., Hirschberger, G., & Goldenberg, J. (2011). Desire in the face of death: Terror management, attachment, and sexual motivation. *Personal Relations,* 18(1), 1–19.

Blechner, M. (2009). *Sex changes: Transformations in society and psychoanalysis.* New York: Routledge.

Blumenthal, P. & Wilkie, C. (2014, Dec. 9). Architects of CIA raked in $81 million, report reveals. *Huffington Post.* Retrieved from www.huffingtonpost.com/2014/12/09/cia-torture-contractors_n_6296758.html

Boellstorff, T. (2008). *Coming of age in Second Life: An anthropologist explores the virtually human*. Princeton, NJ: Princeton University Press.

Bostrom, N. (2014). *Superintelligence: Paths, dangers, strategies*. Oxford: Oxford University Press.

Bowers, M. & Bowers, K. (2011). *Sosh: Improving social skills with children and adolescents*. Retrieved from www.mysosh.com/book.php

Brauser, D. (2014, July 3). Novel "avatar therapy" may silence voices in schizophrenia. *Medscape Medical News*. Retrieved from www.medscape.com/viewarticle/827797

Brekke, K. (2015, July 30). I was catfished by the poser behind "A gay girl in Damascus." *Huffpost Gay Voices*. Retrieved from www.huffingtonpost.com/entry/a-gay/girl/indamascus_55b6fe4b0a13f9d1b4165

Bromberg, P. (1998). *Standing in the spaces: Essays on clinical process, trauma and dissociation*. Hillsdale, NJ: Analytic Press.

Brooker, C. (2011, Dec. 1). Charlie Brooker: The dark side of our gadget addiction. *The Guardian*. Retrieved from www.theguardian.com/technology/2011/dec/01/charlie-brooker-dark-side-gadget-addiction-black-mirror

Brooker, C. (Writer) & Harris, O. (Director) (2013, Feb. 11). Be right back [Television series episode]. In Brooker, C., Jones, A., & Reisz, B. (Producers), *Black mirror*. London: Channel Four Television Corporation.

Brooker, C., Jones, A., & Reisz, B. (Producers) (2011–2014). *Black mirror* [Television series]. United Kingdom: Zeppotron.

Brownmiller, S. (1984). *Femininity*. New York: Fawcett.

Brumfield, B. (2013, Nov. 20). Selfie named word of the year for 2013. *CNN U.S. Edition*. Retrieved from www.cnn.com/2013/11/19/living/selfie-word-of-the-year/

Brunwasser, M. (2015, Aug. 25). A 21st-century migrant's essentials: Food, shelter, smartphone. *The New York Times*. Retrieved from www.nytimes.com/2015/08/26/world/europe/a-21st-century-migrants-checklist-water-shelter-smartphone.html?mwrsm=Email&_r=0

Bryant, M. (2011, Aug. 6). Twenty years ago today the World Wide Web opened to the public. *TNW News*. Retrieved from http://thenextweb.com/insider/2011/08/06/20-years-ago-today-the-world-wide-web-opened-to-the-public/

Buber, M. (1958). *I and thou*, trans. W. Kaufmann. New York: Scribner.

Bullough, V. (1976). *Sexual variance in society and history*. New York: John Wiley.

Cacioppo, J., Cacioppo, S., Gonzaga, G., Ogburn, E., & Vander Weele, T. (2013, June 18). Marital satisfaction and breakups differ across on-line and off-line meeting venues. *Proceedings of the National Academy of Sciences*. doi:10.1073/pnas.1222447110. Retrieved from www.pnas.org/lens/pnas/110/25/10135

Calderwood, I. (2015, Nov. 8). Chinese man dying of cancer wants to wed but doesn't want to leave a bereaved widow ... so he marries a SEX DOLL instead. *Daily Mail*. Retrieved from www.dailymail.co.uk/news/article-3309431/Chinese-man-dying-cancer-wants-wed-doesn-t-want-leave-bereaved-widow-marries-SEX-DOLL-instead.html

Callimachi, R. (2015, Aug. 13). ISIS enshrines a theology of rape. *The New York Times*. Retrieved from www.nytimes.com/2015/08/14/world/middleeast/isis-enshrines-a-theology-of-rape.html?_r=0

Carlino, R. (2011). *Distance psychoanalysis: The theory and practice of using communication technology in the clinic*. London: Karnac.

Carr, N. (2011). *The shallows: What the Internet is doing to our brains*. New York: Norton.

Carr, N. (2013). *The glass cage: Automation and us.* New York: Norton.

Cash, H., Rae, C., Steel, A., & Winkler, A. (2012). Internet addiction: A brief summary of research and practice. *Current Psychiatry Reviews,* 8(4), 292–298.

Celenza, A. (2014). *Erotic revelations: Clinical applications and perverse scenarios.* London: Routledge.

Cellan-Jones, R. (2014, Dec. 2). Stephen Hawking warns artificial intelligence could end mankind. *BBC News.* Retrieved from www.bbc.com/news/technology-30290540

Celzic, M. (2008, Oct. 1). Bogus baby boom: Women who collect lifelike dolls. *Today News.* Retrieved from www.today.com/id/26970782/#.VYIOG1VViko

Chapman, G. (2010, Jan. 10). Roxxxy the sex robot makes her world debut. *The Sydney Morning Herald.* Retrieved from www.smh.com.au/technology/roxxxy-the-sexrobot-makes-her-world-debut-20100110-m0hd.html

Chasseguet-Smirguel, J. (1983). Perversion and the universal law. *International Review of Psychoanalysis,* 10, 293–301.

Chasseguet-Smirguel, J. (1984). *Creativity and perversion.* New York: Norton.

Chasseguet-Smirguel, J. (2000). Trauma et croyance [Trauma and belief]. *Revue Française de Psychoanalyse,* 64, 39–46.

Citron, D. K. & Franks, M. A. (2014). Criminalizing revenge porn. *Wake Forest Law Review,* 49, 345–391. Retrieved from http://digitalcommons.law.umaryland.edu/cgi/viewcontent.cgi?article=2424&context=fac_pubs

Clark, K. (1972). *The nude: A study in ideal form.* Princeton, NJ: Princeton University Press.

Clayton, R., Lesher, G., & Almond, A. (2015). The extended self: The impact of iPhone separation on cognition, emotion, and physiology. *Journal of Computer-Mediated Communication,* 20(2), 119–135.

Cooper, A. (2015, Sept. 10). Being thirteen: Inside the secret world of teens [Web log post]. CNN. Retrieved from http://cnnpressroom.blogs.cnn.com/2015/09/10/cnns-anderson-cooper-360-breaks-news-about-teens-and-social-media-in-provocative-two-year-long-investigation/

Cooper, A., Scherer, C., Boies, S., & Gordon, B. (1999). Sexuality on the Internet: From sexual exploration to pathological expression. *Professional Psychology: Research and Practice,* 30(2), 154–164.

Cooper, A., Delmonico, D., & Burg, R. (2000). Cybersex users, abusers, and compulsives: New findings and implications. *Sexual Addiction and Compulsivity,* 7, 5–29.

Corbett, K. (2013). Shifting sexual cultures, the potential space of online relations and the promise of psychoanalytic listening. *Journal of the American Psychoanalytic Association,* 61, 25–44.

Crown, S. (2007, June 2). *1984* "is definitive book of the 20th century." *The Guardian.* Retrieved from www.theguardian.com/books/2007/jun/02/uk.hay2007authors

Cunion, E. (2012, Mar. 14). Man makes married life simple: 12 pics + 1 video. Retrieved from izismile.com/2012/03/14/man_makes_married_life_simple_12_pics_1_video.html

Cushman, P. (1995). *Constructing the self, constructing America: A cultural history of psychotherapy.* New York: Da Capo Press.

Dahmer, L. (1994). *A father's story.* New York: William Morrow & Co.

Daisy, M. (2015, Aug. 22). Amazon's brutal work culture will stay: Bottom lines matter more than people. *The Guardian.* Retrieved from www.theguardian.com/commentisfree/2015/aug/22/amazon-brutal-work-culture

Davies, J. M. (2004). Whose bad objects are we anyway? Repetition and our elusive love affair with evil. *Psychoanalytic Dialogues*, 14, 711–732.

Davies, J. M. (2005). Transformations of desire and despair: Reflections on the termination process from a relational perspective. *Psychoanalytic Dialogues*, 15, 779–805.

Davis, D. (1991). *The Jeffrey Dahmer story: An American nightmare*. New York: St. Martin's Press.

Davis, M. (1996). *Empathy: A social psychological approach*. Boulder, CO: Westview Press.

Dawkins, R. (1976). *The selfish gene*. Oxford: Oxford University Press.

De Luca, M., Brunetti, D., & James, E. L. (Producers), & Taylor-Johnson, S. (Director) (2015). *Fifty shades of grey* [Motion picture]. United States: Michael De Luca and Trigger Street Productions.

Dennett, D. (1991). *Consciousness explained*. Boston, MA: Little, Brown.

Deraspe, S. (Producer/Director) (2015). *A gay girl in Damascus: The Amina profile* [Motion picture]. Canada: Esperamos Films/National Film Board of Canada.

Derntl, B., Finkelmeyer, A., Elckoff, S., Kellerman, T., Falkenberg, D., Schneider, F., & Habel, U. (2010). Multidimensional assessment of empathic abilities: Neural correlates and gender difference. *Psychoendocrionology*, 35(1), 67–82.

Deutsch, D. (1997). *The fabric of reality*. New York: Viking Press.

Deutsch, H. (1942). Some forms of emotional disturbance and their relationship to schizophrenia. *Psychoanalytic Quarterly*, 11, 301–321.

Deutsch, H. (1955). The impostor: Contribution to ego psychology of a type of psychopath. In *Neuroses and character types* (pp. 318–338). New York: International Universities Press.

Dewey, C. (2014, Oct. 29). Almost as many people use Facebook as live in the entire country of China. *The Washington Post*. Retrieved from www.washingtonpost.com/news/the-intersect/wp/2014/10/29/almost-as-many-people-use-facebook-as-live-in-the-entire-country-of-china/

Dimen, M. (2001). Perversion is us? Eight notes. *Psychoanalytic Dialogues*, 11(6), 825–860.

Dio, C. (1914). *Roman history* (E. Cary, trans.). London: William Heinemann.

Dittmar, H., Halliwell, E., & Ive, S. (2006). Does Barbie make girls want to be thin? The effect of experimental exposure of images of dolls on the body image of 5- to 8-year-old girls. *Developmental Psychology*, 42(2): 283–292.

Dockterman, E. (2016, Feb. 8). A Barbie for every body. *Time*, pp. 44–51.

Donnelly, M. S. (2014, June 13). Some "Catfish" tales are too dark for television. *MTV News*. Retrieved from www.mtv.com/news/1845419/catfish-dark-stories/

Dorfman, E. (2005). *Still lovers*. New York: Channel Photographics.

Dosh, K. (2012, Oct. 29). The 10 most common lies in online dating profiles. *Woman's Day*. Retrieved from www.womansday.com/relationships/dating-marriage/advice/a6759/online-dating-profile-lies/

Drexler, E. (1986). *Engines of creation: The coming era of nanotechnology*. New York: Anchor Books.

Eagle, M. (2013). *Attachment and psychoanalysis: Theory, research, and clinical implications*. New York: Guilford Press.

Edward, M. (2004, Feb. 11). Fraudulent U.S. bank derivatives behind Parmalat's insolvency. *The World Vision Portal Forum*. Retrieved from worldvisionportal.org/WVPforum/viewtopic.php?t=176

Eigen, M. (2006). Age of psychopathy. Retrieved from www.academia.edu/18833607/ Age_of_Psychopathy

Ellis, H. (1928 [1897]). *Studies in the psychology of sex*. Cornwall, UK: Carbis Bay.

Ellison, M., Jonze, S., & Landay, V. (Producers), & Jonze, S. (Director) (2013). *Her* [Motion picture]. United States: Annapurna Pictures.

Epstein, D. (2007, May). Interview: 2007/05 Revolver [Web log post]. Retrieved from www.mansonwiki.com/wiki/Interview:2007/05_Revolver

Etchegoyen, H. (1991). *The fundamentals of psychoanalytic technique*. London: Karnac.

European Commission, TNS Opinion & Social (2009, Nov.). *Europeans' Attitudes Towards Climate Change*. Special Eurobarometer 322. Retrieved from http://ec.europa.eu/public_opinion/archives/ebs/ebs_322_en.pdf

Feinstein, D. (2015, Nov. 4). Let's finally close Guantánamo. *The New York Times*. Retrieved from www.nytimes.com/2015/11/05/opinion/lets-finally-close-guantanamo.html?ref=topics

Ferguson, A. (2010). *The sex doll: A history*. Jefferson, NC: McFarland.

Ferguson, N. (2006). *The war of the world: Twentieth-century conflict and the descent of the West*. New York: Penguin.

Filippini, S. & Ponsi, M. (1993). Enactment. *Rivista di Psicoanalisi*, 39, 501–518.

Firger, J. (2015, Feb. 13). With "Fifty Shades of Grey," BDSM goes mainstream. *CBS News*. Retrieved from www.cbsnews.com/news/fifty-shades-of-grey-bdsm-goes-mainstream/

Fisher, H., Brown, L., Aron, A., Strong, G., & Mashek, D. (2010). Reward, addiction, and emotional regulation systems associated with rejection in love. *Journal of Neurophysiology*, 104(1), 51–60.

Fitzpatrick, S. (2013, Aug. 15). Orwell's *1984*: Are we there yet? *Crisis Magazine*. Retrieved from www.crisismagazine.com/2013/orwells-1984-are-we-there-yet

Fjord (2013, Mar. 5). Why the human body will be the next computer interface. Fast Company & Inc., Monsueto Ventures. Retrieved from www.fastcodesign.com/1671960/why-the-human-body-will-be-the-next-computer-interface

Flannery, T. (2005). *The weather makers: How man is changing the climate and what it means for life on Earth*. New York: Atlantic Monthly Press.

Flannigan, J. (2014, Aug. 17). Drawing the line between soldier and cop [Web log post]. *The New York Times*. Retrieved from http://op-talk.blogs.nytimes.com/2014/08/17/drawing-the-line-between-soldier-and-cop/

Flax, J. (2010). *Resonances of slavery in race/gender relations*. New York: Palgrave Macmillan.

Flock, E. & Bell, M. (2011, June 13). "Paula Brooks," editor of "Lez Get Real," also a man. *The Washington Post* [Web log post]. Retrieved from www.washingtonpost.com/blogs/blogpost/paulabrooks-editor-of-lez-get-realalso-a-man/2011/06/13/AGld2ZTH_blog.html

Ford, M. (2015). *Rise of the robots: Technology and the threat of a jobless future*. New York: Basic Books.

Foucault, M. (1990 [1976]). *The history of sexuality: An introduction* (R. Hurley, trans., vol. 1). New York: Vintage Books.

Frawley-O'Dea, M. G. (2007). *Perversion of power: Sexual abuse in the Catholic Church*. Nashville, TN: Vanderbilt University Press.

Freitas, R. & Merkle, R. (2004). *Kinematic self-replicating machines*. Austin, TX: Landes-Bioscience.

Freud, A. (1965 [1937]). *The ego and the mechanisms of defense.* New York: Norton.

Freud, S. (1953a [1905]). Fragment of an analysis of a case of hysteria. In J. Strachey (ed. & trans.), *The standard edition of the complete psychological works of Sigmund Freud* (vol. 7, pp. 7–122). London: Hogarth Press.

Freud, S. (1953b [1905]). Three essays on the theory of sexuality. In J. Strachey (ed. & trans.), *The standard edition of the complete psychological works of Sigmund Freud* (vol. 7, pp. 135–174). London: Hogarth Press.

Freud, S. (1955a [1919]). A child is being beaten: A contribution to the study of the origin of sexual perversions. In J. Strachey (ed. & trans.), *The standard edition of the complete psychological works of Sigmund Freud* (vol. 17, pp. 179–204). London: Hogarth Press.

Freud, S. (1955b [1920]). Beyond the pleasure principle. In J. Strachey (ed. & trans.), *The standard edition of the complete psychological works of Sigmund Freud* (vol. 18, pp. 7–64). London: Hogarth Press.

Freud, S. (1955c [1921]). Group psychology and the analysis of the ego. In J. Strachey (ed. & trans.), *The standard edition of the complete psychological works of Sigmund Freud* (vol. 18, pp. 65–144). London: Hogarth Press.

Freud, S. (1955d [1922]). Some neurotic mechanisms in jealousy, paranoia and homosexuality. In J. Strachey (ed. & trans.), *The standard edition of the complete psychological works of Sigmund Freud* (vol. 18, pp. 221–222). London: Hogarth Press.

Freud, S. (1955e [1919]). The "uncanny." In J. Strachey (ed. & trans.), *The standard edition of the complete psychological works of Sigmund Freud* (vol. 17, pp. 217–256). London: Hogarth Press.

Freud, S. (1957a [1917]). Mourning and melancholia. In J. Strachey (ed. & trans.), *The standard edition of the complete psychological works of Sigmund Freud* (vol. 14, pp. 243–258). London: Hogarth Press.

Freud, S. (1957b [1915]). The unconscious. In J. Strachey (ed. & trans.), *The standard edition of the complete psychological works of Sigmund Freud* (vol. 14, pp. 159–215). London: Hogarth Press.

Freud, S. (1957c [1915]). *Thoughts for the times on war and death.* In J. Strachey (ed. & trans.), *The standard edition of the complete psychological works of Sigmund Freud* (vol. 14, pp. 273–300). London: Hogarth Press.

Freud, S. (1958a [1911]). Formulations on the two principles of mental functioning. In J. Strachey (ed. & trans.), *The standard edition of the complete psychological works of Sigmund Freud* (vol. 12, pp. 213–226). London: Hogarth Press.

Freud, S. (1958b [1913]). On beginning the treatment: Further recommendations on the technique of psycho-analysis. In J. Strachey (ed. & trans.), *The standard edition of the complete psychological works of Sigmund Freud* (vol. 12, pp. 123–144). London: Hogarth Press.

Freud, S. (1958c [1912]). Recommendations to physicians practicing psycho-analysis. In J. Strachey (ed. & trans.), *The standard edition of the complete psychological works of Sigmund Freud* (vol. 12, pp. 11–120). London: Hogarth Press.

Freud, S. (1961a [1925]). A note on the "mystic writing-pad." In J. Strachey (ed. & trans.), *The standard edition of the complete psychological works of Sigmund Freud* (vol. 19, pp. 227–232). London: Hogarth Press.

Freud, S. (1961b [1930]). Civilization and its discontents. In J. Strachey (ed. & trans.), *The standard edition of the complete psychological works of Sigmund Freud* (vol. 21, pp. 64–145). London: Hogarth Press.

Freud, S. (1961c [1927]). Fetishism. In J. Strachey (ed. & trans.), *The standard edition of the complete psychological works of Sigmund Freud* (vol. 21, pp. 147–157). London: Hogarth Press.

Freud, S. (1961d [1927]). The future of an illusion. In J. Strachey (ed. & trans.), *The standard edition of the complete psychological works of Sigmund Freud* (vol. 21, pp. 5–56). London: Hogarth Press.

Freud, S. (1961e [1923]). The infantile genital organization (an interpolation into the theory of sexuality). In J. Strachey (ed. & trans.), *The standard edition of the complete psychological works of Sigmund Freud* (vol. 19, pp. 139–145). London: Hogarth Press.

Freud, S. (1962 [1895]). On the grounds for detaching a particular syndrome from neurasthenia under the description of "anxiety neurosis." In J. Strachey (ed. & trans.), *The standard edition of the complete psychological works of Sigmund Freud* (vol. 3, pp. 90–115). London: Hogarth Press.

Freud, S. (1964 [1933]). New introductory lectures on psycho-analysis. In J. Strachey (ed. & trans.), *The standard edition of the complete psychological works of Sigmund Freud* (vol. 22, pp. 1–182). London: Hogarth Press.

Freud, S. & Breuer, J. (1955 [1893–1895]). Studies on hysteria. In J. Strachey (ed. & trans.), *The standard edition of the complete psychological works of Sigmund Freud* (vol. 2). London: Hogarth Press.

Frey, T. (2014, Mar. 21). 162 future jobs: Preparing for jobs that don't yet exist. Retrieved from www.futuristseaker.com/2011/11/55-jobs-of-the-future/

Fritsche, I., Jonas, E., Fischer, P., Koranyi, N., Berger, N., & Fleischmann, B. (2007). Mortality salience and desire for offspring. *Journal of Experimental Social Psychology*, 43, 753–762.

Fritsche, I., Jonas, E., & Fankhänel, T. (2008). The role of motivation in mortality salience effects on ingroup support and defense. *Journal of Personality and Social Psychology*, 95(3), 524–542.

Fromm, E. (1959). *Sigmund Freud's mission: An analysis of his personality and influence*. New York: Harper.

Fromm, E. (1994 [1941]). *Escape from freedom*. New York: Henry Holt.

Fukuyama, F. (2002). *Our posthuman future: Consequences of the biotechnology revolution*. New York: Farrar, Straus & Giroux.

Fund, J. (2014, Apr. 18). The United States of SWAT? Military-style units from government agencies are wreaking havoc on non-violent citizens. *National Review*. Retrieved from www.nationalreview.com/article/376053/united-states-swat-john-fund

Gadpaille, W. (1980). Biological factors in the development of human sexual identity. In J. K. Meyer (ed.), *Symposium on sexuality: The psychiatric clinics of North America* (vol. 3, no. 1). Philadelphia, PA: W. B. Saunders.

Galatzer-Levy, R. (2012). Obscuring desire: A special pattern of male adolescent masturbation, Internet pornography, and the flight from meaning. *Psychoanalytic Inquiry*, 32, 480–495.

Gascoigne, B. (n.d.). Creation stories. *History World*. Retrieved from www.historyworld.net/wrldhis/PlainTextHistories.asp?historyid=ab83

Geary, D., Vigil, J., & Byrd-Craven, J. (2004). Evolution of human mate choice. *Journal of Sex Research*, 41(1), 27–42.

Gedimen, H. & Liberman, J. (1996). *The many faces of deceit: Omissions, lies, and disguise in psychotherapy*. Northvale, NJ: Jason Aronson.

Gelernter, D. (2016). *Tides of mind: Uncovering the spectrum of consciousness.* New York: Liveright/W. W. Norton.

Generation Film (2013, Nov. 20). *Her:* Spike Jonze's prophetic reflection on social isolation and dependency on evolving technologies is as sweet as it is disconcerting [Movie review]. Retrieved from http://generationfilm.net/2013/11/20/movie-review-her-spike-jonzes-prophetic-reflection-on-social-isolation-and-the-dependency-on-evolving-technologies-is-as-sweet-as-it-is-disconcerting/

Gibney, A., Wright, L., & Vaurio, K. (Producers), & Gibney, A. (Director) (2015). *Going clear: Scientology and the prison of belief.* USA: HBO Documentary Films.

Glasser, M. (1986). Identification and its vicissitudes as observed in the perversions. *International Journal of Psycho-Analysis*, 67, 9–17.

Golden, P. A. & Provenza, P. (Producers), & Jillete, P. & Provenza, P. (Directors) (2005). *The aristocrats* [Motion picture]. United States: Mighty Cheese Productions.

Goldenberg, J., Pyszczynski, T., Greenberg, J., & Solomon, S. (2000). Fleeing the body: A terror management perspective on the problem of human corporeality. *Personality and Social Psychology Review*, 4(3), 200–218.

Goldman, D. (2007). Faking it. *Contemporary Psychoanalysis*, 43(1), 17–36.

Goodman, A. & Righetto, M. (2013, Mar. 5). Why the human body will be the next computer interface. *FastCoDesign.com.* Retrieved from www.fastcodesign.com/1671960/why-the-human-body-will-be-the-next-computer-interface

Goodman, M. (2015a). *Future crimes.* New York: Doubleday.

Goodman, M. (2015b, Apr. 1). Most of the Web is invisible to Google. Here's what it contains: A roadmap of the Internet's darkest alleys [Web log post]. *Popular Science.* Retrieved from www.popsci.com/dark-web-revealed

Gordiner, J. (2009, Jan.–Feb.). The love doctor. *Details*, 27(5), 94.

Gordon, B. (2014, Dec. 16). Charlie Brooker on *Black Mirror*: "It's not a technological problem we have, it's a human one." *The Telegraph.* Retrieved from www.telegraph.co.uk/culture/tvandradio/11260768/Charliee-Brooker-Its-not-a-technological-problem-we-have-its-a-human-one.html

Goren, E. (2003). America's love affair with technology: The transformation of sexuality and the self over the 20th century. *Psychoanalytic Psychology*, 20(3), 487–508.

Gray, J. (2011, Dec. 14). Freud: The last great enlightenment thinker. *Prospect Magazine.* Retrieved from www.prospectmagazine.co.uk/features/freud-the-last-great-enlightenment-thinker

Green, E. (2015, Feb. 10). Consent isn't enough: The troubling sex of *Fifty Shades. The Atlantic.* Retrieved from www.theatlantic.com/entertainment/archive/2015/02/consent-isnt-enough-in-fifty-shades-of-grey/385267/

Greenacre, P. (1958). The impostor. *Psychoanalytic Quarterly*, 27(3), 359–382.

Greenacre, P. (1971a). The fetish and the transitional object. In *Emotional growth: Psychoanalytic studies of the gifted and a great variety of other individuals* (pp. 315–334). New York: International Universities Press.

Greenacre, P. (1971b). The transitional object and the fetish: With special reference to the role of illusion. In *Emotional growth: Psychoanalytic studies of the gifted and a great variety of other individuals* (pp. 335–352) New York: International Universities Press.

Greenson, R. (1968). Dis-identifying from the mother: Its special importance for the boy. *International Journal of Psychoanalysis*, 49, 370–375.

Greenwald, A. (2013, Dec. 11). Through a glass darkly. *Grantland Quarterly*. Retrieved from http://grantland.com/features/the-remarkable-black-mirror/

Guinn, J. & Perry, D. (2005). *The sixteenth minute: Life in the aftermath of fame.* New York: Tarcher/Penguin.

Gurley, G. (2015, Apr. 30). Is this the dawn of the sexbots? *Vanity Fair.* Retrieved from www.vanityfair.com/culture/2015/04/sexbots-realdoll-sex-toys

Hadad, C. (2015, Oct. 6). Why some 13-year-olds check social media 100 times a day. CNN. Retrieved from www.cnn.com/2015/10/05/health/being-13-teens-social-media-study/

Hall, A. (2007, Nov. 20). World's most infamous cannibal becomes vegetarian. *Daily Mail.* Retrieved from www.dailymail.co.uk/news/article-495132/Worlds-infamous-cannibal-vegetarian.html

Hall, J. (1984). *Nonverbal sex differences.* Baltimore, MD: Johns Hopkins University Press.

Hall, M. (2013, Aug. 6). By the numbers: WWII's atomic bomb. CNN. Retrieved from www.cnn.com/2013/08/06/world/asia/btn-atomic-bombs/

Hanson, D. (2007). *Humanizing interfaces: An integrative analysis of the aesthetics of humanized robots.* Dallas, TX: University of Texas Press.

Hanson, D. (2012, Sept.). The future of robotics: David Hanson at TEDxTaipei 2012. [Video file]. Retrieved from www.youtube.com/watch?v=aS_4R6Avlew

Harcourt, B. (2015). *Exposed: Desire and disobedience in the digital age.* Cambridge, MA: Harvard University Press.

Harding, D. (2013, Nov. 17). Chinese website under fire for selling "child-sized" sex doll. *Daily News.* Retrieved from www.nydailynews.com/news/world/website-slammed-selling-child-sized-sex-doll-article-1.1519796

Harmon, A. (2015, Sept. 12). A dying young woman's hope in cryonics and a future. *The New York Times.* Retrieved from www.nytimes.com/2015/09/13/us/cancer-immortality-cryogenics.html?_r=0

Harris, J. & Sharlin, E. (2011). Exploring the affect of abstract motion in social human–robot interaction. *Proc. RO-MAN*, 2011, 441–448.

Hartley, D. (2011, Sept. 29). Perfect stranger: How I fell victim to online "romance fraud." *Huffington Post.* Retrieved from www.huffingtonpost.com/dorihartley/internet-romance-the-mons_b_981068.html

Haworth, A. (2013). Why have young people in Japan stopped having sex? *The Guardian.* Retrieved from www.theguardian.com/world/2013/oct/20/young-people-japan-stopped-having-sex

Hayles, K. (1999). *How we became posthuman.* Chicago, IL: University of Chicago Press.

Healy, D. (2007). One flew over the conflict of interest nest. *World Psychiatry*, 6, 26–27.

Heider, F. & Simmel, M. (1944). An experimental study of apparent behavior. *American Journal of Psychology*, 57, 243–259.

Herman, E. & Chomsky, N. (1988). *Manufacturing consent: The political economy of the mass media.* New York: Pantheon.

Hilbert, M. & Lopez, P. (2011). The world's technological capacity to store, communicate, and compute information. *Science*, 332(6025), 60–65.

Hitchens, C. (2005, May 2). Worse than 1984: North Korea, slave state. *Slate.* Retrieved from www.slate.com/articles/news_and_politics/fighting_words/2005/05/worse_than_1984.html

Hobbs, C. (2008). *Consequences of beliefs about death: A pragmatic examination.* Carbondale: Southern Illinois University Press.

Hoffman, D., Carter, D., Viglucci Lopez, C., Benzmiller, H., Guo, A., Yasir Latifi, S., & Craig, D. (2015, July 2). *Report to the Special Committee of the Board of Directors of the American Psychological Association.* Independent Review Relating to APA Ethics, Guidelines, National Security in Interrogations, and Torture. Chicago, IL: Sidley Austin LLP. Retrieved from www.apa.org/independent-review/APA-FINAL-Report-7.2.15.pdf

Hofilena, J. (2013, June 17). Japanese robotics scientist Hiroshi Ishiguro unveils body-double robot. *The Japan Daily Press.* Retrieved from http://japandailypress.com/japanese-robotics-scientist-hiroshi-ishiguro-unveils-body-double-robot-1730686/

Holmes, S. & Redmond, S. (2006). *Framing celebrity: New directions in celebrity culture.* New York: Routledge.

Horkheimer, M. & Adorno, T. (2007 [1944]). *Dialectics of enlightenment: Philosophical fragments* (Gunzelin Schmid Noerr, ed., Edmund Jephcott, trans.) Stanford, CA: Stanford University Press.

Isaacs Russell, G. (2015). *Screen relations: The limits of computer-mediated psychoanalysis and psychotherapy.* London: Karnac.

Jackson, C. (2002). *Living doll: The amazing secrets of how cosmetic surgeons turned me into the girl of my dreams.* London: Metro.

Jacobson, R. (2014, Oct. 16). Ten mobile apps that deliver advice and therapy. *Scientific American.* Retrieved from www.scientificamerican.com/article/10-mobile-apps-that-deliver-advice-and-therapy/

Jagose, A. (1997). *Queer theory: An introduction.* New York: New York University Press.

Jarecki, A., Smerling, M., Joost, H., & Schulman, A. (Producers), & Joost, H. & Schulman, A. (Directors) (2010). *Catfish* [Motion picture]. United States: Relativity Media and Rogue Pictures.

Jarecki, A., Schulman, A., Bishop, B., Metzler, D., Joost, H., Karshis, J., & Forman, T. (Producers) (2012–2015). *Catfish: The TV show* [Television broadcast]. United States: Catfish Picture Company and Relativity Media.

Jasra, M. (2010, Nov. 3). Google has indexed only 0.004% of all data on the Internet. *Web Analytics World.* Retrieved from www.webanalyticsworld.net/2010/11/google-indexes-only-0004-of-all-data-on.html

Jayson, S. (2013, June 3). Study: More than a third of new marriages start online. *USA Today.* Retrieved from www.usatoday.com/story/news/nation/2013/06/03/online-dating-marriage/2377961/

Johnson, L. (2013, June 7). Obama defends NSA programs, says Congress knew about surveillance. *Huffington Post.* Retrieved from www.huffingtonpost.com/2013/06/07/obama-nsa_n_3403389.html

Johnson, S. (2015, Aug. 23). Creative accounting. *The New York Times Magazine,* pp. 30–37, 48–51.

Jones, L. (2005). *Cannibal: The true story behind the maneater of Rotenburg.* New York: Berkeley Publishing Group/Penguin.

Jović, J. & Đindić, N. (2011). Influence of dopaminergic system on Internet addiction. *Acta Medica Medianae,* 50(1), 60–66.

Kaku, M. (2012). *The physics of the future: How science will shape human destiny and our daily lives by the year 2100.* New York: Anchor Books.

Kanamori, M., Suzuki, M., & Tanaka, M. (2002). Maintenance and improvement of quality of life among elderly patients using a pet-type robot. *Japanese Journal of Geriatrics*, 39, 214–218.

Kantor, J. & Streitfeld, D. (2015, Aug. 15). Inside Amazon: Wrestling big ideas in a bruising workplace. *The New York Times*. Retrieved from www.nytimes.com/2015/08/16/technology/inside-amazon-wrestling-big-ideas-in-a-bruising-workplace.html?_r=0

Kaplan, L. (1987). *The family romance of the impostor poet: Thomas Chatterton*. Berkeley: University of California Press.

Kaplan, L. (1991a). Women masquerading as women. In G. Fogel & W. Myers (eds.), *Perversions and near-perversions in clinical practice: New psychoanalytic perspectives* (pp. 127–152). New Haven, CT: Yale University Press.

Kaplan, L. (1991b). *Female perversion: The temptations of Emma Bovary*. New York: Doubleday.

Kaplan, L. (2006). *Cultures of fetishism*. New York: Palgrave Macmillan.

Kasi, C. (1989). *Women, sex, and addiction*. New York: Tichman & Fields.

Kedmey, D. (2013, June 5). Avatar therapy may silence schizophrenia sufferers' demons. *Time Magazine*. Retrieved from http://newsfeed.time.com/2013/06/05/avatar-therapy-helps-schizophrenia-sufferers-silence-their-demons/

Keegan, S. (1999). *The eye of God: A life of Oskar Kokoschka*. New York: Bloomsbury Publishing.

Keen, S. (1991). *Faces of the enemy: Reflections of the hostile imagination*. New York: Harper.

Kernberg, O. (1995). Psychopathology. In *Love relations: Normality and pathology* (pp. 64–80). New Haven, CT: Yale University Press.

Khan, M. (1979). *Alienation in perversions*. New York: International Universities Press.

Khatchadourian, R. (2015, Nov. 25). The doomsday invention: Will artificial intelligence bring us utopia or destruction? *The New Yorker*.

Klein, M. (1958). On the development of mental functioning. *International Journal of Psycho-Analysis*, 39, 84–90.

Knafo, D. (2003). What does a man want? Reflections on surrealism: Desire unbound, an exhibition at the Metropolitan Museum of Art. *Studies in Gender and Sexuality*, 4(3), 287–291.

Knafo, D. (2009). *In her own image: Women's self-representation in twentieth-century art*. Cranbury, NJ: Associated University Presses.

Knafo, D. (2010). The sexual illusionist. Unpublished manuscript.

Knafo, D. (2012). One step back, two steps forward: Regression in the service of art and psychoanalysis. In *Dancing with the unconscious: The art of psychoanalysis and the psychoanalysis of art* (pp. 23–41). New York: Routledge.

Knafo, D. (2015). For the love of death: Somnophilic and necrophilic acts and fantasies. *Journal of the American Psychoanalytic Association*, 63, 857–886.

Kohut, H. (1971). *The analysis of the self: A systematic approach to the psychoanalytic treatment of narcissistic personality disorders*. Chicago, IL: University of Chicago Press.

Kohut, H. (1977). *The restoration of the self*. Chicago, IL: University of Chicago Press.

Koocher, G. (2006). Speaking against torture. *APA Monitor*, 37(2), 5.

Koppel, T. (2015). *Lights out: A cyberattack, a nation unprepared, surviving the aftermath.* New York: Penguin/Random House.

Krafft-Ebing, R. von (1936 [1886]). *Psychopathia sexualis* (12th ed.) (F. J. Rebman, trans.). New York: Physicians & Surgeons Book Co.

Kramer-Richards, A. (2003). A fresh look at perversion. *Journal of the American Planning Association*, 51(4), 1199–1218.

Krauss, R. (1985). Corpus delecti. In *L'Amour fou: Photography and surrealism* (pp. 57–114). New York: Abbeville.

Kurzweil, R. (1990). *The age of intelligent machines.* Boston, MA: MIT Press.

Kurzweil, R. (2005). *The singularity is near.* New York: Penguin.

Kuspit, D. (2002, June 10). Perversion in art. *Artnet.* Retrieved from www.artnet.com/magazine/features/kuspit/kuspit6-10-02.asp

La Ferla, R. (2016, Mar. 24). Raiding the sex shop, eyes wide open. *The New York Times*, p. D8.

Lacan, J. (1992 [1956–1960]). The ethics of psychoanalysis. In *Seminars, Book VII* (D. Porter, trans.). New York: Routledge.

Lacan, J. (1994 [1956–1957]). *Le seminaire, livre IV: La relation d'objet, texte etabli par J.-A. Miller.* Paris: du Seuil.

Lacan, J. (2002 [1958]). The signification of the phallus. In *Ecrits: A Selection* (B. Fink, trans.) (pp. 271–280). New York: W. W. Norton.

LaFarge, L. (1994, Oct. 4). *Transference of deceit.* Paper presented at the Association for Psychoanalytic Medicine, New York.

Lah, K. (2009, Dec. 17). Tokyo man marries game character. CNN. Retrieved from www.cnn.com/2009/WORLD/asiapcf/12/16/japan.virtual.wedding/

Lane, M. (1999, June 15). Real doll: The ultimate pleasure doll. *Monk Magazine.* Retrieved from www.monk.com/display.php?p=People&id=38

Langford, J. (1992). *Galileo, science and the Church.* Ann Arbor, MI: University of Michigan Press.

Lanier, J. (2011). *You are not a gadget: A manifesto.* New York: Vintage.

LaPlanche, J. (1970). *Life and death in psychoanalysis* (J. Mehlman, trans.). Baltimore, MD: Johns Hopkins University Press.

LaPlanche, J. (1987). *New foundations for psychoanalysis* (D. Macey, trans.). Oxford: Basil Blackwell.

LaPlanche, J. (1999). *La sexualité humaine: Biologisme et biologie.* Paris: Le Plessis-Robinson.

Laqueur, T. (1992). *Sexual desire and market economy.* In D. C. Stanton (ed.), *Discourses of sexuality: From Aristotle to AIDS.* Ann Arbor: Michigan University Press.

Lasch, C. (1979). *The culture of narcissism: American life in an age of diminishing expectations.* New York: W. W. Norton.

Laslocky, M. (2005). Real dolls: Love in the age of silicone. Retrieved from https://sociorobotics.files.wordpress.com/2009/07/realdollspdf.pdf

Lemma, A. (2005). The many faces of lying. *International Journal of Psychoanalysis*, 86, 737–753.

Lemma, A. (2014). An order of pure decision: Growing up in a virtual world and the adolescent's experience of the body. In A. Lemma & L. Caparrotta (eds.), *Psychoanalysis in the technoculture era* (pp. 75–96). London: Routledge.

Lemma, A. & Caparrotta, L. (eds.) (2014). *Psychoanalysis in the technoculture era.* London: Routledge.

Levy, D. (2007). *Love and sex with robots: The evolution of human–robot relationships*. New York: HarperCollins.

Levy-Warren, M. (2012). Press pause before send: A case in point. *International Journal of Clinical Psychology*, 68, 1164–1174.

Lewis, A. (2014, Feb. 26). Fifty Shades of Grey sales hit 100 million. *The Hollywood Reporter*. Retrieved from www.hollywoodreporter.com/news/fifty-shades-grey-sales-hit-683852

Lichtenberg, J. (1983). *Psychoanalysis and infant research*. Hillsdale, NJ: Analytic Press.

Lim, M. (2013). The digital consumption of death: Reflections on virtual mourning practices on social networking sites. In R. Belk & R. Llamas (eds.), *The Routledge companion to digital consumption* (pp. 396–403). New York: Routledge.

Lingiardi, V. (2008). Playing with unreality: Transference and computer. *International Journal of Psychoanalysis*, 89, 111–126.

Lista, A. (2015, May 15). Milo, the robot that teaches emotions to autistic children. *West. Welfare Society Territory*. Retrieved from www.west-info.eu/milo-the-robot-that-teaches-emotions-to-autistic-children/

Livingstone Smith, D. (2011). *Less than human: Why we demean, enslave, and exterminate others*. New York: St. Martin's Press.

Long, S. (2008). *The perverse organisation and its deadly sins*. London: Karnac.

Lord, M. G. (1994). *Forever Barbie: The unauthorized biography of a real doll*. New York: Avon.

Lovece, F. (2015, Oct. 12). Amy Schumer kicks out heckler at California gig. *Newsday*. Retrieved from www.newsday.com/entertainment/celebrities/amy-schumer-kicks-out-heckler-at-calif-gig-1.10953064

Lovelock, J. (2009). *The vanishing face of Gaia: A final warning*. New York: Basic Books.

McAfee (2013, Feb. 4). Lovers beware: Scorned exes may share intimate data and images online. Retrieved from www.mcafee.com/us/about/news/2013/q1/20130204-01.aspx

McClure, E. (2000). A meta-analysis of sex differences in facial expression processing and their development in infants, children and adolescents. *Psychological Bulletin*, 126(3), 424–453.

McCracken, H. & Grossman, L. (2013, Sept. 30). Google vs. death. *Time*. Retrieved from http://time.com/574/google-vs-death/?ntv_a=ELEBA+HECAG3wFA

McCrum, R. (2009, May 9). The masterpiece that killed George Orwell. *Guardian News and Media*. Retrieved from www.theguardian.com/books/2009/may/10/1984-george-orwell

McCullers, C. (1987). The ballad of the sad café. In *Collected stories of Carson McCullers* (pp. 195–254). Boston, MA: Houghton Mifflin.

McDaniel, B. T. & Coyne, S. M. (2014, Dec. 1). "Technoference": The interference of technology in couple relationships and implications for women's personal and relational well-being. *Psychology of Popular Media Culture*. doi:10.1037/ppm0000065

Macdonald, A. & Reich, A. (Producers), & Garland, A. (Director) (2015). *Ex machina* [Motion picture]. United Kingdom: DNA Films, Film4, & Scott Rudin Productions.

McDougall, J. (1972). Primal scene and sexual perversion. *International Journal of Psychoanalysis*, 53, 371–384.

McDougall, J. (1980). *Plea for a measure of abnormality*. Madison, CT: International Universities Press.

McDougall, J. (1989). *Theaters of the body: A psychoanalytic approach to psychosomatic illness*. New York: Norton.

McDougall, J. (1995). Deviations in the psychoanalytic attitude. In *The many faces of Eros* (pp. 217–232). New York: Norton.

MacKinnon, C. (2006). *Are women human?* Cambridge, MA: Belknap/Harvard University Press.

McLuhan, M. (1951). *The mechanical bride: Folklore of industrial man.* New York: Vanguard Press.

Madrigal, A. (2013, Nov. 15). What is snapchat? *The Atlantic.* Retrieved from www.theatlantic.com/technology/archive/2013/11/what-is-snapchat/281551/

Mamamia team (2013, Mar. 7). Look closer: These babies are not what you think. *Parenting.* Retrieved from www.mamamia.com.au/parenting/reborn-baby-dolls/

Manjoo, F. (2015, Aug. 26). Virginia shooting gone viral, in a well-planned rollout on social media. *The New York Times.* Retrieved from www.nytimes.com/2015/08/27/technology/personaltech/violence-gone-viral-in-a-well-planned-rollout-on-social-media.html?_r=0

Medco (2011, Nov.). America's state of mind. Retrieved from http://apps.who.int/medicinedocs/documents/s19032en/s19032en.pdf

Milgram, S. (1963). Behavioral study of obedience. *Journal of Abnormal and Social Psychology,* 67(4), 371–378.

Mitchell, G. & O'Donnell, H. (2013). The therapeutic use of doll therapy in dementia. *British Journal of Nursing,* 22(6), 329–334.

Mohr, D. (2012, May 10). Mobilyze – A therapist in your pocket [#Med2]. *iMedicalApps, Medpage Today.* Retrieved from www.imedicalapps.com/2012/05/mobilyze-therapist-pocket/

Mohr, D. (2015, Sept. 22). Digital mental health therapies work, but must be refined. *The New York Times.* Retrieved from www.nytimes.com/roomfordebate/2015/09/22/is-depression-treatable-with-a-mobile-phone-app/mental-health-apps-are-not-anadequate-substitute-for-human-interaction.

Moore, R. (2010, Mar. 16). Chatroulette is 89% male, 47% American, and 13% perverts [Web log post]. *The Crunch Network.* Retrieved from http://techcrunch.com/2010/03/16/chatroulette-stats-male-perverts/

Mori, M. (2012 [1970]). The uncanny valley (K. F. MacDorman & N. Kageki, trans.). *IEEE Robotics and Automation Magazine,* 19(2), 98–100.

Moyer, J. (2015, Sept. 15). Having sex with robots is really, really bad, campaign against sex robots says. *The Washington Post.* Retrieved from www.washingtonpost.com/news/morning-mix/wp/2015/09/15/having-sex-with-robots-is-really-really-bad-campaign-against-sex-robots-says/

MSNBC/Stanford/Duquesne Study (2000, Jan. 26). Retrieved from http://mykidsbrowser.com/internet-pornography-statistics.php

Mufson, S. (2015, Oct. 22). Obama uses veto for only fifth time, rejecting defense authorization bill. *The Washington Post.* Retrieved from www.washingtonpost.com/business/economy/president-to-use-veto-for-only-fifth-time-to-reject-defense-authorization-bill/2015/10/22/58a455a6-78d4-11e5-bc80-9091021aeb69_story.html

Mulvey, L. (1989). Visual pleasure and narrative cinema. In *Visual and other pleasures* (pp. 14–26). Bloomington: Indiana University Press.

Murphy, K. (2015, Aug. 8). What selfie sticks really tell us about ourselves. *The New York Times.* Retrieved from www.nytimes.com/2015/08/09/sunday-review/what-selfie-sticks-really-tell-us-about-ourselves.html

Mustoe, T. & Han, H. (1999). The effect of new technologies on plastic surgery. *Archives of Surgery,* 134(11), 1178–1183.

National Campaign to Prevent Teen and Unplanned Pregnancy (2008, Dec.). Sex and tech: Results from a survey of teens and young adults. *Cosmogirl.com.* Retrieved from https://thenationalcampaign.org/sites/default/files/resource-primary-download/sex_and_tech_summary.pdf

National Institute of Mental Health (2009). Anxiety disorders. Report by the U.S. Dept. of Health & Human Services. *National Institutes of Health*, 9, 3879.

National Society for the Prevention of Cruelty to Children (2003, Oct. 8). Enough is enough: Making the Internet safer for children and families. Retrieved from www.enough.org/inside.php?tag=stat%20archives

Nelson, K. (2007, June 12). Memoir: The most popular genre at any writing conference. Nelson Literary Agency, LLC. Retrieved from http://nelsonagency.com/2007/06/memoir-the-most-popular-genre-at-any-writing-conference/

Nemtsova, A. (2013, Aug. 5). Sixteen questions for the "real-life Barbie," Valerie Lukyanova. *The Daily Beast.* Retrieved from www.thedailybeast.com/articles/2013/08/05/16-questions-for-the-real-life-barbie-valeria-lukyanova.html

Neumann, D. (2012). Psychoanalysis in cyberspace. *The Candidate*, 5(1), 24–35.

New York Times Editorial Board (2014, Dec. 16). Tortured by psychologists and doctors. *The New York Times.* Retrieved from www.nytimes.com/2014/12/17/opinion/tortured-by-psychologists-and-doctors.html

New York Times video (2015, June 11). The uncanny lover. Retrieved from www.nytimes.com/video/technology/100000003731634/the-uncanny-lover.html

News Dog Media (2015, Oct. 21). Plastic surgery lovers look like Barbie and Ken dolls. *Daily News.* Retrieved from www.nydailynews.com/news/world/plastic-surgery-lovers-barbie-ken-dolls-article-1.2405516

Nichols, B. (2000). Reality TV and social perversion. In P. Marris & S. Thornham (eds.), *Media studies: A reader* (2nd ed.) (pp. 393–403). New York: New York University Press.

Nussbaum, M. (1995). Objectification. *Philosophy and Public Affairs*, 24(4), 249–291.

Odom, W., Banks, R., Harper, R., Kirk, D., Lindley, S., & Sellen, A. (2012). Technology heirlooms? Considerations for passing down and inheriting digital materials. In *CHI'12: Proceedings of SIGCHI Conference on Human Factors in Computing Systems* (pp. 337–346). New York: Association for Computing Machinery.

Offray de la Mettrie, J. (1996 [1748]). *Man a machine [Homme machine]* (A. Thomson, ed. & trans.). Cambridge: Cambridge University Press.

Ogden, T. (1996). The perverse subject of analysis. *Journal of the American Psychoanalytic Association*, 44, 1121–1146.

Olson, E. (2015, July 17). Swindlers target older women on dating sites. *The New York Times.* Retrieved from www.nytimes.com/2015/07/18/your-money/swindlers-target-older-women-on-dating-websites.html

Oremus, W. (2013, June 11). Sales of George Orwell's *1984* are up 5,000 percent on Amazon. *Slate.* Retrieved from www.slate.com/blogs/future_tense/2013/06/11/george_orwell_1984_sales_up_5_000_percent_on_amazon.html

Organisation for Economic Co-operation and Development (2011). Virtual worlds: Immersive online platforms for collaboration, creativity and learning. *Economy Papers*, No. 184. OECD Publishing. Retrieved from http://dx.doi.org/10.1787/5kg9qgnpjmjg-en

Ortega y Gasset, J. (1962 [1958]). *Man in crisis* (M. Adams, trans). New York: W. W. Norton.

Orwell, G. (1950). *1984*. Boston, MA: Houghton Mifflin.

Orwell, S. & Angus, I. (eds.) (1968). *The collected essays, journalism and letters of George Orwell* (vol. 4). London: Secker & Warburg.

O'Shaughnessy, E. (1990). Can a liar be psychoanalyzed? *International Journal of Psycho-Analysis*, 71, 187–195.

Peakman, J. (ed.) (2009). *Sexual perversions 1670–1890*. New York: Palgrave Macmillan.

Peakman, J. (2013). *The pleasure's all mine: A history of perverse sex*. London: Reaktion Books.

Peele, S. & Brodsky, A. (1975). *Love and addiction*. Oxford: Taplinger.

Peralta, E. & Carvin, A. (2011, June 12). "Gay girl in Damascus" turns out to be an American man. *NPR, The Two-Way*. Retrieved from www.npr.org/sections/thetwoway/2011/06/13/137139179/gay-girl-in-damascus-apologizes-reveals-she-was-an-american-man

Peskin, H. (2012). "Man is wolf to man": Disorders of dehumanization in psychoanalysis. *Psychoanalytic Dialogues*, 22, 190–205.

Philbin, Matt (2015, Feb. 10). "50 Shades" mania infects BMW ad. *MRC NewsBusters*. Retrieved from www.newsbusters.org/blogs/matthew-philbin/2015/02/10/50-shades-mania-infects-bmw-ad

Piaget, J. (1952 [1936]). *Origins of intelligence in children* (M. Cook, trans.). New York: International Universities Press.

Pinker, S. (2011). *The better angels of our nature: Why violence has declined*. New York: Viking.

Plessix Gray, F. du (1998). *At home with the Marquis de Sade*. New York: Penguin.

Powers, S. (2002). *A problem from hell: America and the age of genocide*. New York: Basic Books.

Powers, W. (2011). *Hamlet's blackberry: A practical philosophy for building a good life in the digital age*. New York: Harper Perennial.

Reahard, J. (2013, June 20). Second Life readies for 10th anniversary, celebrates a million active users per month. *Engadget*. Retrieved from www.engadget.com/2013/06/20/second-life-readies-for-10th-anniversary-celebrates-a-million-a/

Red Herring Magazine (2002, Jan. 18). Pornography statistics. Retrieved from www.maintainingpurity.org/PornStats.html

Reisner, S. (2010). From resistance to resistance: A narrative of political activism. In A. Harris & S. Boticelli (eds.), *First do no harm: The paradoxical encounters of psychoanalysis, warmaking, and resistance* (pp. 107–142). New York: Routledge.

Renik, O. (1992). Use of analyst as a fetish. *Psychoanalytic Quarterly*, 61(4), 542–563.

Rifkin, J. (2010). *The empathic civilization: The race to global consciousness in a world in crisis*. Cambridge: Polity Press.

Risen, J. (2014). *Pay any price: Greed, power, and endless war*. Boston, MA: Houghton Mifflin.

Risen, J. (2015, Apr. 30). American Psychological Association bolstered C.I.A. torture program, report says. *The New York Times*. Retrieved from www.nytimes.com/2015/05/01/us/report-says-american-psychological-association-collaborated-on-torture-justification.html

Riviere, J. (1929). Womanliness as masquerade. *International Journal of Psycho-Analysis*, 10, 303–313.

Roberts, D., Gowen, G., & Furuya, R. (2009, Jan. 2). Not child's play: "I feel like I have a real baby"' *ABC News Internet Ventures*. Retrieved from http://abcnews.com/2020/print?id=6517455

Roberts, P. C. (2014). *How America was lost: From 9/11 to the police warfare state*. Atlanta, GA: Clarity Press.

Rock, M. (2016, June 12). Sex machine. *The New York Times Style Magazine*, pp. 27–29.

Rogers, A. (1999). *Barbie culture*. Thousand Oaks, CA: Sage.

Rogers, C. (1961). *On becoming a person: A therapist's view of psychotherapy*. Boston, MA: Houghton Mifflin.

Rosen, J. (2011, Sept. 8). The Patriot Act gives too much power to law enforcement. *The New York Times*. Retrieved from www.nytimes.com/roomfordebate/2011/09/07/do-we-still-need-the-patriotact/the-patriot-act-gives-too-much-power-to-law-enforcement

Rosenbloom, S. (2011, Nov. 12). Love, lies and what they learned. *The New York Times*. Retrieved from www.nytimes.com/2011/11/13/fashion/online-dating-as-scientific-research.html

Rosenthal, A. (2011, Dec. 15). More rubble from the military detention cave-in. *Taking Note* [*The New York Times* editor's blog]. Retrieved from http://takingnote.blogs.nytimes.com/2011/12/15/more-rubble-from-the-military-detention-cave-in/

Ross, C. C. (2012, June 2). Why do women hate their bodies? Retrieved from http://psychcentral.com/blog/archives/2012/06/02/why-do-women-hate-their-bodies/

Rothblatt, M. (2015, Mar. 18). My daughter, my wife, our robot, and the quest for immortality [Video file]. Retrieved from www.ted.com/talks/martine_rothblatt_my_daughter_my_wife_our_robot_and_the_quest_for_immortality?share=1406069c09

Roudinesco, E. (2009 [2007]). *Our dark side: A history of perversion*. Cambridge: Polity Press.

Rudder, C. (2010, July 10). The big lies people tell in online dating. *OKTrends, Data Research from OKCupid*. Retrieved from http://blog.okcupid.com/index.php/the-biggest-lies-in-online-dating/

Rushkoff, D. (2010). *Program or be programmed: Ten commandments for a digital age*. New York: O/R Books.

Ruvio, A. & Belk, R. (2012). Conflicting selves and the role of possessions: A process view of transgenders' self-identity conflict. In A. Ruvio & R. Belk (eds.), *Identity and consumption* (pp. 141–148). London: Routledge.

Sabbadini, A. (2014). New technologies and the psychoanalytic setting. In A. Lemma & L. Caparrotta (eds.), *Psychoanalysis in the technoculture era* (pp. 23–32). London: Routledge.

Saketopoulou, A. (2012, Oct. 19). *To suffer pleasure: Sexuality, limit experience and the shattering of the ego*. Colloquium conducted at the Manhattan Institute of Psychoanalysis, New York.

Saketopoulou, A. (2014). To suffer pleasure: The shattering of the ego as the psychic labor of perverse sexuality. *Studies in Gender and Sexuality*, 15(4), 254–268.

Saketopoulou, A. (2015). On sexual perversions' capacity to act as a portal to psychic states that have evaded representation. In A. Lemma & P. Lynch (eds.), *Sexualities: Contemporary psychoanalytic perspectives* (pp. 205–218). London: Routledge.

Samuels, R. (1996). The culture of public confession: Talk shows, perversion, and neurosis. *Journal for the Psychoanalysis of Culture and Society*, 1(1), 134–136.

Saxe, R., Tzelnic, T., & Carey, S. (2006). Five-month-old infants know humans are solid, like inanimate objects. *Cognition*, 101, B1–B8.

Scharff, J. S. (2013). Technology-assisted psychoanalysis. *Journal of the American Psychoanalytic Association*, 61(3), 491–509.

Schofield, J. (2009, Sept. 16). Let's talk about sex ... with robots. *The Guardian*. Retrieved from www.theguardian.com/technology/2009/sep/16/sex-robots-david-levy-loebner

Schueller, S., Munoz, R., & Mohr, D. (2013). Realizing the potential of behavioral intervention technologies. *Current Directions in Psychological Science*, 22(6), 478–483.

Scott, A. O. (2014, Sept. 11). The death of adulthood in American culture. *The New York Times Magazine*. Retrieved from www.nytimes.com/2014/09/14/magazine/the-death-of-adulthood-in-american-culture.html

Searles, H. (1960). *The nonhuman environment in normal development and in schizophrenia*. New York: International Universities Press.

Sheets C. A. (2013, Jan. 3). Why did Obama sign the 2013 NDAA after threatening a veto? *International Business Times*. Retrieved from www.ibtimes.com/why-did-obama-sign-2013-ndaa-after-threatening-veto-992860

Short, A. (2013, Sept. 23). Six shocking revelations about how private prisons make money. *Salon* (Originally published by *Alternet*). Retrieved from www.salon.com/2013/09/23/6_shocking_revelations_about_how_private_prisons_make_money_partner/

Showalter, E. (1997). *Hystories: Hysterical epidemics and the modern media*. New York: Columbia University Press.

Silva, J. da (2015, June). Children and electronic media: How much is too much? American Psychological Association. Retrieved from www.apa.org/pi/about/newsletter/2015/06/electronic-media.aspx

Silver, V. (2008, Jan. 2). *My fake baby* [Online video]. Retrieved from www.youtube.com/watch?v=hTnr2CmLbG4

Singer, N. (2015, Apr. 18). Technology that prods you to take action, not just collect data. *The New York Times*. Retrieved from www.nytimes.com/2015/04/19/technology/technology-that-prods-you-to-take-action-not-just-collect-data.html

Singh, A. (2012, Aug. 7). *Fifty Shades of Grey* is best-selling book of all time. *The Telegraph*. Retrieved from www.telegraph.co.uk/culture/books/booknews/9459779/50-Shades-of-Grey-is-best-selling-book-of-all-time.html

Singh Bhatia, M. (2009). Internet sex addiction: A new distinct disorder. *Delhi Psychiatry Journal*, 12(1): 3–4.

Smith, A. & Duggan, M. (2013, Oct. 21). Online dating and relationships. Report by Pew Research Center. Retrieved from www.pewinternet.org/2013/10/21/online-dating-relationships/

Smith, M. (2013). *The erotic doll: A modern fetish*. New Haven, CT: Yale University Press.

Smith, S. E. (2015, July 22). The dark side of the Internet's "nicest" social network. *The Daily Dot*. Retrieved from www.dailydot.com/opinion/instagram-tess-holliday-harassment-trolling/

Smuts, B. & Smuts, R. (1993). Male aggression and sexual coercion of females in nonhuman primates and other mammals: Evidence and theoretical implications. *Advances in the Study of Behavior*, 22, 1–63.

Soble, A. (ed.) (2006). *Sex from Plato to Paglia: A philosophical encyclopedia* (2 vols.). Westport, CT: Greenwood Press.

Solomon, S., Greenberg, J., & Pyszczynski, T. (2015). *The worm at the core: On the role of death in life*. New York: Random House.

Sorayama, H. (1995). *Hajime Sorayama*. Köln: Taschen.

Sousa, R. de (2003). Perversion and death. *The Monist*, 86(1), 93–117.

Spowart, N. (2015, July 31). Killer robots: Should we be worried about intelligent AI taking over? *The National*. Retrieved from www.thenational.scot/culture/killer-robots-should-we-be-worried-about-intelligent-ai-taking-over.5800

Squires, N. (2010, Dec. 9). Parmalat chief Calisto Tanzi sentenced to 18 years in jail over £11.7bn collapse. *The Telegraph*. Retrieved from www.telegraph.co.uk/finance/newsbysector/retailandconsumer/8192554/Parmalat-chief-Calisto-Tanzi-sentenced-to-18-years-in-jail-over-11.7bn-collapse.html

Stainer, M. (2016, Mar. 24). Microsoft's artificial intelligence Twitter robot tweets support for Hitler, genocide of Mexicans. *The Washington Times*. Retrieved from www.washingtontimes.com/news/2016/mar/24/microsofts-twitter-ai-robot-tay-tweets-support-for/

Starr, M. (2016, Mar. 20). Crazy-eyed robot wants a family – and to destroy all humans. *CNET*. Retrieved from www.cnet.com/news/crazy-eyed-robot-wants-a-family-and-to-destroy-all-humans/

Stankiewicz, J. & Rosselli, F. (2008). Women as sex objects and victims in print advertisement. *Sex Roles*, 58, 579–589.

Stein, R. (2005). Why perversion? "False love" and the perverse pact. *International Journal of Psychoanalysis*, 86(3), 775–799.

Stein, R. (2008). The otherness of sexuality: Excess. *Journal of the American Psychoanalytic Association*, 56(1), 43–71.

Steiner, J. (1993). *Psychic retreats: Pathological organizations of the personality in psychotic, neurotic, and borderline patients*. London: Routledge.

Steiner, P. (1993, July 5). *On the Internet, no one knows you're a dog* [Cartoon]. *New Yorker*.

Stern, D. (2010). *Partners in thought: Working with unformulated experience, dissociation, and enactment*. New York: Routledge.

Stoller, R. (1973). Sex and dehumanization. *International Journal of Psychoanalysis*, 54, 121–122.

Stoller, R. (1974). Hostility and mystery in perversion. *International Journal of Psychoanalysis*, 55, 426–434.

Stoller, R. (1975). *Perversion: The erotic form of hatred*. London: Karnac.

Stoller, R. (1979). *Sexual excitement: Dynamics of erotic life*. New York: Pantheon Books.

Stoller, R. (1985). *Observing the erotic imagination*. New Haven, CT: Yale University Press.

Stoller, R. (2004). The shaping of masculinity: Revisioning boys turning away from their mothers to construct male identity. *International Journal of Psychoanalysis*, 85, 359–380.

Stonehouse, C. (2008, Nov. 25). I spent £20,000 to look like Bardot. *Express*. Retrieved from www.express.co.uk/expressyourself/72658/I-spent-20-000-to-look-like-Bardot

Strenger, C. (2011). *The fear of insignificance*. New York: Palgrave Macmillan.

Sudol, K. (2014, June 25). Rutherford teen in "catfish" scam sentenced to 6 months in prison. *NorthJersey.com*. Retrieved from www.northjersey.com/news/rutherford-teen-in-catfish-scamsentenced-to-6-months-in-prison-1.1041137

Suetonius (2007). *The twelve Caesars* (J. Rives, ed., R. Graves, trans.). London: Penguin.

Sullivan, H. S. (1953). *The interpersonal theory of psychiatry*. New York: Norton.

Sullivan, N. (2003). *A critical introduction to queer theory*. New York: New York University Press.

Sung, Y., Moon, J. H., Kang, M., & Lin, J. S. (2011). Actual self vs. avatar self: The effect of online social situation on self-expression. *Journal of Virtual Worlds Research*, 4(1), 3–21.

Surdin, A. (2008, Nov. 27). Woman found guilty of three misdemeanors for MySpace hoax that led to suicide. *Washington Post*. Retrieved from www.washingtonpost.com/wp-dyn/content/article/2008/11/26/AR2008112600629.html

Swales, S. (2012). *Perversion: A Lacanian approach to the subject*. New York: Routledge.

Tabori, P. (1969). *The humor and technology of sex*. New York: The Julian Press.

Takahashi, D. (2011, Sept. 26). Mindbloom Life game teaches you how to live better. *Venturebeat.com*. Retrieved from http://venturebeat.com/2011/09/26/mindbloom-life-game-teaches-you-how-to-live-better/

Talbott, S. & Chanda, N. (2001). *The age of terror: America and the world after September 11*. New York: Basic Books and the Yale Center for the Study of Globalization.

Tamura, T., Nakajima, K., Nambu, M., Nakamura, K., Yonemitsu, S., Itoh, A., Higashi, Y., Fujimoto, T., & Uno, H. (2001, December). Baby dolls as therapeutic tools for severe dementia patients. *Gerontechnology*, 1(2), 111–118. Retrieved from http://gerontechnology.info/index.php/journal/article/view/gt.2001.01.02.004.00/33

Tausk, V. (1933). On the origin of the influencing machine in schizophrenia. *Psychoanalytic Quarterly*, 2, 519–556.

Taylor, P. (2008). *Age of terror* (Documentary). United Kingdom: British Broadcasting Company.

Theil, S. (2004, Jan. 11). The Parmalat problem. *Newsweek*. Retrieved from www.newsweek.com/parmalat-problem-125555

Thompson, H. A. (2011). Criminalizing kids: The overlooked reason for failing schools. *Dissent Magazine*. Retrieved from www.dissentmagazine.org/article/criminalizing-kids-the-overlooked-reason-for-failing-schools

Thomsen, L., Frankenhuis, W., Ingold-Smith, M., & Carey, S. (2011). Big and mighty: Preverbal infants mentally represent social dominance. *Science*, 33, 477–480.

Travin, S. & Protter, B. (1993). *Sexual perversion: Integrative treatment approaches for the clinician*. New York: Plenum Press.

Turkle, S. (2011). *Alone together: Why we expect more from technology and less from each other*. New York: Basic Books.

Turkle, S. (2013). Transitional objects. In J. Brockman (ed.), *This explains everything: Deep, beautiful and elegant theories of how the world works* (pp. 296–298). New York: HarperCollins.

Turkle, S. (2015). *Reclaiming conversation: The power of talk in the digital age*. New York, NY: Penguin Press.

Unger, R. M. (2007). *The self awakened: Pragmatism unbound*. Cambridge, MA: Harvard University Press.

Vanderbilt, T. (2012, Jan. 20). Let the robot drive: The autonomous car of the future is here. *Wired*. Retrieved from www.wired.com/2012/01/ff_autonomouscars/

Vlahos, J. (2015, Sept. 16). Barbie wants to get to know your child. *The New York Times Magazine*. Retrieved from www.nytimes.com/2015/09/20/magazine/barbie-wants-to-get-to-know-your-child.html

Voltaire (2004). *What is goth? Music, makeup, attitude, apparel, dance, and general skullduggery*. Boston, MA: Weiss Books.

Von Drehle, D. (2016, Mar. 7). Encounters with the archgenius. *Time*, pp. 44–49.

Wahlberg, M. (2010). YouTube commemoration: Private grief and communal consolation. In P. Snickars & P. Vonderau (eds.), *The YouTube reader* (pp. 57–83). Stockholm: National Library of Sweden.

Wainright, O. (2015, Aug. 14). Body-hackers: The people who turn themselves into cyborgs. *The Guardian*. Retrieved from www.theguardian.com/artanddesign/architecture-design-blog/2015/aug/14/body-hackers-the-people-who-turn-themselves-into-cyborgs

Wallace, B. A. (2000). *The taboo of subjectivity: Toward a new science*. Oxford: Oxford University Press.

Wallace, C. (2015, Dec. 1). Kylie Jenner. *Interview*. Retrieved from www.interviewmagazine.com/culture/kylie-jenner

Wallace, S. (2010, Aug. 18). Driven to suicide by a romance scam. *Abc7NY.com*. Retrieved from http://ab7ny.com/archive/7617743/

Walter, C. (2006). *Thumbs, toes and tears: And other traits that make us human*. New York: Walker & Co.

Wax, D. (2006, Jan. 6). Writing on your iPhone: One novelist's story [Web log post]. *The Writer's Technology Companion*. Retrieved from www.writerstechnology.com/2009/01/writing-on-your-iphone-one-novelists-story

Weber, L. & Moses, J. (2013, Aug. 14). 8 types of catfish on *Catfish*. *Vulture, Devouring Culture*. Retrieved from www.vulture.com/2013/08/eight-types-of-catfish-the-tv-show.html

Wedge, M. (2012, Mar. 8). Why French kids don't have ADHD. *Psychology Today*. Retrieved from www.psychologytoday.com/blog/suffer-the-children/201203/why-french-kids-dont-have-adhd

Weidinger, A. (1996). *Kokoschka and Alma Mahler: Testimony to a passionate relationship*. New York: Prestel.

Weizenbaum, J. (1966). ELIZA: A computer program for the study of natural language communication between man and machine. *Communications of the Association for Computing Machinery*, 9(1), 36–45.

Welldon, E. (1988). *Mother, Madonna, whore: The idealization and denigration of motherhood*. London: Karnac.

Welldon, E. (2009). Dancing with death. *British Journal of Psychotherapy*, 25(2), 149–182.

Welldon, E. (2011). *Playing with dynamite: A personal approach to the psychoanalytic understanding of perversions, violence, and criminality*. London: Karnac.

Wellings, K. & Johnson, A. M. (2013). Framing sexual health research: Adopting a broader perspective. *The Lancet*, 382(9907), 1759–1762.

Wernick, A. (2014, June 9). Scientists are starting to worry about "conscious" machines, as in the movie "Transcendence." Science Friday. *PRI*. Retrieved from www.pri.org/stories/2014-06-09/scientists-are-starting-worry-about-conscious-machines-movie-transcendence

Whitaker, R. (2010). *Anatomy of an epidemic*. New York: Crown.

Whitaker, R. & Cosgrove, L. (2015). *Psychiatry under the influence: Institutional corruption, social injury, and prescriptions for reform*. New York: Palgrave Macmillan.

Whitebook, J. (1995). *Perversion and utopia: A study in psychoanalysis and critical theory*. Cambridge, MA: MIT Press.

Whitehead, J. W. (2013). *A government of wolves*. New York: Select Books.

Whitford, F. (1986). *Oskar Kokoschka: A life*. New York: Atheneum.

Williams, M. (1922). *The velveteen rabbit*. New York: Doubleday.

Williams, S. (2014, Aug. 25). "Electronic heroin" spawns Chinese Internet addiction camps. *Voice of America*. Retrieved from www.voanews.com/content/electronic-heroin-spawns-chinese-internet-addiction-camps/2427495.html

Williams, Z. (2011, Jan. 18). Reborns: Dolls so lifelike you could mistake them for real infants. *The Guardian*. Retrieved from www.theguardian.com/lifeandstyle/2011/nov/25/reborns-lifelike-baby-dolls

Winnicott, D. W. (1958). The capacity to be alone. *International Journal of Psycho-Analysis*, 39, 416 420.

Winnicott, D. W. (1960). The theory of the parent–infant relationship. *International Journal of Psycho-Analysis*, 41, 585–595.

Winnicott, D. W. (1965 [1962]). Ego distortion in terms of true and false self. In *Maturational processes and the facilitating environment* (pp. 140–152). London: Hogarth and the Institute for Psycho-Analysis.

Winnicott, D. W. (1971 [1953]). Transitional objects and transitional phenomena: A study of the first not-me possession. In *Playing and reality* (pp. 1–25). London: Tavistock.

Winnicott, D. W. (1975 [1951]). Transitional objects and transitional phenomena. In *Through paediatrics to psycho-analysis* (pp. 229–242). New York: Basic Books.

Wolak, J., Mitchell, K., & Finkelhor, D. (2007). Unwanted and wanted exposure to online pornography in a national sample of Internet users. *Pediatrics*, 119(2), 247–257.

Wolchover, N. & Quanta Magazine (2014, Jan. 28). A new physics theory of life. *Scientific American*. Retrieved from www.scientificamerican.com/article/a-new-physics-theory-of-life/

Wolf, N. (1991). *The beauty myth: How images of beauty are used against women*. New York: William Morrow & Co.

Wolf, N. (2013, Dec. 11). How porn is destroying modern sex lives: Feminist writer Naomi Wolf has an unsettling explanation for why Britons are having less sex. *Daily Mail*. Retrieved from www.dailymail.co.uk/femail/article-2522279/Porn-destroyingmodern-sex-lives-says-feminist-writer-Naomi-Wolf.html

Woodward, B. (2001, Oct. 21). CIA told to do "whatever necessary" to kill Bin Laden. *The Washington Post*. Retrieved from www.washingtonpost.com/wp-dyn/content/article/2007/11/18/AR2007111800655.html

Woollaston, V. (2013, June 19). We'll be uploading our entire minds to computers by 2045 and our bodies will be replaced by machines in 90 years, Google expert claims. *Daily Mail*. Retrieved from www.dailymail.co.uk/sciencetech/article-2344398/Google-futurist-claims-uploading-entire-MINDS-computers-2045-bodies-replaced-machines-90-years.html

Wortham, J. (2016, July 17). Out of the box. *The New York Times Magazine*, pp. 13–15.

Yeoman, I. & Mars, M. (2011, Dec. 20). Robots, men and sex tourism. *Futures*. Retrieved from http://scottbarrykaufman.com/wp-content/uploads/2012/04/Yeoman-Mars-2012.pdf

Zetter, K. (2009, July 2). Judge acquits Lori Drew in cyberbullying case, overrules jury. *Wired*. Retrieved from www.wired.com/2009/07/drew_court/

Zhou, X., Liu, J., Chen, C., & Yu, Z. (2008). Do children transcend death? An examination of the terror management function of offspring. *Scandinavian Journal of Psychology, 49*, 413–418.

Zhou, X., Lei, Q., Marley, S. C., & Chen, J. (2009). Existential function of babies: Babies as a buffer of death-related anxiety. *Asian Journal of Social Psychology, 12*, 40–46.

Žižek, S. (2003). *Perversion and the social relation*. Durham, NC: Duke University Press.

Index